SOCIAL WORK PRACTICE WITH
THE FRAIL ELDERLY AND THEIR FAMILIES

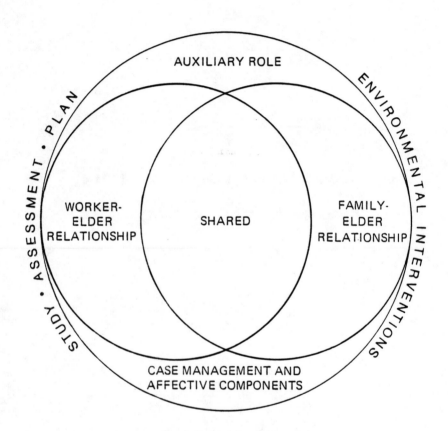

AUXILIARY FUNCTION MODEL

SOCIAL WORK PRACTICE WITH THE FRAIL ELDERLY AND THEIR FAMILIES

The Auxiliary Function Model

By

BARBARA SILVERSTONE, D.S.W.

Executive Director
The Benjamin Rose Institute
Cleveland, Ohio

and

ANN BURACK-WEISS, M.S.S.W.

Training Consultant
Brookdale Institute on Aging and Adult Human Development
Lecturer, Columbia University School of Social Work
Columbia University
New York, New York

With a Chapter by

Mario Tonti, D.S.W.

CHARLES C THOMAS • PUBLISHER

Springfield • Illinois • U.S.A.

Published and Distributed Throughout the World by

CHARLES C THOMAS • PUBLISHER
2600 South First Street
Springfield, Illinois U.S.A. 62717

©*1983, by* CHARLES C THOMAS • PUBLISHER
ISBN 0-398 04851-7
Library of Congress Catalog Card Number: 83-576

With THOMAS BOOKS careful attention is given to all details of manufacturing and design. It is the Publisher's desire to present books that are satisfactory as to their physical qualities and artistic possibilities and appropriate for their particular use. THOMAS BOOKS will be true to those laws of quality that assure a good name and good will.

Library of Congress Cataloging in Publication Data

Silverstone, Barbara, 1931-
    Social work practice with the frail elderly and their families.

    Bibliography: p.
    Includes index.
    1. Social work with the aged.   I. Burack-Weiss, Ann.
II. Tonti, Mario.   III. Title.
HV1451.S57   1983   362.6   83-576
ISBN 0-398-04851-7

Printed in the United States of America
SC–R–3

To Our Husbands: Stanley Silverstone and Roy L. Weiss

CONTENTS

Section I
Framework for the Auxiliary Function Model

Section II
Implementing the Auxiliary Function: The Worker-Client Relationship

ACKNOWLEDGMENTS

Our deep thanks and appreciation reach out to clients, students, teachers, colleagues, and families who over the past decade gave root to our ideas, nurtured our thinking, and supported the writing of this text.

Elderly clients and their families at the Community Service Society and the Jewish Home and Hospital for Aged in New York and The Benjamin Rose Institute in Cleveland provided the core professional experience for this text. Among the old people served were home care recipients, day program participants, and nursing home residents. A frail but feisty group of consumers, they taught us much about a time of life we have yet to face. Our gratitude is, foremost, to them.

Next are graduate students of the Columbia University School of Social Work, fifty of them over the years this book was in process, who fulfilled their field work requirements in community and institutional settings for the aged. Case examples of their practice fill these pages. The enthusiasm and questioning they brought to work with frail elders and families and their thirst for skills to enhance helping efforts provided the catalyst for formulation of the auxiliary function model.

Students taught in the classroom also provided an impetus to us. Of particular note are those who participated in the 1982 Summer Workshop of the University of West Virginia, where the content of our text was shared and important feedback received. Professor Nancy Lohmann is to be thanked also for her encouragement and aid.

At the Columbia University School of Social Work, Professors Irving Miller and Renee Solomon, who developed the field work program in its early stages, and Professor Abraham Monk, who lent the support of the Brookdale Institute on Aging and Adult Human Development and developed the program further, provided a climate in which educational and service ideas could grow.

At the agencies in which we practiced, Silvia Abramsky, Frances Coyle Brennan, Gertrude Elowitz, Rose Goldstein, Jessica Getzel, Charlotte Kirschner, Sandra Lavin, Walter Poulshock, Alyce Rudden, Mario Tonti, Jim Stilson, Alice Brightup, and Anna Zimmer were a continuing source of practice wisdom. Mario Tonti, Director of Community and Family Services at The Benjamin Rose Institute, contributed a key chapter to this text.

Also to be acknowledged are our teachers, past and present: George Brager, Alex Gitterman, Florence Hollis, Eugene Litwak, Carol Meyer, Helen Harris Perlman, Irving Sternschein, Charlotte Towle. With different areas of expertise but similar commitments to professional knowledge building, they provided an example of what can be done.

Two librarians, Karen Bensing of The Benjamin Rose Institute and Celestine Tutt of the Columbia University School of Social Work contributed to our bibliographic material from their store of knowledge. The secretarial staff at The Benjamin Rose Institute, JoAnn Lunar, Patricia Walter, and Fern de Arango, were quite clearly indispensable. Special thanks to the valuable information provided by Ruth Green of the New York League for the Hard of Hearing and Dolores Caviglia of the Neurological Institute of Columbia Presbyterian Hospital.

Readers who offered many helpful suggestions and insights to the work in process were Dr. Stanley Silverstone, psychoanalyst, Professor George Getzel of the Hunter College School of Social Work, and Rose Goldstein, Director of Social Service at the Kingsbridge Center of the Jewish Home and Hospital for Aged. Responsibility for the ideas in the final manuscript is, of course, wholly our own.

This text is dedicated, in thanks and love, to our husbands, Stan and Roy. Through the years of this project, they have patiently withstood the trials and enthusiastically shared the joys attendant to "the Book."

Barbara M. Silverstone
Ann Burack-Weiss

INTRODUCTION

To the growing literature on aging, we add yet another book. To the social work profession, we add yet another practice model. As a text grounded in two camps is responsible to both, we anticipate many questions. Not only will the reader want to know how the model relates to state of the art knowledge in gerontology and what it offers that is unique, he or she will also ask how it fits into the current practice perspective of the profession. We so begin by briefly addressing each of these issues, or themes, that intertwine to comprise the body of this text.

The frail elderly, a distinct subgroup of the aging population, is a group apart in many ways. Present in all socio-economic and ethnic groups, they are defined here as the old-old (75 years and above), whose general condition interferes with functioning, and/or those over sixty who suffer chronic conditions of an incapacitating nature. They are an at-risk population.

Frailty is by no means a ubiquitous gerontological condition, and care must be taken that the designation is not inappropriately applied. The majority of older persons are not frail. Frailty may be temporary or permanent, partial or total. Although closely associated with advanced age, illness, and loss, frailty is not the sum of these. It is rather the functional consequence—a state of reliance on someone else, most often the family but frequently unrelated others, to fulfill everyday tasks once handled independently. Depletions arising from the aging process itself (a general slowing down, heightened sensory thresholds that diminish input from the environment, the weakening of intersystemic boundaries that undermine resiliency) combine with external losses (ego sustaining relationships and roles) to confound attempts at mastery. At the end of life the frail elder is an individual facing a major battle with diminished resources. The stake is survival. The means is adaptation. Whether it is the spirit or the flesh or both that is weak, the frail older person can maximize adaptation with the prosthetic boost of a supportive environment that includes significant others. We call this the auxiliary function model.

Depletions (multiple, cumulative, and interactive) require a strategic approach to the frail older person specifically designed to counteract their force. What is most often lost is the sense of control and meaningful connection to the mainstream of life that makes survival worth the effort. The auxiliary function is, in essence, a loan transaction in which the frail elder borrows what is needed for as long as it is needed from a significant other or others. As an auxiliary lighting system is triggered to action by the failure of a permanent system and fades when power is restored, so the person assuming the auxiliary role fills in for inner and outer resources that have proved functional for the client throughout life. Thus while the goal with the environment often is change, the goal with the frail elder is more often replenishment of what was and conservation of what is.

Relationship is the medium through which the auxiliary function is provided. This emotional bond and attachment with caring figures is as crucial at the end of life as at its beginning. Feelings of worth and self-esteem, eroded by failing powers and increased dependencies, are buttressed by the concern and borrowed strength of others. The auxiliary role may overlap or be distinct from physical caregiving functions. It is most commonly carried out by the family, who also provides the great bulk of care to the frail elderly and to whom the elderly usually turn at times of crisis. The social worker may perform the auxiliary role, share it with other members of the helping team, or assist family members or other informal supports in assuming the role. Who serves as the significant other is less important than the fact that affective as well as instrumental needs of the frail elder are met.

While concrete service needs of the frail elderly are generally recognized, the needs for emotional bonding are less frequently considered. It is seldom recognized that, regardless of the adequacy of the environment achieved at any point in time, internal processes are underway that can invalidate the "fit" in a moment. Unlike the younger, more able person who has a store of inner strength and outer resources upon which to draw in time of stress, the frail elder lives on the margin. A relatively small upset in any area of life can affect others without timely and individualized attention. The relationship is not only a means to effective utilization of services, it also in itself may be therapeutic. The empathic encouragement of a worker, alone or in conjunction with others, may help a discouraged and anxious elder regain a modicum of self-esteem and hope eroded by cumulative physical, psychological, and/or social losses.

The frail elder cannot, of course, be viewed in isolation. As a family member, the elder's life is inextricably bound with other generations. Our practice perspective therefore calls for a familiarity with both the commonalities and differences in the family system at each stage of the life cycle. No less important are the community and bureaucratic levels of organization that impinge upon the lives of the elderly and their families. The frail elder is at risk and in need of social work services when transactions with the family and environment are maladaptive.

The past decade has witnessed major changes within the social work profession, i.e. recognition of the reciprocal adaptation of man and environment. The contributions of open systems theory (von Bertalanffy, 1968) have served to unify casework, groupwork, and community organization in a common base of practice. Consequently, most recent texts have been generic in scope. Some propose middle range models, which integrate major contributions of each area and apply these to a wide range of clients and situations (Germain & Gitterman, 1980; Pincus & Minahan, 1973). Others address the aged population only, either across the continuum of need and care (Lowy, 1980) or as related to practice setting (Brody, 1977). All are recommended. Together they reflect the knowledge base on which this book, in gratitude, freely draws.

At the same time, we see a need as yet unmet for even greater specificity. We have been curious about the frail elderly, seeking the differences between them and the well elderly, the commonalities across practice settings, the particular value dilemmas posed by their dependence in a society that prizes autonomy, and, most important, the skills that best speak to their condition. As Meyer (1976) has suggested, it is the particular circumstances of the client group, rather than any a priori methodology, that has dictated the approach chosen. Thus, the auxiliary function model evolved. It is the result of several decades of our combined practice experience in community and institutional settings. It is deeply indebted to scores of graduate students, agency staff, frail elders, and families who shared their troubles, giving and receiving help. From their needs the conceptual framework grew, and a workable methodology followed.

We define direct social work practice with the frail elderly as comprising two overlapping processes: a broad based assessment and a conscious, strategic use of the helping relationship in groups or individually to enable elders and families to function optimally on their own and through service utilization. Optimally these direct services are integrated by the worker with environmental and organization interventions into a comprehensive case plan. The auxiliary function model is applicable to all settings where the frail elderly are encountered.

While this text directs primary attention to the skills required in direct practice with frail elders and their families, we unequivocably support and also address social work efforts directly aimed at alleviating noxious environmental influences and developing resources that give needed support. In many cases, the provision of these services may be the primary task of the social worker. Such interventions range from contracting for services and coordinating them to organizing self-help groups to advocating for needed organizational or policy changes.

We view this text as an adjunct to a generic social work knowledge base. The possession of direct practice skills is a necessary condition for forming helping relationships that extend to a wide variety of frail elders and the situations they face. The auxiliary role further differentiates these skills and often overlaps. It is the differentiation that is critical. The conscious, strategic use of the relationship requires self-awareness on the part of the worker, particularly in regard to his or her own aging and feelings toward the elderly. It requires knowledge of the psychodynamics of elders and families, particularly in relation to their feelings about disability and needing to use services. It requires a sensitive awareness of the rebounding effects of environmental threats and deprivations. It requires generic skills necessary to interact in an enabling fashion as well as specific adjustments necessary with the frail. As the frail elder presents a mixture of instrumental and affective needs, the enabling relationship cannot be separated from concrete service provision either in conception or in practice. The auxiliary function model does not distinguish between these but rather sees a meshing at each stage of the process.

The strategic use of the enabling relationship between worker and elder is also not viewed as the exclusive function of the professional social worker. While we strongly advocate that complex tasks such as the psychosocial assessment are best carried out by a trained worker (and the elderly have a right to this skilled help), we recognize that many kinds of relationships, formal and informal, can enrich the lives of the frail elderly. As skill and knowledge can be imparted to these helpers, many more vulnerable elderly will be served.

Thus, while this text is addressed to the graduate level of practice, it is hoped that others will profit from some or all of its sections and that the professional social worker will utilize its content in teaching, supervising, and expanding helping resources for the frail elderly. A caveat is in order, however. As Greengross (1981) noted in an article advocating the training of community volunteer counselors for the vulnerable elderly under the supervision of trained workers, "the personality of the counselor has been found to be of fundamental importance. Empathy, warmth, and non-possessiveness are among the essential qualities, as is an optimistic attitude and belief that the work is worth attempting because one is able to achieve beneficial results."

Finally, we wish to stress that our approach is a dynamic one open to change and development as clinical experience and research evaluation dictates. Pieces of the model are still missing; for example, skills with groups are less fully developed than with individuals and families. We welcome the reaction of practitioners to our text and hope that the hypothesis upon which this model rests stirs the interest of theoreticians and researchers. While this text summarizes our accumulated practice wisdom from the past, it has also been developed as a model that can be adapted to changing needs and times.

In Section one, the framework of the auxiliary function model is set forth. Chapter 1 examines the client population identified as the frail elderly, presents the rationale for individualized services and the values undergirding them, and sets forth the practice perspective that has generated the auxiliary function model.

Chapter 2 is devoted to the construction of the *study, assessment, and plan*: the information that must be gathered in order to make an assessment, the knowledge base that directs the worker's inquiries, and the means by which these culminate in a plan.

With an eye on locating services where events in the life of the client intersect with institutional processes, we shall in Chapter 3 describe the various settings in which the auxiliary function model can be practiced. Included are a variety of health and social service settings: nursing homes, hospitals, congregate housing, day centers, case management agencies, and others.

Section two, Chapters 4 through 8, focuses on the implementation of the auxiliary function model through the worker-client relationship, with the worker performing the auxiliary role. We move from the initial through middle and termination phases of the work. Addressed are interviewing techniques, themes, issues, and individual and group interventions with the frail elderly. Problematic conditions, including cognitive and sensory impairment, that place special demands on the social worker in terms of communication and management are also discussed.

Section three deals with the environmental interventions critical to implementing the auxiliary function model. Chapter 9 addresses the physical and social environments of the elderly. The role of informal helping networks is explored as well as the common problems encountered in service organizations. Strategies for intervention in both the informal and formal systems are discussed.

Chapter 10 focuses exclusively on the family environment and the auxiliary role of the family in relation to the frail elder. A problem-solving strategy for the worker that aids in involving the family in planning as well as the issues related to assuming or continuing an auxiliary role are outlined.

The Epilogue addresses the personal and professional issues that constitute the social worker's challenge.

Appendix A categorizes the wide range of resources upon

which this text has drawn. The student, practitioner, or teacher is urged to utilize these and other resources for a deeper understanding of the complex variables contributing to the condition of and services to the frail elderly and their families. Readings are listed in social work, gerontology, personality theory, role theory, organizational theory, rehabilitation, physical environments, social welfare, health care, and landmark writings that have contributed significantly to our understanding of the frail elderly and their families. Appendix B lists pamphlets, books, and other materials that have been prepared for the consumers of service but are useful to the professional as well. Appendix C summarizes some of the diseases commonly found in the frail elderly.

SOCIAL WORK PRACTICE WITH
THE FRAIL ELDERLY AND THEIR FAMILIES

SECTION I

FRAMEWORK FOR THE
AUXILIARY FUNCTION MODEL

Chapter 1

THE PRACTICE PERSPECTIVE

This text is founded on a firm commitment to the basic human rights and dignity of the frail elderly as well as to a practice perspective based on clinical experience and gerontological knowledge. The practice perspective, here defined as the auxiliary function model, serves as an organizing theoretical framework for the assumptions, knowledge, and values upon which our interventive decisions are based. This model was constructed from the inside out; the salient characteristics of frailty and the responses required by the environment to counteract its force forming the core of our practice perspective.

This chapter describes the condition of frailty and the client population designated as frail, examines the relevance of contemporary social work practice models for this population, and presents the auxiliary function model as a critically needed refinement. In closing, we cite the enduring professional values that undergird our approach.

THE CLIENT POPULATION

The frail elderly have recently emerged as important consumers of social work services. They are generally defined as the old-old (over 75) and other persons over sixty who suffer from impairments or ennervating conditions that can temporarily or permanently interfere with autonomous functioning. While there are elderly over seventy-five who are not frail and those under seventy-five who are, there is little doubt that frailty dramatically increases in the very late years.

The elderly, as a whole, comprise almost 11 percent of the population in contrast to 3 percent at the turn of the century. The number of people who are old, a time of life that can span thirty-five or more years, has been growing faster than the number who are young. This is particularly true in the seventy-five and older bracket, those elderly most vulnerable to frailty and disability. The control of communicable disease in the past century and the improvement in health care for all generations has resulted in increased longevity for many. As a result, people are living longer with the disabling effects of chronic illness.

The Bureau of the Census now projects that the dramatic growth in the elderly population during the past few decades will slow considerably, but again mushroom in the early twenty-first century when the baby boom generation of the 1950s becomes elderly. Projections regarding the over seventy-five population are less clear, but present trends suggest that increasing numbers of persons will survive into very old age. Whereas, only one in twenty elders were over eighty-five in 1950, one in six will be over eighty-five in the year 2050 (United States DHHS, 1981).

The disparity between the number of older men and women, due to the shortened life expectancy of males, becomes more striking in the old-old population. For every 100 men in the over sixty-five age bracket, there are 147 women; in the over eighty-five group, 220 women. Since men tend to marry younger women, the disparity between the number of widows and widowers is noteworthy. In the over seventy-five age bracket 70 percent of women are widows; whereas approximately the same percent of men are married (U.S. Census, 1980).

Unquestionably, a sizeable number of disorders that afflict the elderly are chronic and irreversible. For the very old, the energy sapping effects of the aging process itself must be considered, as well as a general slowing down. Sensory thresholds are heightened affecting sight, hearing, touch, and taste. Diseases such as arthritis and arteriosclerosis, to name a few, are progressive in nature, and medical interventions have not yet been discovered to reverse their course. A significant number of disorders are often dramatically amenable to clinical interventions. Noteworthy here are the acute organic brain syndromes, cataracts, certain sclerotic conditions, and cancer (see Appendix C).

Interwoven with the reversible and irreversible conditions

afflicting the old (which seldom exist in isolation from one another) are emotional ones—depression and anxiety states—which occur among the elderly in greater proportions than the young. Often these conditions are reactions to disabling disease and illness or the loss of loved ones, status, and roles. Sometimes they have accompanied the old person through his or her life cycle in addition to other disorders such as schizophrenia and alcoholism. In and of themselves, these emotional conditions can be disabling.

The National Institute of Mental Health (1980) estimates that 15 to 28 percent of the elderly have "significant symptoms of mental disorder," 5 to 6 percent senile dementia, and 10 percent clinically diagnosed depression. The majority of nursing home patients exhibit symptoms of mental disorder, and the suicide rate of older people is disproportionately higher than the rate for the total population (Hendin, 1982).

Compounding this already complex clinical picture, and of particular meaning to the social worker, is the fact that the disabled and frail old are more vulnerable to external influences owing to their increased dependence on others. The capacity of an elder to mobilize help and support or withstand external threats is often the decisive factor in survival. This capacity can vary greatly among the old as a result of contrasting personality structures, life experiences, and cultural backgrounds.

When personal frailty occurs in the context of inadequate financial resources, housing, and transportation, adaptation becomes all the more difficult. Poverty, a fact of life for many, when coupled with disability can be of overwhelming impact. As internal and external resources are significantly reduced for the elderly, a composite picture of multiple needs emerges. The elderly in general have lower incomes than younger persons. While there have been significant improvements in recent years in the economic condition of the old, 14 percent have incomes below the official poverty line and another 23 percent have incomes hovering near the poverty line. Blacks and females are disproportionately represented among the elderly poor or near poor (Brotman, 1979).

The proportion of elderly living alone has increased from 19 percent of the noninstitutionalized elderly in 1960 to 30 percent in 1979 (United States DHHS, 1981). The increase in single households has been most significant for the over seventy-five population: 50 percent of women and 21 percent of men in this old-old age category lived alone in 1979 (U.S. Census, 1980). Only 27 percent of women over seventy-five and 10 percent of men lived with relatives other than spouse. The fact that large numbers of noninstitutionalized women over the age of seventy-five live alone suggests that many are capable of independent living. By the same token, it may also reflect a lack of needed assistance in their lives.

The number of elderly living in nursing homes was 1.1 million in 1977; 81 percent of them over the age of seventy-five. Most were women and widowed. Admissions were from their own homes, hospitals, and mental institutions. While the number of elderly sixty-five and over in nursing homes is only 5 percent of the population, it has been estimated that one in four will enter a nursing home at some time, a projection consonant with the fact that 20 percent of the over eighty population is in nursing homes (Kastenbaum and Candy, 1973).

The young-old for the most part are active and even vigorous. While most older persons (65+) suffer from at least one chronic condition, these are not necessarily disabling. A significant proportion of persons sixty-five and over report functional limitations due to a chronic condition, but it is not until age seventy-five that a majority report such limitations. Only 20 percent of non-institutionalized elders seventy-five to eighty-nine years of age report limitations in major activities due to chronic conditions, 31 percent of those over eighty-five (United States DHHS, 1981). However, when these reported functional limitations are coupled with the extensive mental health problems of the elderly as well as poverty and social isolation, the scope of frailty widens. Current estimates that place high risk elderly at 18 percent of the total elderly population may not be exaggerated.

The need for services among the frail elderly is difficult to ascertain. Clearly, they are heavy users of health services. While only representing 11 percent of the total population, the elderly account for 29 percent of total personal health care expenditures. They see physicians 50 percent more often than younger people and have about twice as many hospital stays that last twice as long than hospitalizations for younger persons (Brotman, 1978).

They use outpatient mental health services, however, at a far lower rate than the general population, comprising only 4 to 5 percent of outpatient caseloads. If general expenditure figures are any indication, their utilization of social services is also low, less than 8 percent of total health and social care funding going to social services (Silverstone, 1981).

Utilization rates, however, obscure need. So do recent surveys of the reported service needs of elders. The National Center For Health Statistics (1980) reports that only 24 percent of the over seventy-five population need help with dressing and 15 percent with bathing and far less with eating and toileting. The need for counselling, case management, help in money management, shopping, housekeeping, and psychiatric care has not been ascertained, although it is known that social and health agencies provide these services to some elderly.

The most dependable resource for the elderly is the family. Families provide most of the care to the elderly, and it is the family to whom elders usually turn at times of crisis (Shanas, 1979). Family care, most usually given by the spouse and/or adult child, is influenced by the nature of marital and intergenerational relationships and characteristic coping styles (Silverstone, 1982). In turn, family relationships are affected by the challenge of caregiving and the aging and deterioration of the elder. Current research studies find families managing to cope with caregiving tasks; however, they are under stress, particularly in relation to mental impairment (Poulshock & Noelker, 1982).

Childlessness for elderly women has been declining and will continue to do so for the next several decades, a trend that may increase family caregiving. Reflected here are the low birthrates of the depression years and the ensuing baby boom of post war years. Measured against this trend, however, is the movement of women into paid employment and the probability that childlessness may rise again when the present baby boom generation becomes old.

The older population is a diverse and changing group. There is a wide disparity within current cohorts of elderly on cultural, socio-economic, educational, and personal parameters. Approximately 5000 Americans turn sixty-five every day. New cohorts with different life histories are constantly entering the ranks of the elderly. One of the most striking changes forecast for the elderly of the future is their educational level. In 1978, 46 percent of older Americans had not completed one year of high school. Less than 10 percent will lack a high school education after the year 2000. The possible implications of this change for a reduction in poverty and increase in coping capacities are noteworthy (Brotman, 1979).

In summary, mental and physical frailty as a significant condition for the older population has been well established. Chronic illnesses proliferate for the over sixty-five population, but they are translated into impairing conditions for only a minority until the later years. It is the over seventy-five population that makes heavy use of nursing homes. The majority of the old-old in the community need some support due to mental problems, social isolation, widowhood, and functional impairment. The burden of care falls largely on the family, who also needs support and perhaps supplementation in meeting the needs of its elder members. Without doubt, a population at-risk has emerged and will continue to grow, requiring social work attention.

CONTRIBUTIONS OF THE PAST AND PRESENT

The restructuring of social work thinking in the past decade has had positive and negative consequences for practice with the frail elderly. The auxiliary function model is an attempt to integrate the best of past and present practice perspectives as applied to this specific client population.

The ecosystems perspective, as defined in the life model (Germain & Gitterman, 1980), has proved valuable in conceptualizing the reciprocity of man and environment, the interrelatedness of all aspects of the client's field, and the notion of adaptive fit. To discuss the frail elder without such external referents would now seem absurd. Their primacy in determining assessment and intervention has become a given. Similarly, the developmental view of tasks and growth opportunities at each stage of the life cycle is fully congruent with our view that the aged, no matter how impaired, have cause for hope and reason for survival (Erikson, 1959; Peck, 1956; Pincus, 1967).

Contributions from ego psychology, particularly those having to do with efficacy and competence, are relevant to the old and frail who are provided far too few opportunities for mastery and in turn the enhancement of self-esteem (White, 1963; Hartman, 1958). Crisis intervention obviously holds a priority position in the base of knowledge and skills of those who work with a vulnerable client group for whom developmental or situational life events of even a minor nature have potential for immediate and devastating consequences (Parad, 1958; Rapaport, 1971).

Problem-solving and task oriented models of practice alert the profession to the importance of focus, direction, and goal-setting (Perlman, 1957; Reid & Epstein, 1972). This accountability of worker practice and mandate for client involvement in planning are too frequently overlooked in cases of frailty and disability.

Underlying all these contributions is a systems view as opposed to a linear view of human behavior. Seeing the client as not in the situation but of it has made possible a generic base of social work practice. Ideas of reciprocal interaction in life situations have served to remove some of the stigmatizing or value laden approaches to elders in need that prevailed in early years of the profession. Information and collaboration from many fields of inquiry and professional disciplines are now possible, and all that is to the good. However, as ideas of prevention and change have moved social workers away from the now scorned "medical model," something has been lost. Illness has been replaced with wellness as the new social work metaphor. The past of the client, no longer explored for historical roots of pathology, has now become simply irrelevant.

Such accents on the positive, the present, and the productive have been an inevitable consequence of the growth of practice research and empirical measures of effectiveness. Operative words are increasingly energetic such as "action" and "change" (Lowy, 1979; Pincus & Minahan 1973; Compton & Galaway, 1975). Relationship is seen as arising from the task at hand, ceasing when the task is completed. Indeed, as regretfully noted by Perlman (1979), the very term has fallen into disrepute with its past associations to undesirable dependency of client on worker. The client's ability to manage his or her own life, if provided with opportunity and skills to do so, is our new belief system, a business-like contract is the new means of insuring client autonomy.

As gerontologists, social workers, and mortals afraid of our own eventual decline, we have embraced each new research finding that disproves negative stereotypes of aging. Reassuring ourselves and each other that the decremental model is not inevitable we have highlighted the positives and all but eliminated the negatives of aging. As a desirable consequence, much prejudice against the field has been overcome. Medical science has offered us hope that in the future we will all be healthier longer. Societally imposed limitations on the aged appear capable of redress.

As a consequence, workers and students of today are increasingly being drawn to practice with the aged. Yet, armed with expectations about the promise of the later years and faced with frail elders in the field, they are often hard put to apply theory to practice. Frustrated, they may fault their clients for not assuming a more active role in the helping process or themselves for not being professional enough in handling the demands for personal attention placed upon them. In fact, what is lacking is a differential approach to the very old and impaired that can enhance service delivery and professional satisfaction.

Unlike a younger, healthier population, change for the frail elderly is often change for the worse. In the face of declining powers, conservation and maintenance of the status quo may be a more appropriate intervention. For the isolated elder, relationship with the worker may well be an end in itself, as crucial to the maintenance of personal well-being as any concrete work accomplished. While the past is not turned to for roots of pathology, it remains of key importance in the identification of strengths and as a source of self-affirmation. Coping capacities obscured by the present situation may well be revealed in tales of the long ago. By the same token, the frail elder may well be dependent for the remainder of his or her life.

Decrements in health and functioning are real. Denial of the impact of these in the name of eschewing the medical model does the frail elder a great disservice. Yet, focusing only on impairment does the elder a greater one. The dilemma is how to revive what is relevant to practice with the frail elderly from the discard heap of social casework and how to integrate it with the holistic approach to social work practice to which the profession is now rightfully committed. While many have written well and extensively about social work practice with the frail elderly, few have devoted exclusive texts to the subject. A comparison of a pioneering text with one of current vintage may highlight the problem and point to its resolution.

It has been little more than twenty years that the profession has evinced more than a passing interest in direct social work practice with the aged. An early pioneer, Edna Wasser (1966) was a caseworker who integrated emerging research findings in the then new field of social gerontology and insights from the also new field of geriatric psychiatry into her work. Applying the person-in-situation diagnostic perspective to the old, she advocated a bio-psychosocial approach with recognition accorded developmental tasks facing the aging individual and the aging family. She recognized the significant impact of loss on many elderly and the importance of grieving, mourning, and redefining values "which emphasize continuing reorganization of the self to give meaning to one's life and to help face one's death" (Wasser, 1966). Wasser was one of the first to suggest modifications of the traditional professional role needed with the aged, recognizing that touch, social conversation, and concrete demonstrations of caring must often precede or accompany traditional casework. Most importantly, she advocated flexibility and innovation in exemplifying ways in which agencies serving the aged should be modified in policy and procedures by the needs of the population.

Although she wrote only of casework and did not differentiate the old-old from the young-old or the active from the disabled, her contribution to the field has been long-lasting. Wasser was informed at each step by practice experiences of workers in family agencies. It was this faithfulness to the observed needs of the aged that gives the text its continuing authenticity.

Writing within the cognitive set of today, Lowy (1979) has performed the formidable task of incorporating current knowledge about the aged with a generic view of social work practice in a comprehensive guide to the entire field. State of the art gerontological knowledge and social work skills, holistically conceived, are applied to a wide variety of situations encountered in work with the elderly. The process-action model is presented with case examples illustrative of what is known and what can be done. It is a hopeful book in its presentation of the wide range of possible interventions and their helpfulness in improving the lives of the old. As an expansion and update of Wasser's formulations, much of importance has been added. Yet, in the breadth of scope, concepts specific to work with the frail elderly are sometimes obscured.

Wasser's work has alerted us to the differential needs of the aged, Lowy's to the many ways in which social work can help. We focus our view more narrowly on the needs of the frail alone. We have worked inductively from practice experience and deductively from the theoretical contributions of a systems perspective. Together they have indicated the particular mix of contributions from past and present that underlie our practice perspective.

THE AUXILIARY FUNCTION MODEL

The auxiliary function model is a logical extension of past wisdom and recent developments in social work thinking. It is a practice model undergirded by a systems approach that specifically addresses the why and how of our help to frail elders and their families. It addresses their individuality as well as the broad range of services and interventive strategies available to us. The auxiliary function model is an organizing framework, a structure for ordering what is currently known about and effective with the frail elderly and their families as well as what we are continuing to learn.

The name of the model is based on metaphor—the image is that of an auxiliary lighting system triggered to action by failure of a permanent system, fading when power is restored. An auxiliary adds to, fills in for, and bolsters that which is depleted.

The auxiliary function model of social work practice is bounded by the professionally drawn study, assessment, and plan and environmental interventions on behalf of the frail elder. The model encompasses the auxiliary role that is filled by significant others, most often the family, by the social worker in cases where there is no available family, and sometimes is a shared responsibility.

Depletion and Loss: A Systems Approach

Central to the auxiliary function model are the depletions and losses underlying frailty that require intervention in terms of a specific relationship, the auxiliary role, and environmental supports. Depletion and loss take an emotional and functional toll on frail elders and can seriously affect their ability to negotiate the environment.

A *systems approach*, which provides the framework for contemporary social work practice, aids in our understanding of depletion and its rebounding effects on the emotions as well as the physical, mental, and social functioning of the elder. It identifies common characteristics of all living systems that influence adaptation: their intrinsic capacity for growth and differentiation given sufficient input from the environment, throughput and output capabilities that enable the system to carry on transactions with the environment, and decline and dedifferentiation resulting ultimately in the entropic process we know as dying.

Social work practice of today that is based on a systems approach places heavy emphasis on the transactions between the individual and the environment implicitly relying on the human organism's innate capacity for growth and differentiation to achieve a better fit given a more responsive environment. However, it does not address conditions where the processes of degrowth, dedifferentiation, and entropy have overtaken growth processes. It is these conditions and the chronic impairments accompanying them that underly frailty in the elderly. They can be exacerbated or ameliorated by the environment but not reversed.

We have chosen to identify the cumulative insults that are the results of biological changes and the concomitant diminution of meaningful roles and relationships as *primary and secondary depletion*. The concept of depletion is central in understanding how the frail elderly differ from other adult clients encountered in social work practice. Defined as a "lessening markedly in quantity, content, power, or value," depletion of inner and outer resources necessitates direct replenishment if the elder's condition is not to deteriorate further (Cath, 1963).

Primary depletion, as we define it, has its roots in the biological entropic changes that characterize aging. External physical changes are readily apparent, but internal changes are also in process. Physiological studies point to cellular loss in bodily organs sufficient to sap needed backup reserves that sustain adaptation at times of stress. Also documented is decline in the immunological system, rendering the human organism more susceptible to acute and chronic disease. While modern science has not unraveled the key to human aging, it has documented these and other depleting processes that take place in all humans with wide chronological variation among individuals and between organ systems (Finch & Hayflick, 1977).*

Secondary depletion refers to losses experienced by the old that accompany biological aging or are imposed by the age structure of our social system and other environmental deficits. Secondary depletions are not confined to the frail elderly, but can be experienced with less frequency by the younger elderly as well. Cohort loss, particularly of the spouse, is a profound depletion for some, particularly common for women who tend to outlive men. The young-old and the old-old are both affected by changes in status, work and familial roles and finances. All of these may be experienced as *loss*. The marked lack of response of the service system to the heightened needs of the frail is another case in point.

Our concept of depletion may not be popularly regarded. For some, it may only seem to corroborate the common stereotype of the old as involved in irreversible decline. To ignore depletion in the old, however, to view it as merely a transactional phenomenon, or to coat it in developmental euphemisms denies a hard reality and limits our thinking on the problem. The important point to keep in mind is that chronological aging is not the earmark of depletion. While depleting processes tend to intensify in the over seventy-five population, they are not applicable to all in this age category. In less frequent circumstances, they can apply to younger persons. Furthermore, depletion can occur with great individual variation and intensity, calling for careful study and assessment in each individual situation.

---

*For a clear statement on the biological parameters of human aging, the reader is referenced to the text *Vitality and Aging* by James Fries and Lawrence Crapo, 1981.

As noted, a systems view helps us understand the process of depletion by recognizing subsystems that comprise the human system as well as those external to its boundaries. Primary depletion heightens intersystemic effects in the aged. Various physical and psychological problems blend into one another resulting in a complexity of symptoms not seen in the young. Furthermore, these intersystemic changes are rapid. An old frail person can quickly lapse into a confused episode if nutrition is poor. By the same token, a confused state of mind will often clear rapidly if the individual is placed without too much delay on a nutritious diet.

Simultaneously occurring are the common diminishments in sensory acuity, a general slowing down, and a far greater susceptability to disease, which result in physical and mental impairments with their ominous effects on daily functioning. Depletions in executive functions of the ego — sensory, perceptual, and cognitive — can have particularly devastating effects on overall performance (Birren & Schaie, 1977).

Blending a systems perspective with a psychodynamic one further illuminates the consequences of depletion. Wasser (1966) and Cath (1963) have identified the mourning reactions that are an expected and indeed necessary response to losses in old age. Depression over depletion of inner and outer resources and anxiety and fear over diminished ability to control aspects of one's environment are omnipresent. The effects of these heightened emotional reactions on transactions with the environment can, of course, be profound.

Adaptation of the Frail Elder

A systems perspective with an adaptive evolutionary view of human beings in constant interchange with all elements of their environment highlights the consequences of depletion. Paradoxically, just as the elder becomes less able to receive, process, and handle input from the environment, he or she becomes more dependent on it. It is at this juncture that the affective (caring, hope, empathy) and instrumental (problem-solving, coordination) components of the auxiliary function are activated to maximize adaptive fit.

Just as the extent and meaning of depletion must be assessed in each individual situation, so must the type of adaption. The auxiliary function model is based on the premise that for the frail elderly, adaptation to depletion and loss takes different forms. *Restitution, compensation,* and *accommodation* are the terms we use to identify the ways in which adaptation takes place. Each necessitates a differential exercise of the auxiliary function model, determining the type of help needed, the time frame in which it is offered, and the degree of worker involvement.

Restitution and *compensation* are the first options for maintaining systemic integrity when depletion occurs. Each of these types of adaptation results in the individual regaining a loss or prior level of functioning even if at a slightly diminished level. *Restitution* refers to the restoration of a function or object that has been lost either through healing, spontaneous remission, or external intervention or replenishment. Examples of restitution in the frail elderly are recovery from a hip fracture to the extent that mobility is regained or cataract surgery that restores eyesight.

Compensation refers here to the substitution of a function that has been lost by increased functioning of an unimpaired part of the organism or by the substitution of a lost object. Compensation in the frail elderly is exemplified by the use of prosthetic devices such as a walker or wheelchair, which divert functioning from the legs to the arms. Compensation is also an important adaptation in the case of secondary depletion. New relationships can be formed to ease the loss of spouse and old friends. Leisure time activities fill in for the void left by cessation of the work role.

While far less available to the very old than to younger persons, restitution and compensation are possible adaptations for the frail elderly. Decline is not necessarily linear or nonselective. The life course comprises a series of plateaus and spurts in growth as well as depletion. Although these plateaus and spurts in growth are far more difficult to achieve in the late years because of system decline and cumulative losses, there is repeated evidence of restorative and compensatory behavior on the part of very old persons that belies a designation of frailty. Recovery is slower than for younger persons, but still a very real phenomenon.

For the frail elderly, restitution and compensation are usually adaptations to a limited degree or in relation to specific functions.

They should not be negated simply because total recovery is not achieved, but rather recognized for the still intact capacities they represent. The most striking example is seen in the case of catastrophic illness such as a stroke or hip fracture that can immediately result in the loss of mobility and mental alertness. Immobility may be permanent, but mental symptoms reversible. In the case of multiple losses, partial restoration or substitution of some functions and objects is often possible.

Restitutive and compensatory adaptations rely heavily on resources of the environment. In the case of primary depletion, the environment can provide medical and surgical care, rehabilitative interventions, and the interpersonal relationships so critical to motivation on the part of the elder. Similarly, environmental obstacles such as physical barriers, negative social attitudes, and ignorance of the aging process can block recovery.

The potential for restitution and compensation on the part of frail elders must constantly alert the worker to the possibility of rehabilitation. In addition to replenishment of what has been lost, restitution and compensation require encouraging and enabling responses built on the expectation of improvement. The potential for a higher level of performance underscores the auxiliary nature of the function, which is a subsidiary one, filling in for, and only for, those abilities that are impaired for only as long as the condition lasts. An element of physical risk may be involved. In order to achieve a higher level of functioning the elder and others may have to live with the uncertainty that success may not be possible (Stevenson, 1981).

For many frail elders, restitution and compensation are not or cannot be achieved. Mental and physical disabilities become chronic. In such instances, depletion is particularly marked and the level of functioning significantly diminished. *Accommodation* to these changes must be effected by elder and environment. A passive acquiescence or an active adjustment to a new life-style and life space are polar extremes of a wider range of successful and unsuccessful accommodations. Like restitution and compensation, each accommodation will result from an individual blend of the elder's coping capacities, the quality of the environment, and the transactions between them at any point in time.

Because of the heightened and prolonged dependence inherent in accommodation, the auxiliary function takes on paramount importance. On the most basic level, services and other supports must be tapped from the environment to sustain the frail elder's functioning. Instrumental tasks, including the arrangement, provision, coordination, and monitoring of concrete services, become critically important components of the auxiliary function.

Accommodation to both internal changes and environmental conditions is accomplished with wide individual variation. Sometimes helping seems futile, and we question if auxiliary support is appropriate. A very depressed elder, unreconciled to a permanent loss of physical function, may remain depressed regardless of the attempts of the environment to accommodate his or her losses. Here, it is not the instrumental but rather the affective component of the auxiliary function that comes into play, not as means to an end, but rather as an end in itself supplying the missing measure of affirmation and hope. In cases where depletions in executive functions of the ego place the elder at great risk, the auxiliary function becomes crucial to accommodation. Provided to the elder as a loan transaction are the sensory, perceptual, and/or cognitive skills of a significant other.

Accommodation to frailty does not rule out restitutive or compensatory behaviors that can function simultaneously or consecutively. An elder may accommodate to impairing arthritis by moving to a barrier-free living facility. At the same time, compensation for the loss of peers can be realized by making new friends. This blend of adaptations calls for flexibility in the performance of the auxiliary function.

An issue crosscutting the range of accommodations made to depletion and loss is the elder's capacity to utilize auxiliary aid. Increased dependence on others can result in very different behaviors. Some elders are only able to accept help and emotional support from one significant other such as a spouse, a particular adult offspring, or worker. Others can respond easily to several persons sharing the auxiliary role, and there are those who seem to care little about who or how many fill the role as long as it is implemented. Personality and family patterns spun out over a lifetime usually determine the behaviors that must be weighed in planning the type of auxiliary aid to be given.

Dimensions of the Auxiliary Function Model

The auxiliary function model, based on a systems approach, defines the purpose of social work practice as expediting a loan transaction in which the elder borrows what is needed for as long as is needed to supplement diminished powers. The processes of primary and secondary depletion and loss, and the resulting adaptations set the parameters of the model.

Depletion and loss experienced by the frail elder require replenishment on affective and instrumental levels. Since a toll is taken on the emotions of the old, warmth, hope, and empathy conveyed by a significant other are as essential to a sense of well-being as any concrete assistance provided.

Depletion and loss take their toll on the functional capacities of the elder as well. The instrumental component of the auxiliary function comprises specific tasks related to negotiations with the environment: lending cognitive sensory and perceptual skills to the elder, assisting in problem-solving, carrying out case management tasks in relation to concrete services, or expediting changes in the physical and social environment.

The types of adaptation possible further delineates the tasks to be performed. When restitution and compensation are possible, rehabilitation and environmental change are foremost considerations. When accommodations must be made, environmental resources are harnessed and sustained. In cases where more than one type of adaptation is possible, diversified responses from the worker and/or environment are necessary.

The enabling relationship, or the auxiliary role, bridges the instrumental and affective components of the auxiliary function; the two closely intertwined, reinforcing the other. While the auxiliary function model is implemented by the social worker, others may perform the auxiliary role. It may be filled totally by the family, involve a partnership between the family and social worker, or be enacted by the social worker and/or other service provider. This determination will depend on the resources available and the capacities and choice of the elder.

In summary, we have outlined the auxiliary function model of practice with the frail elderly and their families bounded by the study, assessment, plan, and environmental interventions. It encompasses the auxiliary role, a critical relationship for the frail elder that is normally filled by the family but out of necessity may be filled by or shared with the social worker and others. The cornerstones of the auxiliary function model, based on a systems approach, are the depletions and losses suffered by the frail in varying degrees and the varied adaptations to these changes which require a highly individualized approach.

VALUE ISSUES

Important values underly the professional relationship. Foremost are the elder's right to self-determination, confidentiality, and treatment with dignity. Violations of rights are rampant in the care of the frail, impaired elderly. In the case of the mentally impaired, this can extend, sometimes justifiably, to the legal abrogation of rights through guardianship or commitment. In other circumstances, however, rights are unnecessarily withdrawn, withheld, or interferred with under the guise of protection or providing good care.

The helplessness faced by some frail elders brought about by physical and mental impairment is not necessarily accompanied by a loss of judgment in regard to their own welfare or their ability to make decisions for themselves. In the case of severe memory loss, confusion, or psychosis this may be true, but these cases are in the minority. As an adult member of society, the aged person's right to self-determination is indisputable. The family's right to decide the degree and type of involvement with a frail elder is also a manifestation of self-determination that must be respected by the worker.

Rights include the frail elder's active involvement in the client-worker relationship and assessment of the problem and the formulation of a plan of care. Families who seek help for an elder and omit that person from the planning process, particularly in the case of nursing home placement, violate a human right. If joined by the social worker in this omission, professional ethics have also been violated. Confidentiality requires the same assiduous attention in the professional relationship. Contacting family, neighbors, agencies, or other professionals without client permission is antithetical to professional values.

Ethical issues coincide with important practice issues. The enabling relationship that reflects client rights is conducive to rehabilitation on the elder's part. Decision making is the first step to improved overall functioning regardless of the cluster of impairments suffered by the elder. The often corrosive fear of loss of control over one's own life that disability can arouse can be a barrier to help and services. It must be actively combated with a meticulous, patient involvement of the elder in decisions regarding his or her welfare.

It is the underlying value base of the social work profession that differentiates the auxiliary function model from the approaches of other disciplines. Empirically validated models for changing elder behavior, while unquestionably effective and obviously well-meant, can slip into manipulation if indiscriminately applied. Self-determination and self-reliance are not to be confused. The frail elder may choose to rely upon others and in so doing exercise self-determination. At the same time, a hasty refusal of all assistance cannot be viewed as self-determination if the elder has not been provided opportunity to consider the plan. The auxiliary function model, which is essentially an extension of the elder's unique coping mechanisms, is in fact the embodiment of self-determination.

Mutuality and Reciprocity

The tension between the giving and taking of help that exists in all social work relationships is highlighted in practice with the frail elderly. The balance of power is skewed to the worker's side to an extent unmatched by other populations, except perhaps the very young. The primary and secondary depletions of age, economic and societal inequities, and their resulting dependencies may render the elder a helpless pawn in the hands of caregivers. Grateful for whatever assistance he or she receives, the elder's individuality is sacrificed. The elder who protests the terms of help may protect integrity but at the cost of needed care. The auxiliary function model is predicated upon mutuality and reciprocity in this potentially most uneven of relationships. Goals and the means of achieving them are never reached unilaterally. No matter how impaired the elder, he or she is capable of some degree of involvement. In most cases, the elder can participate far more than expected if given time and patience on the part of the worker.

We must never forget that it is the frail elder who must live out the consequences of any actions taken. Sharing of the case plan and its implementation is an ongoing process, requiring repetition, simplification, and clarification at each stage. The worker who bypasses the elder in the mistaken belief that he or she can move more quickly alone is not only abrogating the elder's rights but placing an unfair burden on him or herself as well. Thus, mutuality and reciprocity are values that serve both elder and worker under the auxiliary function model.

This chapter and the following chapters define and operationalize the auxiliary function model along with the tasks and values inherent in it. The study and assessment critical to determining the dimensions of the model, identifying who is to fill the significant other component of the auxiliary role, and developing an individualized care plan are integral parts of the whole. To be discussed are the skills required in engaging the elder in the assessment plan and in ongoing individual contacts and groups, the interventions important in engaging and/or helping others share in or fill the auxiliary role, and the harnessing of environmental resources to support these efforts.

Chapter 2

THE STUDY, ASSESSMENT, AND PLAN

OVERVIEW

The auxiliary function model of social work addresses the processes of depletion and loss that characterize frailty and the wide variation in the way individuals experience and adapt to depletion within an environmental context. An individualized approach is imperative to insure that the worker's use of self, as well as other services provided to the client, is appropriately measured and adjusted.

The individualized service plan, which should be constructed for and with every client regardless of the setting and/or time limitations, is an explicitly stated set of long-range objectives and short-range goals based upon a clearly stated assessment of the client's total field, which in turn is based upon a careful study of the client's situation.

As a written statement, the *study, assessment, and plan* is an organizing tool for the social worker, a basic ingredient of record keeping and accountability, and an important means of inter-professional communication. It can be readily adapted for medical charts, is used in conjunction with standardized functional assessment instruments, and is the very basis of the social work record. Conciseness and clarity are necessary if others are to fully utilize it.

The fact that many agencies that elders and/or families approach offer limited services increases the chance that client need will be narrowly studied and assessed in terms of what the agency can provide. The broader need for help or alternatives to care may be left unexplored. This could be true of the home care agency, which does not recognize the need for socialization that might be

25

filled by a day program, or the long-term care facility, which does not include exploration of community resources in the intake process. Thus, the study outline determines the parameters of the social worker's professional interest, regardless of whether or not the particular agency setting can meet all the problems and needs uncovered. The plan enables the social worker to explore other resources for this purpose.

The following chapter outlines the ingredients of and rationale for the *study, assessment, and plan.* It focuses on the *study* — the relevant information gathered and organized about the elder, the family, and the environment. It includes the facts as well as client and family feelings about the facts, or the reality as they perceive it. The *assessment* is a summary and interpretation of this information for the purpose of identifying the problems that need to be addressed. The *plan* summarizes the long-range objectives and short-range goals that will address these problems, the interventions necessary to reach these goals, and the assignment of auxiliary and other service tasks.

While discussed here individually, it is understood that the processes involved in implementing the *study, assessment, and plan* are most often concurrent rather than sequential. The study itself may prove a useful intervention, and interventions might begin before all the facts are in or the meanings clear. Practice demands place a special responsibility on the worker to continually reassess as new information becomes available and is recorded in the case record.

The Knowledge Base Needed: A Broad-Based Approach

There are two types of knowledge that are essential for making a *study, assessment, and plan.* The first is a general knowledge base relating to human behavior and the social environment with particular focus on the aging population. The second is specific knowledge of the case at hand. It is the meshing of these two areas of knowledge that results in a professional *study, assessment, and plan.* The general knowledge base directs the worker's inquiries resulting in specific information and facilitates the coherent organization of that information.

The General Knowledge Base

Acquisition of professional knowledge cannot be obtained once and for all, surely not within the context of a time-limited course of study. It is an ongoing process, dependent upon a self-disciplined approach to continuing education in its formal and informal manifestations. There are two basic reference groups with which the practitioner will identify, each an ongoing provider of information on important developments in the field. The first is the social work profession. The second is the multidisciplinary field of gerontology. Appendix A lists for the reader suggested basic readings in each of these areas further subdivided by relevant topics.

Within the field of social work, textbooks and journals generic to the profession and specific to aging are valuable resources. Much that is applicable to direct practice with the frail elderly may be noted first in work with other dependent populations. Therefore, readings in such areas as long-term care and rehabilitation may be useful. The tunnel vision often fostered by agency affiliation must be counteracted, for client need is not so sharply compartmentalized. Community and institutional workers would do well to become familiar with each other's practice. Both should be cognizant of policy issues at local, state, and national levels that directly impinge upon service delivery and be prepared to buttress advocacy efforts with documentation from the field.

The wider field of gerontology is an important source of ongoing education. Research has been extensive in the past few decades. Findings have been well organized into basic texts and handbooks which provide an overview of the entire aging population vis-à-vis particular lines of inquiry. Valuable literature is available through regional and national organizations and university-based centers on gerontology. While it is important to place the frail elder within the context of the later years, all may not be applicable. The very old may have been widowed for as many years as they were married. The event of retirement may be ancient history. Thus, discretion is necessary for application.

An understanding of human development and behavior is essential. From whatever sources it is gleaned, knowledge of expected tasks and predictable resolutions at each stage of the life cycle helps the worker evaluate client strengths and capacities at the end of life. Recently, the overemphasis on the developmental tasks of youth has been balanced by theoretical formulations and research efforts that address the later years of individuals and families. Intergenerational mutuality (Rhodes, 1977), integrity (Erikson, 1959), and filial responsibility (Blenkner, 1965) are among the numerous concepts that have been formulated to describe development in the later years.

The deeper and more extensive is this knowledge of human behavior, the better equipped the social worker is to deal with the complexities inherent in work with aged clients. Ego psychology illuminates the coping and adaptive patterns used by individuals in dealing with their environment, both functional and dysfunctional, conscious and unconscious (Hartmann, 1958; White, 1963). Object relations theory and the concept of narcissism speaks to the nature of the human bond critical to understanding the psychological components of the elder's dependence on others (Loewenstein, 1977).

Role theory provides a coherent framework for understanding the effects of social status and interaction on behavior (Gross et al., 1966). Research studies concerned with the concepts of excess disability (Brody, 1979), learned helplessness (Hooker, 1976), and perceived control (Schulz, 1976) relate directly to the frail elderly. Placing family behavior within a theoretical context requires familiarity with sociological, systems, and treatment literature.

One cannot work with the frail elderly without an intelligent understanding of the physical and mental depletions that define their status. This knowledge is essential in any consideration of a total plan of care. When formal training has not been received, the worker will have to conduct a self-educative effort beginning with each specific case encountered. Constant reference to a medical dictionary (for understanding the diagnosis as given) and *Physicians Desk Reference* (for understanding the drugs prescribed to treat it) is the first step. Ongoing consultation with physicians, nurses, and therapists in various areas of specialization will expand on this beginning understanding. This, in turn, can be linked to ongoing reading in the gerontological literature (see list of common conditions in Appendix C).

With time and experience, knowledge about the more common frailities of age and their customary treatments will become second nature. Marked deviations from this picture will arouse concern and the seeking of medical clarification. Comparisons between the functional responses of clients with the same organic diagnoses should arouse further curiosity, questioning, and learning.

Legal issues are increasingly relevant to practice with frail elders. Regulations and judicial interpretations of protective services will be important for those who work with the mentally impaired (Regan, 1977). Those who work in specific locales will note environmental themes underlying the problems of many clients. These must be broadly conceptualized and acted upon; for example, if unsanitary, unsafe, or unavailable housing is the issue, the auxiliary function of the worker dictates work on these areas—work based on understanding and participation in legal processes. While this is too specific an area to be addressed here, local legal aid offices are often a source of information and guidance. Entitlements must be known by all as the provisions of Social Security and SSI, the coverage of Medicare and Medicaid policies directly affect the lives of every elder under care.

Frail elders are often in thrall to organizations. Institutionalized in hospital or nursing home, the older person is intruded upon in every area by the organization. Even in the community, decisions about home care or food purchases may come from other authority. In order to help organizations work for people, the worker must understand the functional properties of organizations, the uses of power, and how change can be implemented and institutionalized (Brager & Holloway, 1978).

In addition to the foregoing, knowledge of the political, economic, cultural, and social framework of the recent past is essential. The personal recollections of the elderly are set on the backdrop of a time quite different from today. Recognition and genuine appreciation of the differences between the past and the present are necessary if the worker is to understand the life history of the client.

Knowledge of ethnic traditions, religious beliefs, and social values found in the population served is imperative. As persons grow older, they tend to place increasing value on the practices of family and country of childhood, even though such beliefs may appear to have been abandoned years before. This is illustrated by the frequent return to a native tongue at times of stress. Understanding the client requires an understanding of the client's perception of the world, however different from the worker's own.

Specific Knowledge

Specific knowledge is related to the individual client and situation. Construction of the *study, assessment, and plan* for the frail elder is a complex process, involving the integration of many factors. Knowledge of biological, psychological, socio-economic, and cultural aspects of the individual's life, the environmental context in which they occur, and the transactions between them is essential. Identification of the areas of depletion, the adaptive processes already in motion, and existing strengths to be mobilized must be extracted, comprehended, and organized so that problems can be identified and a plan of intervention formulated. Relevant information from the past, specifically the resolution of developmental tasks and reactions to prior life crises, may also be required.

The interrelatedness of many problems experienced by the frail elder often results in a labyrinth from which it is difficult to untangle discrete elements. A hairline fracture may be experienced without pain and interpreted by the client as simple fatigue. The older person who presents as confused and in need of protective services may be overmedicated and capable of more independent functioning if drug usage is reviewed and adjusted. The depressive episodes that follow rapidly on the heels of physical illness and physical problems that develop at times of stress are further illustrations. Lack of socialization may be related to the relationship capacities of the individual, but it may also be related to absence of opportunities in the environment. Nothing can be taken at face value.

Behavior must be viewed in sociocultural as well as psychodynamic terms in assessing the frail elder. Ethnic customs and dietary habits are obvious manifestations. Attitudes toward the roles of adult children, medical care, and institutionalization are other areas in which client preferences must be viewed within a cultural context. The fact that so many of the very old in America today are immigrants to this country or members of minority groups who retained or reverted to old customs makes this a special consideration for the frail elderly. This understanding is necessary not only in assessment but also in engaging the client in the helping process. It may offer clues as to the best point of entry into a case or the service provider most likely to be accepted by virtue of cultural similarity.

Study data gathered at a time of crisis (when most frail elderly are first seen) may lead to a faulty assessment and inappropriate case plan. Although elderly clients in crisis typically evidence deterioration in many areas, the worker must recognize that even in the very old there is hope for restitution and compensation and the reemergence of coping capacities. The well-functioning eighty-five-year-old who is hospitalized for a hip fracture may well be able to return to her own home following a period of rehabilitation. However, if family sees this as the first step in an inevitable irreversible decline and the elder in her weakened state agrees, the worker may be asked to arrange an institutional placement. Months later when the client is capable of maintaining herself more independently, there may be no home to which to return.

Simplistic assessments and plans, based on inadequate information or an abbreviated process, can only be avoided if the worker allows enough time for all salient aspects to emerge. Seeing the elder several times, at least once in his or her home, may be necessary. A month's time will usually yield an understanding of what is fluctuating and what is enduring in the client situation as well as allow opportunity for the gathering of needed information from other sources. When demands of the setting are such that this is not possible, the assessment and case plan should be recognized as limited by the sparseness of the study data and not overreach it. The making of irrevocable decisions at a time of crisis is a prime example of such overreaching.

That the scope of the study and assessment is determined by the uses to which it will be put is an obvious, but frequently overlooked, consideration. Information is not gathered indiscriminately, but rather as part of a problem-solving process. It is gathered strategically to fill in what is missing and needed to adequately understand the situation faced by elder and family.

At the present time, functional measurements are widely used to describe the elder's physical, mental, economic, and social resources; the capacity to handle activities of daily living; and the areas in which help is needed. Two such instruments are the OARS, Older Americans Resources and Services (Pfeiffer, 1977), and PACE, Patient Appraisal and Care Evaluation (DHEW, 1982). To the extent that standardized functional assessment tools promote service provision and delivery, they are valuable for the social worker. Community as well as individual need can be documented, and resource allocation planned accordingly.

There are, however, many gaps in necessary information unfilled by current tools. Qualitative information is lacking. Unaddressed are the past of elder and family, the relative importance of current abilities and disabilities, and the way in which these interact. Also omitted is the idiosyncratic dynamic interplay between the client and environment so germane to adaptation. For these reasons, the following outline of a *study, assessment, and plan* is offered as an adjunct, to be used in part or in full with standardized forms.

The Worker-Client Relationship

The formulation of the *study, assessment, and plan* is the core of the auxiliary function model. When elder, family, and worker are equally involved in the process, all are well on the way to problem resolution. By the same token, in some cases trust in the worker may have to be established before a *study, assessment, and plan* can be carried out. This is particularly the case with the mentally impaired or suspicious client.

A mechanically conducted *study, assessment, and plan*, following a questionnaire or prescribed interviewing schedule without regard to engaging the client, sidesteps a unique opportunity for implementing the auxiliary role. It can come immediately into play with a focus on the elder's state of depletion and needs for help in adaptation or relating to another area of concern to the client. In addition to engaging the client on an affective level, the worker may undertake concrete steps during the study, such as arranging a medical examination, which in and of itself is an important auxiliary intervention.

Chapter 4 discusses in detail the interviewing skills required to engage the client, compile necessary information about the elder's situation, clarify and redefine the problem, and begin to evolve a plan with the client. Process has been arbitrarily separated from content in this text, although in reality they are intertwined. Our purpose is to underscore the necessity for a documented empirical approach—a written organization of the information gathered and the worker's impressions and rationale for present and future interventions.

The following outline of the *study, assessment, and plan* is directly related to the auxiliary function model: gathering information about the extent of client depletions and losses, the adaptations made reciprocally by client and environment in the present and past, auxiliary resources and roles required by the client and their availability in the total field, the worker's formulation of the problems, the goals to be achieved, and the necessary steps involved.

If the social worker is the only professional involved in assessing the frail elder's situation, a great deal of additional information may have to be gathered in terms of functional and health care needs. When the worker is fortunate enough to be a member of a multidisciplinary evaluation team, focus on issues directly relevant to implementation of the auxiliary function will supplement input from rehabilitation and health care professionals. The *study, assessment, and plan* is outlined on page 34. The following sections spell out each of the components in detail with a case example.

THE STUDY

Overview

The overview presents a brief description of the case as initially viewed by the worker and contains information usually gathered in the first interview. It describes the elder and/or family as they initially present themselves and their problems. It sets the direction for further inquiry as well as offering basic demographic data and cites the number of contacts made by the worker and

OUTLINE OF STUDY, ASSESSMENT, AND PLAN

1. STUDY
   A. Overview.
      (1) Presenting problem and precipitating event.
      (2) Referral Source.
      (3) Client profile (face sheet).
         (a) Age, sex, marital status, race, religion.
         (b) Family constellation.
         (c) Socioeconomic and cultural influences.
         (d) Environmental influences.
      (4) Client and family behavior in interview situation.
      (5) Professional contacts and consultation arranged.
   B. Depletion and Losses.
      (1) Primary: physical and mental.
      (2) Secondary: social and economic.
   C. Current Adaptation (Restitution, Compensation, and/or Accommodation).
      (1) Individual functioning.
         (a) Activities of daily living.
         (b) Problem-solving capacities.
         (c) Affective and interpersonal behaviors.
      (2) Environmental Functioning.
         (a) Physical surroundings.
         (b) Family: resources and problem-solving capacity.
         (c) Service organizations.
         (d) Other informal resources.
   D. Previous adaptation.
      (1) Developmental and situational crises.
      (2) Life-style.
      (3) Family exchange patterns.
2. ASSESSMENT
   A. Summary of Study.
   B. Interpretation: Reformulation of Problem.
3. PLAN
   A. Long Range Objectives.
   B. Short Range Goals.
   C. Social Work Tasks.

other professionals. The overview serves to organize the worker's approach to a case and provides the reader with the preliminary background necessary for understanding the ensuing sections of the study.

This is a self-referral to the senior center social worker by Mr. Marshall, eighty-three, who was seeking nursing home placement for his seventy-nine-year-old wife, due to the fact that she was becoming increasingly difficult to care for. He learned of the social worker's services through a center newsletter. Clearly in conflict about the move, he had spent a sleepless night following an angry scene with his wife who was reportedly both confused and incontinent.

Mr. and Mrs. Marshall are a black couple, originally from Alabama, and married for sixty years. The husband is a former postal employee now retired for eighteen years. His wife is a former part-time sales clerk who retired with her husband. They are supported adequately by a government pension and Social Security. For the past three years the couple have lived in a public housing project for seniors after the neighborhood they had resided in all their married years had been razed. Devout Baptists, the Marshalls have not attended church since moving to their new home and have no contact with their neighbors.

The couple have two middle-aged married sons, a lawyer living in Atlanta and a businessman living in Chicago. They visit their parents a few times a year and talk with them weekly on the phone. There are six grandchildren, but no other close family members. Mrs. Marshall's sister, who lived nearby, died one year ago.

One office visit with Mr. Marshall, two home visits with the couple, and one telephone call to each son (with the Marshalls' permission) were conducted for the purpose of assessment and planning. A medical examination was obtained for both Mr. and Mrs. Marshall who had not seen a physician in many years. A psychiatric examination and nursing consultation were also arranged for Mrs. Marshall.

Mr. Marshall appeared quite frail in the interviews. Although he seemed alert and socially appropriate, he was openly distraught that he could no longer manage on his own. In interviews, Mr. Marshall appeared at times angry and at times quite tender toward his wife, who appeared physically well cared for, confused, ingratiating, and inappropriately cheerful and unconcerned about their circumstances.

The source of the referral, presenting problem, and precipitating event as well as the client's initial behavior provide a wealth of important information. A self-referral, such as in the Marshalls' situation, suggests a readiness on the husband's part for some kind of help. When clients are not self-referred, immediate questions arise about their knowledge or view of a situation and the need to involve them as quickly as possible. This is the case when families seek help without the elder's knowledge.

The problem as initially presented clues the worker into the elder's perception of and current adaptation to the situation. Mr. Marshall viewed the problem as his wife's and, as is often the case, presented the problem in terms of a proposed solution (immediate placement of his wife in a nursing home.) The precipitating event, however, a piece of information usually not difficult to elicit from clients, immediately throws additional light on the problem. In the Marshalls' case the immediate precipitant, a sleepless night following an angry scene with the wife, defines the problem as a mutual one.

Demographic data are also usually readily available. In the case of the Marshall couple, preliminary information was already known. As residents of the housing project in which the senior center was located, the living situation was deemed modest but safe and comfortable. As the ethnic, financial, and cultural characteristics of the population were familiar, the problem presented could immediately be placed within a framework of norms, reasonable expectations, and available resources. In the Marshalls' case, the fact that the previous neighborhood they had lived in for many years was in a black community while their present one was predominantly white suggests problems of fit in the new neighborhood and the absence of formal and informal supports. It also suggests the desperation Mr. Marshall must be feeling to reach beyond his ethnic mores and seek agency help in institutionalizing his wife, rather than resolving it within church or family.

Demographic data usually overlap face sheet data, which should be supplemented as necessary. In the application form used by this agency, space was provided for "health care affiliation." The fact that Mr. Marshall left this blank was interesting in view of the existence of obvious medical problems. Other fact sheet data such as age, marital status, and the presence of family members are always significant. With this baseline of factual data, salient issues emerge and unanswered questions in areas needing exploration become clear.

It is important that client behavior in the interview situation be described early in the study since it offers valuable clues to understanding the problem and in working with the client. The behavior of Mrs. Marshall suggested the possibility of serious impairment and emotional problems. In Mr. Marshall's case, his personal pride, distraught condition, obvious frailty, and apparent ambivalence toward his wife were noted. They quickly alerted the worker to the fact that this was a jointly shared problem.

Before proceeding further with the study, the worker should have a list of questions that need to be answered. Later information may negate the importance of these questions and many new questions may emerge, but much valuable time is saved if full advantage is taken of the knowledge gained in the first interview and summarized in the overview. In the Marshalls' case, the following questions would be asked:

1. How have the Marshalls managed in the three years since they left their old neighborhood and church?
2. What was the impact of the sister's death?
3. Why are the sons not more involved in the present crisis?
4. What has been the nature of the marital relationship over the years in view of the present tensions?
5. Why does Mrs. Marshall view her problems inappropriately?
6. Why have the Marshalls apparently not had medical care, particularly in view of their present condition?

Current Depletions and Losses

The highlighting of depletion and loss in the auxiliary function model necessitates that this issue be confronted early in the study if possible. It usually serves as the focal point for engaging the client. There are some elders, however, who do not wish to focus on this aspect of their situation immediately or who may try to avoid the subject indefinitely.

Skillful interviewing and timing are of paramount importance here. In the case of Mr. Marshall, who was a self-referral, the discussion of the subject although a painful one was possible from the beginning. Past health history, if attainable, is an important baseline.

Primary Depletions

The health problems of Mr. and Mrs. Marshall apparently first appeared in old age. The husband and later his wife responded openly to an exploration of their current depletions and losses, at which time they expressed willingness to undergo necessary medical examinations if arranged by the worker. Mr. Marshall, in fact, seemed quite relieved, and was able to then talk about the death of his sister-in-law who had been an important support and his regret that he had not kept his sons abreast of the situation.

Psychiatric and medical examinations revealed that Mrs. Marshall's major problem was the presence of moderate organic brain disease manifested chiefly by confusion for time but not place and person and a form of urinary incontinence that could be controlled by frequent use of the toilet. Visual impairment attributable to glaucoma was also detected and eye drops prescribed. Neither of the couple was aware of this sensory defect.

Although Mr. Marshall had not originally sought help for problems other than the care of his wife, he too was suffering from physical problems. Medical examination revealed arteriosclerotic heart disease, sensorineural hearing loss, and beginning evidences of osteoarthritis. Mr. Marshall was surprised at the presence of these conditions, particularly the hearing loss.

Secondary Depletions

Social losses for the couple included the change in their own relationship, the death of Mrs. Marshall's sister, who was an important caring figure, and relocation from their old neighborhood and church, where they had received a great deal of emotional and social nurturance. Urban relocation had forced this move three years ago. While they greatly missed their religious and church activities and former neighbors, they moved nearer to the sister who filled part of the void for them. Providing much concrete care for Mrs. Marshall and emotional support to Mr. Marshall, her death one year ago was experienced as a major loss.

Once the subject of depletion and loss was "on the table," the study proceeded rapidly into other areas. Mr. Marshall was no longer alone with his problem. A medical examination and nursing consultation were accepted by the couple on the condition that the worker would make all arrangements. This was done including transportation in the Center van and the accompanying attendance of a paraprofessional, on this one time only basis. Although Mr. Marshall could probably afford a taxi, he was reluctant, now as in the past, to make such an uncharacteristic expenditure and had some trepidation about making the trip alone. Thus the worker lent an auxiliary boost to the medical expedition while recognizing that in better times in the future he might be able to handle it independently.

Often older people, such as the Marshall couple, attribute remediable health problems to "just old age." Fear, ignorance, or a lack of access to medical care contributes to unidentified medical problems that could be restituted or compensated for, improving the psychosocial situation considerably. It was a surprise to the Marshalls that they suffered from sensory deficits, a discovery all the more significant in that difficulties with sight and hearing contributed greatly to the interactions between them.

The gathering of the above information is often time-consuming and, particularly in the case of the Marshalls who had not received medical attention for some time, a process involving much planning and coordination. The affective and instrumental components of the auxiliary role of the worker had come immediately into play with her acknowledgement of Mr. Marshall's current manifestation of depletion and need for medical care. His flagging energies to cope with the overwhelming situation were buttressed by the worker's infusion of energy, hope, and availability to make the necessary arrangements.

As the biological and psychological components of the frail older person's situation are so crucial, every study should include information from health professionals already involved as well as suggest those of other disciplines who should be approached where possible. Knowledge and understanding of the organic and functional aspects of each diagnosis in regard to prognosis, medication, rehabilitation possibilities, custodial needs if any, and anticipated effects on the elder's total life situation must underscore all planning.

The social worker's responsibility for collecting these data is most common in a community context where the client presents concrete service needs, but may also be true in institutional settings. In the absence of administratively sanctioned mechanisms such as team meetings for information sharing and decision making, the worker is usually charged with integrating the viewpoints of all involved professionals into the study. Determining the weight to be given to each view requires that the worker neither overrate the expertise of his or her own profession nor slavishly follow the dictates of others but rather think each case anew prioritizing among multiple needs.

As with many frail elders, cumulative social losses left a void for the Marshalls that could not be filled in their present situation. Attention to the dates and chronology in which losses occur adds greater precision to the study. In this case, the loss of neighborhood and church could be borne while one significant other, the care-taking sister, remained available. The study already determined that the auxiliary role of the worker was to fill in not only for the overtaxed inner resources of Mr. Marshall by handling the concrete aspects of obtaining health care but also to supply some of the affective responsiveness previously provided by the sister. The worker's appreciation of their religious beliefs and openness to discussing them thus filled a void vacated by the sister, validating to the Marshalls the functional areas of their life worth preserving.

Finally, it is important to note those situations in which depletion and loss are apparent but not real. Depressive reactions, for example, are often mistaken for conditions of frailty and impairment. Specificity in delineating areas of dysfunction, using outside consultants as necessary, minimizes this risk.

Current Adaptation

This section of the study summarizes the worker's observations and findings regarding the way in which the client is adapting to depletions and losses. Situations of restitution, compensation, and successful accommodation are noted as well as problematic accommodations. The measuring of strengths as well as weaknesses is an important component of the study.

Elder Functioning

This couple's accommodation to the wife's deterioration has been characterized by her increased dependence and the husband's increased efforts on her behalf since the death of the sister. Mrs. Marshall's dependent behavior does not match her demonstrated ability to perform the activities of daily living. While she is unable to shop or cook, she can dress and bathe herself and do light household tasks. Her major problem seems to be that of incontinence if she is not directed to the bathroom frequently during the day. There have been no efforts to restore functioning in this area.

It is demands in this area as well as with other tasks and her confusion that seem most burdensome to the husband. He has recently stopped reading aloud to her from the Bible (which she enjoyed) although they continue to listen together to church broadcasts. Mr. Marshall performs all activities of daily living, although his energy level has waned considerably and he tires easily. His hearing loss, which is not obvious in the interview situation, does prevent him from hearing his wife call from another room.

The problem-solving efforts of this couple have been limited to a day-to-day effort to survive. There has been ignorance and/or denial of their depletions, which has made it difficult for them to identify and understand the problem. Mr. Marshall has been able to respond to the worker's focus on their depletions, but Mrs. Marshall continues to minimize their importance.

Since her sister's death, Mrs. Marshall has become more querulous and complaining to her husband. Her presentation to others, however, her sons and the worker, is quite different. She does not view herself as having any problems and is quite comfortable in her present circumstances. In contrast, Mr. Marshall sees his wife as worse off than she actually appears to be. His discussion of her problems is colored by a great deal of anger coexisting with painful outbursts that "after sixty years it has come to this" and expressed fears about his own deterioration.

Environmental Functioning

The sons have established very separate lives from their parents, although they call regularly and feel a responsibility to their parents. Little has been shared with them about their mother's deterioration and their father's weakened condition. When told by the worker about their mother's and father's plight, the sons were greatly surprised, for the father consistantly provided an "everything under control" facade and did not seek their support, even at those times when the sons visited.

Other informal supports are nonexistent in the present life space of the Marshalls since the move away from their old neighborhood. Their only contact with an agency came with this self-referral to the nearby senior center that had sent Mr. Marshall a regular newsletter informing him of social work services.

Their internal physical surroundings are pleasant and safe and easy to negotiate for both husband and wife. The sister had arranged furniture, handrails, and other devices in the home that are helpful to both of them. While shopping is accessible in their neighborhood, which is also relatively safe, Mr. Marshall has found it increasingly difficult to manage this task and orders groceries over the phone from a small relatively expensive neighborhood store.

Information about the ways in which clients manage activities of daily living helps measure the extent of depletion and physical and mental deficits, yet tells us far more about their adaptive capacities. Clients with similar degrees of depletion and loss can function quite differently. In the case of Mrs. Marshall, efforts at restitution and compensation seemed minimal. Accommodation by others to her condition was the chief form of adaptation.

Even when obvious life-threatening consequences do not result, the individual elder who cannot recognize and mourn the depletion and losses he or she has experienced often makes a premature or ineffective accommodation to a situation in which restitution or compensation is possible. On the other hand, denial may serve a useful function for the frail in intractable situations, helping them endure what cannot be changed.

Certain restitutive and compensatory adaptations may have been utilized by the Marshalls if they had been more aware of and less denying of their depletions; remediation for hearing loss, medical care for his heart condition, and her incontinence being cases in point. Mr. Marshall had attempted, but failed, to compensate by overextending himself and his resources (ordering groceries over the phone). While restitution is often not possible, the compensatory capabilities of the frail elderly are extraordinary as well as their ability to successfully accommodate to losses and impairments. The auxiliary role of the worker or family is called into play as with the Marshalls when these adaptive efforts are nonexistent or unsuccessful.

It is crucial to identify problem-solving capacity, affective and interpersonal behaviors, and factors in the environment that lead to dysfunctioning. The varieties of defenses that are utilized by younger people at times of stress are less available to the frail elderly due to depletion and loss. Anxiety can be overwhelming for the frail or totally denied, as in the case of Mrs. Marshall. When viewed in conjunction with her cognitive impairments, this suggested to the worker that Mrs. Marshall would have difficulty in addressing her problems and not be able to participate fully in planning.

In considering the current adaptation of the frail elder attention must be paid to both the objective and subjective realities; or to put it in another way, differentiation must be made between the external press of outside factors and the internal stress caused by reactions to them. The individual experience is then viewed against a professionally accepted consensus of what falls within the expected or typical range of responses in given circumstances and what is evidence of breakdown in either the individual or the environment. With Mrs. Marshall, we see a discrepancy between her dependent behavior and demonstrated ability, making it essential to separate out the reality from its distortions, the cause from the effect. This is a crucial distinction in planning interventions.

The important role of sensory deficits, often undetected, may be overlooked. Does Mr. Marshall always hear his wife call? Does Mrs. Marshall always see her way to the bathroom? Practical questions raised by the discovery of these impairments in the study process yield further areas for exploration before the objective reality and its potential for change can be determined.

Exploration of the extent of coping capabilities, often neglected by problem-focused workers, can yield important information and prognostications for the future. Although Mr. Marshall's problem-solving capacities were taxed under stress, they appeared basically sound, as suggested by his search for aid and readiness to follow through. While Mrs. Marshall showed significant deficits in cognition and capacity for problem identification and solution, her dependence on care giving figures facilitated the worker's exercise of the auxiliary role.

The interplay between the client's coping capacities and environmental factors adds another ingredient to understanding the current adaptation. Information is needed about the extent to which physical and social environments are abetting or detracting. Chapter 9 elaborates on the environmental factors that impinge on the lives of the frail elderly. They include the immediate physical surroundings, barriers and supportive features. The social environment—formal and informal—must be evaluated in terms of the ability of significant others to perform the auxiliary role and the social and recreation sources available. The service environment, if present, must be identified and evaluated in terms of coordination required. In the Marshalls' case, this environment was depleted until the time that Mr. Marshall reached out to the social worker. The worker was the first on the scene and, with her efforts in arranging medical care, began to establish a service environment for the Marshalls. If she had been called in later, initial consultation with other providers to prevent duplication and coordinate efforts would have been essential.

Previous Adaptation

Past patterns of adaptation are often, but not always, indications of what can be expected in the immediate future. In the case of the elderly, some situations are being faced that have never been encountered before. The frail elder is also facing these situations at a different stage of life marked by the weaknesses of age and the strength of experience. Nevertheless, past patterns may identify potential strengths obscured by frailty as well as predictable difficulties.

Developmental and Situational Crises

The past was discussed easily by Mr. and Mrs. Marshall, who looked back on former days as a happier, more carefree time. Prior to the death of the sister and their own depleting conditions, they noted no unanticipated crises in their life. Mr. and Mrs. Marshall reported having been "happily" married for sixty years; the first marital stress having been experienced only recently. Mrs. Marshall an attractive, fun-loving woman always lived under the protective arm of her husband and sister. After each birth, she became more dependent on them. Neither of her sons experienced her as being closely involved in their upbringing, and their move to other cities when they were adults was not protested by the parents. Gracious and charming in a childlike manner when talking about her past, Mrs. Marshall's recollections dwelled excessively on possessions and on people in terms of what they could do for her, concerns that seemed to be present from early life.

Mr. Marshall, on the other hand, focused more on his ability to manage and cope throughout life and never to be a burden on his sons.

He was pleased to expand on how he had risen through the ranks in the Postal Service, and obviously he had been a steady and valued worker. He was the main bread-winner, although his wife worked occasionally. He was proud that he could be the mainstay of the family, a chief support for the sons, and the protector of his wife. He apparently was very close to both sons and very involved in their parenting since they were born. The sons viewed their father as always dependable and proud, but since leaving home in early adulthood, contacts have been limited to several visits a year and regular phone calls. Mr. Marshall's adjustment to retirement appeared to be a good one until evicted from his old neighborhood. The death of Mrs. Marshall's sister seemed to have had greater impact on Mr. Marshall than on his wife, for Mrs. Marshall transferred her demands immediately to her husband, yet he had no one nearby to turn to.

Life-Style

The life-style of the Marshalls had been, up until five years ago, largely centered around work and church activities. Mrs. Marshall was reportedly greatly admired for her contributions to church life, particularly in the choir. After his retirement, Mr. Marshall was also able to participate more in church activities, particularly task-oriented projects. The Marshalls have always prized their privacy and have had few visitors in their home. Their social life centered around church activities.

Family Exchange Patterns

For most of their married life, Mr. Marshall has been his wife's protector and caretaker, a role later shared with the sister. He has been gratified by her attractiveness, vivaciousness, talent, and great affection and admiration for him. Apparently the sister also found the relationship with Mrs. Marshall to be emotionally gratifying in spite of her dependence.

The sons, on the other hand, upon achieving adulthood have been alienated from their mother and while dutiful in their telephone calls and visits, have not been dependable figures in her life. Their concerns have focused more on the father, whom they openly admire and love, but who has not sought out their support. In terms of their own immediate family responsibilities, Mr. Marshall proudly speaks of them as having been hard working, devoted husbands and fathers.

For the Marshalls, past history was more readily accessible than discussion of current problems. In addition to revealing much about their life-style and family exchange patterns, it uncovered a lifelong pattern of exaggerated dependence on Mrs. Marshall's part and proud self-reliance on the husband's part until he became frail and more dependent on the sister. This suggested to the worker that while the behavior of husband and wife had been mutually reinforcing for many years, that modest changes might be possible in their interaction given a different set of expectations.

While a general health history is essential and useful to the health care team, more important to the social worker is the way in which help and other crises were handled by the client. If the critical episodes of life were handled fairly smoothly and independently, this might be a pattern that can continue. If the client reacted poorly to life crises and losses or became much more dependent at these times, this pattern might have to be respected. As noted, new patterns of behavior can arise for the first time in response to the onslaughts of age. In the case of the Marshalls, earlier crises appear to have been few. Of note is the fact that the birth of the children resulted in increased dependence on Mrs. Marshall's part and a stronger role for Mr. Marshall.

Prior occupation and avocations are important clues to adaptation. Not only a prime indicator of past socio-economic status, the work histories of many aged reveal capacities and coping skills. Mr. Marshall's capacity to attend to details was an asset in his work, although it also contributed to his present dilemma. For Mrs. Marshall, who depended so much on the admiration of others, loss of socialization opportunities now mattered more than inability to perform housekeeping tasks.

The past history of the family, particularly in terms of patterns of reciprocity and parenting, may disclose the extent to which younger family members will assume the auxiliary role. In the Marshalls' case, nurturance and support were apparently provided primarily by the father, whom the sons continue to view as strong and in control. While lack of response on the part of the sons to the current plight of their parents is due in part to the father's failure to communicate his needs, past patterns of family exchanges may also play a role. Alienated from their mother since early adulthood because of her reportedly inadequate parenting, the Marshall sons would not be expected to respond enthusiastically now to her needs. Yet, in view of a longstanding strong relationship with the father and their own present life stage, the sons could possibly become an important resource. Past history can offer important clues to the type of family interventions to be made. In the case of the Marshalls, the husband's pride and wish to remain in control would be a primary consideration.

The life-style and past habits of aged clients are important pieces of information since planning for the frail elderly at times involves dramatic changes in their living situation. While the elderly have the capacity for changing old life-styles, depletion of cognitive and sensory abilities may limit new adaptations. Caution or rigid adherence to old ways is a frequent and understandable response. A person who has relished privacy all his life, like Mr. Marshall, might feel assaulted by having to share a room in a nursing home. His capacity to utilize the sister's help, however, suggests that services cautiously introduced might be brought into the home.

THE ASSESSMENT

The assessment is a bridge between the study and plan; an ordering and interpretation of the information gathered to date pointing to the problems that must be addressed and a course of action. The problems identified in the assessment should be justified by the data collected. At the same time, it is open to amendment as new information is uncovered and as circumstances change.

Brevity and precision are desirable in the assessment, challenging the worker to conceptualize the situation at the appropriate level of abstraction and thus define the problem(s) as accurately as possible. The assessment of the Marshall's case illustrates this point.

Summary of Study

Mr. and Mrs. Marshall, ages eighty-three and seventy-nine respectively, are a long-married black couple, self-referred by the husband for the ostensible reason of placing his wife, whose confusion and demands for toileting and other types of personal care were overwhelming and angering him. Mr. Marshall, a proud man and former postal employee, earlier in life had handled the self-absorbed behavior of his wife with relative equanimity. Increased frailty on the part of both and mental and physical impairment on the part of the wife had been ignored and denied, but once recognized and accepted opened the door to needed medical care. Mr. Marshall's image of self-sufficiency is not inflexible, having until a year ago depended on the emotional and practical support of a now deceased sister-in-law. This projected image, however, has kept at a distance two interested adult sons, who have historically not responded to the demands of their self-absorbed mother. A sparseness of family support and socialization extends to the new neighborhood, which lacks the cultural and religious resources that have sustained the couple in the past.

Interpretation

The Marshalls have made tenuous adaptation to the decrements and losses of advanced age. The contributing problems are (1) psychological: a life-long exaggerated dependence on part of the wife now exacerbated by frailty and impairment, overprotectiveness by the husband, which has reinforced the wife's behavior and sapped his own flagging energies, and a tendency toward denial of frailty on both their parts preempting effective adaptive strategies and use of health and social resources and (2) social: inadequate neighborhood resources in terms of meeting cultural, support, and religious needs and depleted family resources since the death of the sister.

The severity of these problems is tempered by Mr. Marshall's demonstrated coping capacities over the years, his commitment to his wife, and the presence of sons who express filial responsibility if not a desire for increased closeness with the mother. With encouragement, Mrs. Marshall might function a little more autonomously and/or deflect some of her dependency needs onto someone other than her husband. The potential for maintaining this couple in the community for at least a time is, therefore, good given an increase in affective and concrete supports and small efforts on the part of Mrs. Marshall. Mobilization of these resources, including the sons, should parallel time-limited counselling with the couple, who are still confused about their situation and their expectations of each other.

The presenting problem couched in terms of the need for nursing home placement has now been reformulated by the worker. Broader systemic, dynamic, and developmental issues are at stake. Conclusions are tentative, for there are still unknowns: the capacity of the sons to fill the auxiliary role, which appears limited by distance and past patterns; the availability of other social resources that have yet to be tapped; the couple's ability, tested over time, to utilize services; Mrs. Marshall's capacity for modest restitution.

The assessment should be shared with the clients in a nonjudgmental, understandable fashion and reactions reached for. In this case, the Marshall couple recognized things were better when "Sister Betty" was alive, could agree that no one could take her place, but that other helpers might perform her roles. Other elders might disagree with a worker's assessment, seeing the problem in quite a different light. If so, more discussion is necessary until agreement is reached. Mrs. Marshall, for example, disagreed adamantly that she could do more for herself, but was willing to talk further with the worker.

Labels such as "Alzheimers," "senile," "neurotic," etc. should be avoided in the assessment, since they can become self-fulfilling prophecies and limit the view of the total situation. By the same token, anecdotal and/or oral reports, which proliferate in congregate settings, may obscure important patterns. Adherence to a written assessment buttressed by study data serves as a corrective to overgeneralizations and unsubstantiated impressions.

THE PLAN

The plan addresses the situation defined by the assessment. It summarizes long-range objectives and short-term goals in maximizing adaptation. It identifies who will fill instrumental and affective components of the auxiliary role, what resources in the service network must be tapped, and what interventions are required by the worker.

Long-range objectives set the parameters of the problem-solving framework and become the critical ingredients of the worker-client contract. They are the outcomes that the worker and client are seeking to achieve and should be specific enough to be understood by the clients and lend themselves to empirical validation at an appointed time in the future. Overgeneralized and open-ended objectives such as "psychosocial adjustment," "environmental fit," or "stable adaptation" are desirable but impossible to measure.

Unless specified, such objectives undermine the credibility of the worker's plan and certainly have no meaning for the client.

Long Range Objectives

For the Marshalls, these objectives might be as follows:

(1) Auxiliary support and in-home services to maintain the Marshalls in their present situation with less strain and upset as expressed by Mr. Marshall.

(2) Restoration (to extent possible) of Mrs. Marshall's functioning in relation to bladder control and lessening of her demanding behavior.

(3) Linking of couple with outside organization — preferably church — for some socialization and religious activities and concrete support as needs arise; i.e. shopping.

(4) Increased supportive communication between sons and couple so that sons may share auxiliary role.

Long-range objectives should not be overly ambitious for the frail elderly. Their needs and wants may be realistically modest yet important to them. Small progress in each of the stated objectives may be sufficient. For the Marshalls, remaining in their apartment was all important. For Mr. Marshall, help with daily routines and emotional respite so that he felt less upset and tired were important. The worker, in addition, sought to involve the sons more, reestablish linkages with a church, and improve Mrs. Marshall's functioning. While these were not the stated objectives of the couple, she obtained tentative agreement from Mr. and Mrs. Marshall to pursue them.

Short-term goals address the continued engagement and exploration necessary for achieving the long-term objectives. These should be very specific and time limited and determined by the worker's knowledge and experience. Fear that such time limited goals might be too restrictive with frail clients is not uncommon. Yet without such yardsticks, the worker may not be able to measure the impact of his or her efforts. If goals are not achieved within a specific time frame, then the situation is reassessed and the worker's interventions examined. New or continued goals and objectives can then be established.

Short-Term Goals (6 months)

There are seven goals:

(1) Preparation for in-home care: focus worker-client relationship with Mr. Marshall on sharing burdens and accepting his own legitimate needs for help and care (2 months).

(2) Preparation for in-home care: beginning acceptance by Mrs. Marshall of her own real limitations and her husband's needs and motivating her to function more independently (6 months).

(3) Introduction of a home-health aide twice a week (2 months).

(4) Identification of community supports, particularly the church.

(5) Establishment of regular medical care and transportation for that care (immediately).

(6) Family meeting with sons (4 months).

(7) Introduction of rehabilitation specialist for Mrs. Marshall (5 months).

In the case of the Marshalls, short-term goals were established within a six month framework to enable the worker to prepare the couple for services and rehabilitation. While homemaker-home health aide services and medical care were immediately needed, the couple's difficulties in the past in facing their problems warned the worker to move ahead cautiously, particularly with Mrs. Marshall, who was reluctant to shift her demands from her husband. Per the request of Mr. Marshall, a family meeting was postponed until a time when he himself could call such a conference.

The final section of the plan focuses exclusively on direct social work interventions necessary for implementing goals and objectives. Since the auxiliary function model of social work practice seeks to involve others in planning, the implementation of goals and objectives may also be shared. Specification in advance of the worker's use of self and the reason for this involvement is an important ingredient in time utilization and measurement of input. In the case of the Marshalls, their difficult situation called for heavy worker involvement at least in the first six months. In other less complex cases, family members who live nearby might implement goals with help from the worker.

Social Work Tasks (6 months)

The tenuousness at this juncture of other social supports, the geographical distance of sons, the difficulties between the couple, and the condition of the wife suggest long-term but gradually modified auxiliary involvement of worker.

(1) *Weekly one and one-half hour visits are to be made to the Marshalls, continuing until one month after semiweekly homemaker-home-health aide services are instituted. Semimonthly visits to continue until rehabilitation instituted with Mrs. Marshall.*

(2) *Several phone contacts and one family meeting with sons.*

(3) *Collateral contacts with medical clinic, home health aide, and rehabilitative specialist to commence immediately until service regularized and Mr. Marshall and/or sons able to coordinate and supervise.*

(4) *Search and contact with neighboring church or senior services for volunteer help in shopping, transporting, and socialization.*

Following this six month period the social worker, in conjunction with measuring the achievement of short-term goals, reviews the necessity of her involvement. In the case of the Marshalls, the worker was able to reduce her contacts to bimonthly ones because of the emotional and concrete support given by the homemaker-home-health aide, increased attention from the sons, and a linkage with a local church auxiliary. Her own contacts served mainly the purpose of reinforcing Mrs. Marshall's attempts to do more on her own.

WHEN NURSING HOME PLACEMENT IS A REALISTIC OPTION

In the case of the Marshalls, the nursing home option was quickly forgotten by the husband when he experienced the support and helpfulness of the worker. He and his wife were very committed to remaining in their home in spite of their problems. Mr. Marshall's impulsive move toward nursing home placement was later seen as an act of desperation.

In other situations, it can be far more difficult for all to reach a decision about institutional placement. The complexity of the situation, the availability or unavailability of decent nursing home care, and the fears and anxieties of client and family may cloud the situation.

When the plan involves nursing home placement, it is irrevocable unless there are sufficient financial and social resources that enable the elder to return at a later time to the community. Therefore, the study and assessment process, both in terms of obtaining accurate information and working closely with client and family in examining all options and alternatives, may need to be extended.

If there is indecisiveness about nursing home placement, the plan developed by the worker may be indefinite in terms of long-range objectives, but it should include further exploration of the total situation in tandem with the elder and family. When all options are explored and the resources of family and client are carefully measured, a decision can be made. Chapter 10 on problem-solving with the family addresses this process in detail. The same type of problem-solving, in which all options are explored, can be carried out with the elder who has no family and must make this decision on his or her own.

The *study, assessment, and plan* serves as an organizing and conceptual tool for the social worker and to some extent for clients and families. It most certainly provides the basis for the contract upon which social worker and client agree. The *study, assessment, and plan* should also be the core of the case record. This clarity and precision lends itself to the scrutiny of others and measurement of achieved goals over time. The establishment of time frames in the execution of goals is not an unrealistic endeavor. Rather, it sets a parameter by which the social worker can measure the effectiveness of interventive efforts.

The following chapters describe the practice skills needed for making a *study, assessment, and plan* and continuing ongoing work. The arbitrary delineation we have made between substance and process is not always consistently held, and materials in the following chapters will be helpful to the worker in conducting a study and making an assessment and plan, just as the material covered in this chapter serves as important guidelines for intervention strategies.

Chapter 3

THE SETTINGS FOR SOCIAL WORK
PRACTICE WITH THE FRAIL ELDERLY

A CONTINUUM OF CARE

Social work services to the frail elderly and their families are scattered among a number of different organizational settings. Ideally, these settings offer a rational continuum of care, ranging from services that address crisis situations confronting the frail elderly and their families in the community to "round the clock" institutional services for the severely impaired. In practice, this is rarely the case. Gaps and inequities in the service system are a commonly experienced frustration for worker and client. Nevertheless, understanding of the continuum and all the settings for practice is essential to the social worker, regardless of where he or she is located in the total scheme.

A large portion of social work services to the frail elderly falls within the parameters of *long-term care*, which "refers to one or more services provided on a *sustained* basis to enable individuals whose functional capacities are chronically impaired to be maintained at their maximum levels of health and well-being" (Brody, 1977). The auxiliary function model of social work practice with the frail elderly, however, extends beyond long-term care to short-term, time-limited interventions where the condition of the elder sufficiently improves and/or where formal and informal auxiliary services, other than social work, can sustain the permanently impaired older person at maximal functioning.

A sharp look at the long-term care system is in order, for it is crucial to the well-being of frail elders and families and affects social work practice, time-limited or extended. Chapter 9, which examines the service environment of the elderly, explains this issue in depth. The point to be made at this juncture is that long-term care services are oriented to institutional care and sorely lacking a comprehensive coherent and coordinated system of community care. The disproportionate availability of institutional resources is related to a paucity of quality community-based health and social services even for those elders and families who can purchase them. Furthermore, within institutional settings, social services are limited.

Under these circumstances, the auxiliary function model of practice can be a difficult one to operationalize, for there is a shortage of settings in which social workers are employed and resources that they can garner on behalf of their frail clients. Existing services may be splintered and beset with irrational eligibility requirements. Social work staffing, if present at all, may be meager. Furthermore, these settings may have organizational goals dissonant with social work goals. Regardless of disarray or shortages, however, the social worker has a responsibility to provide skilled services.

Here and there, with great variation from community to community and state to state, organizations exist or are sprouting up that are consonant with an auxiliary function model of service. They include family service agencies, senior centers, nursing homes with rehabilitation and daytime programs, and home care programs, which attempt to meet the needs of the frail elderly and their families before problems become overwhelming. Some other more traditional settings, such as the acute hospital, are updating social services to the frail elderly and their families. In these, the worker's task is facilitated.

This chapter examines the social worker's auxiliary role as differentiated by practice setting, which can generally be divided into health and social service organizations. The acute hospital setting, perhaps the single most important entry point for the frail elderly into the system of long-term care, will be examined first followed by the nursing home, the rehabilitation center, and community health (and mental health) settings, including home health care services. Social services settings include family service agencies, public welfare agencies, home care agencies, senior centers, offices on the aging, and case management or "channeling" agencies. Day programs and congregate housing for the elderly will each be treated separately. Chapter 9 will return to a discussion of these settings within the context of the service environment that affects the adaptation of the frail elder and strategies for change that can be undertaken.

HEALTH SETTINGS

While all health organizations support the physical, psychological, and social well-being of their patients, the operational goals that govern their operations clearly focus on medical and skilled nursing care. The priority that health settings give to the psychosocial problems of their patients is varied and most commonly reflected in the administrative hierarchy and staffing patterns.

The most important differential feature of social work practice in health settings is that of interdisciplinary collaboration. The auxiliary role of the worker consists of bringing psychosocial concerns into clear focus and interpreting individual needs. Since primary attention to medical and skilled nursing needs is organizationally sanctioned, an important feature of the social worker's auxiliary function—to be present through the medium of the professional relationship to fill in for those activities the client could and would do for him or herself only as long as the client is unable to do so—is providing the interpretive linkage between the frail client, family, and health professionals.

The Acute Hospital

Hospitalization is always a time of crisis for clients and their families. For the frail elderly, it can also be a turning point in their lives. The disabling effects of the conditions that led to their hospitalization in the first place such as catastrophic illness (stroke or hip fracture) may strike previously well-functioning elders, rendering them far less able to manage on their own; or an acute illness such as pneumonia may strike with the potential of being the "straw that broke the camel's back," leading to rapid intersystemic changes. Hospitalization for the frail elderly may also result from gradual or rapid deterioration, such as in cases of malnutrition.

From a social perspective, hospitalization of a frail older person is often the occasion for family decision-making in regard to the elder's future. Family intervention, if thwarted in the past by the elder, may now appear to be sanctioned by the crisis situation. The crisis situation itself may demand action that had never been considered before by either the older person or his or her family. Thus, hospitalization may provide families and other community caregivers or agents with the opportunity needed to make what they consider to be better plans for the elder. The acute hospital is the site of important decision-making, frequently influencing the rest of the client's life.

The utilization of the hospital for this social function, while often unavoidable, does pose certain dilemmas. The first of these is that the client whose life is being planned is in poor condition for participation in the process. Problem-solving may be left to others. The second is that the acute nature of the setting permits only a short planning period for what are usually long-term plans.

Social work practice in the hospital setting is aimed at redressing the psychosocial dislocation that occurs for clients and their families when illness strikes. The profession has gone far in establishing standards for social work practice in hospitals and has identified the elderly as a high-risk population requiring social work services (Berkman, 1981). A significant portion of this practice is part of "discharge planning," which is defined as "a centralized, coordinated, interdisciplinary process that ensures a plan of continuing care for each patient" (American Hospital Association, 1980).

Discharge planning fulfills individual and institutional objectives. Ideally, it is the result of rational problem-solving that focuses on continuity of care for elders in recognition of their right to retain control over their lives or share control with caring others. For the institution, discharge planning enables compliance with bed utilization requirements that ensure economical use of the facility. In practice, institutional and individual objectives in the discharge planning process often collide with each other, for "appropriate" bed utilization often places severe time constraints on planning.

Older patients in acute care hospitals make few requests for social services. Referrals are usually made by a staff person or member of the patient's family. A "Classification of the Social Needs of the Hospitalized Elderly Patient" (Berkman & Rehr, 1972) has been developed and is being used in some hospitals as a screening mechanism for early identification of high risk patients and families who need social services. In the meantime, hospital social workers must rely on interdisciplinary referrals and their own outreach efforts to ensure that needy clients are reached in time for effective planning.

There are several differential features of social work practice with the frail elderly in the hospital setting. In addition to the previously mentioned need for close interdisciplinary collaboration with the health care team (and sometimes a separate discharge planning department) whose goals may be at odds with the worker's, it is necessary to work with elders and their families at a time of great emotional, physical, and social stress—even confusion and disorientation. Often there is heavy pressure to resolve planning issues that have been pending for a long time. The frail older person's debilitated condition underscores the auxiliary role of the social worker—to establish a relationship that enables options to be clearly spelled out to the client and his or her opinions and desires transmitted to staff and family.

Another differentiating factor is the severe time constraint often placed upon the helping process. This time constraint poses a tremendous challenge to skilled social work intervention. The psychosocial assessment, as with the medical diagnosis, is difficult to carry out in situations of such fluidity and crisis. It is further complicated by the symptomatic vagaries of the very old. A rushed process also precludes establishing the kind of relationship necessary for effective assessment and planning. Under these circumstances, insuring an appropriate time span for the planning period becomes an extremely important social work intervention. Even in cases in which it is clear that restitution and compensation are impossible, the wide variety of options for maximizing the client's long-term accommodation demands discharge solutions that do not "burn bridges" behind the client and family. Nursing home placement combined with giving up of the client's home in the community is a prime example of such precipitous action.

There are circumstances, of course, in which a frail elder and family have made a long-term contingency plan in the event of a disabling illness. More often, however, particularly in the cases that come to the attention of the social worker, plans have not been made, and hospitalization is truly a time of family crisis.

Mrs. Morris's daughters had been worried for some time about their mother's increasing inability to care for herself and inordinate dependence on them. Yet the elder had consistently refused to consider living anywhere but in her own home. When she broke her hip and was hospitalized, the daughters consulted with the social worker regarding nursing home placement and their desire to close the mother's home and use the period of hospitalization as a period of transition. Several interviews with Mrs. Morris convinced the worker that taking over in this manner would only enrage and further deplete her. She advised the daughters to include the mother in all planning efforts, but waiting until she was stronger. To this end, they decided to maintain her present home and place her in an extended care facility for several months.

Skilled Nursing and Intermediate Care Facilities

The term "nursing home" here is used to describe skilled nursing and intermediate care facilities, government designated terms for two levels of reimbursable care. Historically derived from homes for the aged, these institutions have developed into medical facilities owing to the growing number of sick and impaired older people and extensive Medicaid funding.

Many nursing homes, particularly long-standing voluntary facilities, have maintained their identification as "homes." While meeting nursing and medical standards, they usually place strong emphasis on the psychological and social needs of their clients, who are referred to as residents not patients. Their administrators may be social workers. Other nursing homes resemble minihospitals, institutional in ambiance and sparse in the psychosocial features of care.

Social service functions, as spelled out by some state regulations, are sufficiently broad so that the social worker can, given other supports, participate in intake, residential services, and discharge planning. The standards of social work practice in long-term care facilities, adopted by the National Association of Social Workers in

1981, provide a suitable framework for the exercise of the auxiliary function model.

If intake into a nursing home is a sanctioned social service function (and it often is not), the social worker has an excellent opportunity for intervening effectively at a time of crisis for clients and families. A full study and assessment can be conducted. The frail elder and family can be helped to review the steps along the way that led to the desire for nursing home placement. They may clarify if their decision is the correct one, or they may simply be exploring options for the future. In either case, the auxiliary function model dictates that the social worker provide clarification, information, and guidance in keeping with client need, whether or not placement is the end result. When intake into a nursing home overlaps with discharge from a hospital, the pressure felt by the hospital social worker can be transmitted to the nursing home setting. Again, biding for time can be an important task for the social worker. Arranging for admission on a temporary trial basis may be a viable solution.

Enlightened nursing home administrators welcome this client-oriented approach, for it helps prevent inappropriate admissions that can become problematic in the future as well as smoothing the traumatic impact of entry. Through rational problem-solving, encouraged in intake, the auxiliary function of the social worker is exercised, maximizing participation of all clients, including the mentally depleted, in the planning process.

For the frail resident whose placement is a permanent one, the challenge to the social worker clearly extends beyond work with individual residents and families. One-to-one interventions are essential in the early days of placement in order to establish a working relationship and amplify the psychosocial assessment. Thereafter, with the exception of highly problematic individual and family cases, social work interventions must be directed at the group and organizational levels. An environment that provides participatory and socialization opportunities, privacy, and recreation tailored to the individual needs of residents and families must be developed or sustained. New roles and opportunities for involvement need to be carved out to enhance the family's usefulness.

Economics alone necessitates organizational and group interventions. The social needs of all residents and families are paramount in a nursing home, since long-term adjustments must be made. The utilization of extensive social work relationships to fill social voids in the lives of some residents is a disservice to the resident and to others. If a resident can establish a good relationship with a social worker, he or she can be helped to do so with other staff, residents, and volunteers, who can be sensitized to the resident's deficits and play an auxiliary role, if necessary. To continue in such a manner with the social worker perpetuates a dependence which can be met elsewhere within the system.

It is only the resident with severe relationship problems to whom the social worker should be directing ongoing individual attention. The auxiliary role of the social worker suggests the monitoring of certain residents closely due to continuing depletions and maladaptive behavior.

Owing to several illnesses, Mr. Sand was blind and incontinent upon admission to the home. He was hostile to most staff and disruptive with other residents. His own mistrust and shame were so severe that he refused to socialize or even eat with others. The social worker painstakingly established a fragile relationship with him over a period of two months, tentatively approaching him on the most concrete of issues. His anger and disruptiveness finally abated, and although he still preferred to remain distant from others, his overall adjustment improved. The social worker, however, continued to visit with him once a week, serving as an outlet for his angry feelings and as mediator with other staff.

The differential features of the auxiliary function model in the nursing home include interdisciplinary collaboration and client/family problem solving, common to the hospital. In addition, it includes intervention at the group and organizational levels to ensure a sustaining environment for long-term care residents, with individualized auxiliary assistance restricted to those for whom adaptation remains problematic.

Rehabilitation Centers

Some nursing homes are also identified as rehabilitation centers, providing both short and long-term accommodations. Others are freestanding rehabilitation centers usually serving the disabled of all ages. For the elderly, short-term institutionalization for rehabilitation purposes is one of the services more readily covered by Medicare (in contrast to nursing home care beyond 100 days, which only Medicaid subsidizes).

The social worker's auxiliary role in relation to the rehabilitation resident is clearly targeted to discharge planning. The explicit purpose of a rehabilitation stay is geared to a return of previous physical and social functioning or accommodation to a different level of functioning that will sustain the client at home or in a modified environment.

Since the goals of a rehabilitation setting are so closely aligned to the auxiliary function model, the social worker's view is usually consonant with that of the interdisciplinary staff. The major interpretive function takes place beyond the institution. Family, neighbors, and community agencies must be readied to sustain the frail elder upon discharge (Silverstone, 1983).

Community Health Settings

Community health settings include outpatient clinics, emergency rooms, health maintenance organizations, home care agencies, and hospice settings. Referrals to the social worker in these circumstances are usually made in relation to chronic problems of the frail elderly and their families. An immediate crisis situation may be looming, but the time constraints are far less severe since the client is situated in his own home in the community. The pressure of family and neighbors, of course, may be intense.

Outpatient Clinics

Referral to the social worker in a clinic, including the emergency room, is usually for the purpose of dealing with a difficult personal or family problem, intervening in a poor living situation, or acquiring needed services. Not infrequently, the social problem is defined in advance for the social worker, whose auxiliary function demands a much closer scrutiny of the situation than was made heretofore.

In recent clinic visits, eighty-year-old Mrs. Shea, under treatment for high blood pressure, had appeared to grow confused and disoriented.

Referral was made to the clinic social worker for nursing home placement. Having ruled out an acute brain syndrome, the physician saw the medical problem as the beginning stage of senile dementia and the social problem as an inappropriate living situation for a woman so impaired. Mrs. Shea, depressed and anxious over her deteriorating condition, was not able to partialize and articulate the problems she was facing. The social worker, after several interviews, was able to determine that the major problem faced by Mrs. Shea was an inability to organize household chores and finances. Otherwise, she felt she could continue managing in her own home for the present. This opinion and wish of the client was interpreted to the referring physician and plans for community social services made accordingly.

The differential aspects of social work practice with the frail elderly in the outpatient health setting involve clarification and interpretation of the social problem as mutually defined by client and worker. As in all health settings, the interpretive function of the social worker is an important one, insuring that the elder's preferences are heeded. In the community health setting, it can be the crucial link to the social service system.

Community Mental Health Centers

The mental health setting introduces the social worker, most often, to those elderly who have been discharged from state hospitals and are being treated on an outpatient basis. A few settings offer mental health services, diagnostic and therapeutic, to elderly with more recent psychiatric problems. The social worker is usually viewed as an important member of the health care team, whose interventions are as crucial to the well-being of the patient as medical ones. Counselling and/or environmental interventions are viewed as legitimate. Thus, the worker has sanction, although not necessarily time, to implement the auxiliary role for frail elders with mental problems.

There are of course mental health settings that provide only the most perfunctory of services and give low priority to elderly patients, particularly those with organic impairment; but even under these circumstances, auxiliary tasks can be performed. The typical clinic office visit format for the frail client is not appropriate.

Home visits must be part of the mental health worker's repertoire of interventions.

Home Health Care Settings

These settings include a variety of community and hospital-based agencies under voluntary, public, and proprietary auspices that offer nursing and personal care services to patients in their homes. Owing to the reimbursement features of Medicare, these programs for the frail elderly are largely tied into time-limited, posthospitalization care, although some clients may purchase on-going services. Social workers are employed by some agencies usually as consultants for intervention in highly problematic cases. However, a fuller involvement is now being advocated by the profession; the action of the 1981 National Association of Social Workers Delegate Assembly is a case in point.

In most settings, psychosocial functions are shared with the nurse. This offers an opportunity for the social worker to demonstrate the effectiveness of the auxiliary function model. One of the important advantages of this setting is its social goal: to maintain the frail in their own homes. While other health settings claim holistic goals, time or funding constraints may limit agency efforts to a focus on the cure of disease or amelioration of symptoms.

SOCIAL SERVICE SETTINGS

In contrast to health settings, social service settings are administered by nonmedical personnel and have an explicit primary goal of meeting social needs (although health care needs are often attended to by ancillary medical staff). In theory, social service settings provide a congenial host environment for the social worker who assumes the primary role of assessing, planning, and coordinating care. On a practical level, social service agencies or settings for the frail elderly are not in abundance, tend not to employ professional social workers and, thus, while philosophically supportive of the auxiliary function model, often cannot provide the backup resources needed for effective interventions. Agency capacities, of course, vary greatly, but the fact is that government funding for social services to the frail elderly under

Title XX of the Social Security Act and Title III of the Older Americans Act is limited now and will probably be further reduced in the future.

Those social service settings that do have sufficient resources can provide easy access for frail elderly persons into the long-term care system or short-term help at times of crisis. For the frail elderly in dire circumstances, such as the protective service case, the worker can intervene in nonthreatening ways. Thus, an important differential for the operationalization of the auxiliary role of the social worker in social service settings is an opportunity to be the first professional on the scene and set the pace for establishing a relationship and ongoing problem-solving. The worker also assumes primary responsibility for recognizing unidentified medical problems of the elder and making appropriate referrals for health care.

Family Service and Other Voluntary Agencies

Some family service agencies in various localities throughout the country provide social work and other support services to the frail elderly. Most operate under voluntary auspices. Often they have on staff teams of homemakers, home health aides, and nurses to supplement the efforts of the social worker in maintaining an elder in the community. Family agencies are particularly tuned into an intergenerational approach to the needs of the frail elder. With the considerable resources these agencies often have to offer, social work intervention can be gratifying and fruitful. Some voluntary agencies have developed special service units specifically targeted to the needs of older clients and their families.

The auxiliary role of the social worker can reach its full potential in such settings. Not only are the goals of the agency consonant, but resources are on tap for providing necessary support. The professionalism of these agencies also enables social workers to conduct a full psychosocial assessment to ascertain the restitutive, compensatory, or accommodating potential of clients within the perspective of the individual's life history and the current or projected environment. Time is allowed for the development of a working relationship particularly in situations where client reluctance may be very high.

The agency had been alerted by the police to the plight of Miss Elliot, an eighty-year-old recluse, whose large collection of dogs and cats was becoming a nuisance to the neighbors and a potential health hazard to her. On her first visit, the worker knocked on the door and left her card. After several more visits, she was able to lure Miss Elliot to the door and spoke with her through it. It took three more visits until the worker was admitted, and this was accomplished with the offer of a basket of Easter eggs.

The skills that these agencies have developed in working with the family as a whole can also be particularly conducive in mobilizing informal resources as well as external formal resources; but just as social problems can be obscured in the health setting, so can medical or psychiatric problems be overlooked in the social service setting. A depression suffered by an old man might be interpreted by the family as prolonged mourning. Viewing the problem as a psychosocial one, the family might seek out a counselling agency. Yet the problem may have physical roots that must be addressed. It is incumbent upon the social worker to be alert to situations of depletion in the frail elderly and direct the family and elder to other than psychosocial explanations of behavioral problems. Whether or not the medical condition of the elder is a factor, a physical examination is important for anyone in this age group. The social worker who is familiar with the wide variety of restitutive medical interventions that might be possible will greatly enhance the help offered to client and family.

There is another differential aspect of the auxiliary role in comparatively resource-rich social service agencies—the tendency to do too much for the elder. The obvious depletion of frail clients evokes an immediate desire for replenishment on the part of the helping person. With resources readily at hand, they may be offered before sufficient thought is given as to whether or not the client really needs as much help as is available. It is far more difficult for the social worker or family members to withhold support services when they are available than when they are not. Yet, a crucial balance must be maintained between giving too much and giving too little care to the frail elderly, who, in common with younger persons, need some challenge in order to maintain optimum functioning levels.

Public Welfare Agencies

An abundance of resources does not characterize most public welfare agencies that provide social services to the frail elderly. Many public welfare agencies have homemakers and home health aides on their staffs. However, as intake cannot be closed, they are often overwhelmed with long waiting lists and unable to provide what is considered to be a modicum of services. It is usually in the public welfare agency that the social worker will come face-to-face with the protective service client. At times, protective service clients are served by voluntary social service agencies or even health settings, but it is the public agency that has ultimate responsibility for those whom no one else is able or willing to help.

The pressures on protective service workers to take actions that will safeguard the elder can be intense. For the social worker attempting to carry out the auxiliary role, the dilemma posed by being asked to take control away from clients, even to the extent of guardianship, is painful and real. In such an adversary climate, the interpretive role of the social worker is important to forestall precipitous action. In the case of severe mental impairment, temporary or permanent, the worker must move in quickly to begin establishing trust and an understanding of the needs and wishes of the client. This must then be interpreted to those who view the frail elder's behavior as deviant. If they can be helped to understand that medical and social interventions may improve the situation and persuaded to allow a sufficient trial period, legal action may be forestalled.

Public welfare settings in the United States are quite different from the publicly supported personal social service system found in England. The separation in the 1960s of casework services from income maintenance dealt a particularly severe blow to the provision of social services to the frail elderly. This was underscored by the federally administered SSI program of 1974. Before that time, early case finding was possible, as old people receiving public assistance were assigned an investigator who visited regularly, if sparingly, and so could identify emerging problems.

Regardless of the resources available in the public welfare

agency, some believe that the elderly client receives short shrift in comparison to younger clients. There is merit to this argument in view of the fewer number of professional social workers who choose to work exclusively with the elderly. However, in any setting that encourages skilled professional practice with the old, age integrated services need not be deleterious to the elderly and can be advantageous from a family perspective.

Offices on Aging and Senior Centers

The Older Americans Act amendments of 1975 provides monies for the provision of social services to the elderly under Title III. These include a variety of locally distributed services, such as homemakers, home health aides, and chore services. The delivery of these services, while limited in nature, varies greatly from community to community. Some offices on aging provide their own social services. Others contract with voluntary agencies. Senior centers, which are supported by the Older Americans Act in some instances, draw on Title III funds and provide social services to those older clients who are frail.

The staffs of these programs are often not social work professionals. However, an important cadre of workers has entered the aging field from a variety of backgrounds, relating well to the social work model of service. More professional social workers are entering the aging network via administrative and supervisory roles, a welcome trend that can be supportive of the auxiliary function model. While resources are limited, there is a strong commitment in these agencies to maintain older people in the community. Unlike public welfare agencies, morale is usually high, and the increasing ability of these agencies to reach out to the frail elderly in the community is exemplary.

The differential features of implementing the auxiliary function model in offices on aging and senior centers are similar to those of other social service agencies, particularly in regard to the need for establishing linkages to the health care system. Since these agencies are mandated to serve the elderly, they may overlook the needs of the family. Caution must be exercised to consider and involve the informal network as appropriate.

Case Management Agencies

A new crop of agencies that provides case management services targeted to the frail elderly has developed, supported in the main by federally sponsored demonstration grants. Some of these programs are short-lived and have not been extended beyond their demonstration contracts. Others have been continued under separate auspices. The most recent and ambitious thrust of the federal government, the "Long-Term Care Demonstration Project," more popularly known as "Channeling," is being carried out in eight states from 1981 to 1985.

Each of these demonstrations reflects a heightened government interest in the chronically sick and impaired elderly due to their increasing numbers and heavy reliance on expensive nursing home care. The central focus of most of these agencies is on case management. While there is no uniform definition of case management, it generally encompasses the tasks of assessment, formulating a case plan, coordination of the necessary services elders need to remain in the community, monitoring of these services, and adjusting them as the needs of the elderly change. "Management" is presumably not of the person but of services which, in some situations, case managers can "purchase" through Medicare and Medicaid waivers.

There is controversy over whether case management is a social work function. The reality is that other professionals, particularly nurses, are performing case management functions. An issue more pressing than professional auspices is the affinity between case management and the auxiliary function model. This issue is highlighted by the fact that counselling is not uniformly accepted as a function of case management. Some agencies view counselling as a service to be contracted for by the case manager (Steinberg & Carter, 1983). The worker-client relationship is discounted as a service except for those special cases in which counselling may be needed. Thus, case management and the auxiliary function model can be incompatible, for the relationship with a significant other, which at least temporarily involves the worker, is a crucial ingredient of the latter.

Our view is that case management is a component of the auxiliary function model. It represents several of the instrumental tasks (assessment, coordination, monitoring of services) to be carried out in conjunction with affective tasks. Our model also involves significant others in implementing all of these tasks with the exception of assessment, which remains the province of the professional worker.

There are, of course, some case management agencies that view counselling as an essential component of the overall plan of care and recognize the importance of a helping relationship in the maintenance of frail older persons. These agencies look to the social worker for individualizing and enriching the functional and health assessment. In such situations, the opportunity for exercising the auxiliary role is excellent, enhanced by the worker's access to and control over service resources. Our only objection would be in labelling the dynamic interplay between elder, worker, and significant others as "case management," a term that denotes control and authority of the worker and dehumanization of the client. Whatever the terms used, the social worker in the case management agency, by being alert to the components of the auxiliary function model, can contribute greatly to the development of these important services.

Private Practice

Social workers are entering private practice in increasing numbers and will face more older clients in their caseloads as future cohorts of the elderly and their families, more receptive to psychotherapy, seek help. Present generations of the frail elderly and their families are now seeking help with planning for crisis situations. Some social workers are actually specializing in geriatric practices. They have been particularly helpful to families who live a distance from their elderly relatives. Some work with physicians who are seeking help for their elderly patients.

Social workers must be prepared if they work with frail elderly clients and their families in the private setting to extend their boundaries. Home visits are necessary as well as ongoing work with collaterals: physicians, psychiatrists, and home care agencies. For the salaried worker in an agency setting, this is not a problem. The private practitioner, however, must give this consideration in his or her time allocation and setting of fees. Demands on time may also extend beyond regularly scheduled appointments, as emergency situations requiring an immediate response occur with some frequency. For this reason, the worker who develops such a practice can rarely do it successfully on a part-time basis unless he or she can be "on tap" for timely responses.

Day Programs

Day programs for the frail elderly are not widely established in this country. Usually referred to as day-care or day hospitalization, these programs include a repertoire of therapeutic, rehabilitative, recreational, and nutritional services scheduled in the daytime hours for the elderly who live in their own homes in the community.

Progressive nursing homes have begun to convert part of their facilities for day programs for the elderly, utilizing built-in rehabilitative, nursing, recreational, and dietary services for these nonresidents. A few programs are free-standing or found in senior centers. Specialized transportation is a critically important feature of these programs due to the impairments of the participants.

Day programs offer the frail elderly the diversion, socialization, and stimulation sometimes missing in the isolation of their own homes, as well as a cluster of necessary services under one roof. In addition to these features, a compelling argument for day programs is the respite offered to those families who can maintain and care for their frail relatives in the evenings and weekends, but need daytime support, or those families who simply need relief from the burden of twenty-four-hour a day caring.

The social worker is a necessary feature in day programs for the frail elderly, for it is often only within the context of the helping relationship that the frail elderly will risk involvement. Leaving their own homes, if only for part of the daytime hours, will be viewed as hazardous by many in spite of the poor adaptation they are making and the need for an improvement in their lives.

The auxiliary function of the social worker in day programs, when trust has been established with the client, is largely one of challenge and encouragement while providing the necessary support to sustain involvement. The home environment must also be assessed and consideration given to the need for prosthetic devices or homemaker services. Monitoring of the home environment is also essential if discharge from a day program is contemplated.

Congregate and Domiciliary Housing

Congregate housing refers to private or publicly subsidized housing for the elderly in which additional services are provided. These usually include one or two meals per day served in a central dining room and recreational activities. In some instances, social and nursing services are available. Congregate housing to date has largely served the independent elderly. Thus, at one time social and nursing services were not seen as necessary. More emphasis of late has been given to housing for the physically disabled elderly. In view of this interest and the fact that the elderly do not always remain independent, social and nursing services are being given higher priority.

Domiciliary homes are congregate facilities directly subsidized by local welfare authorities. They resemble boarding houses more than apartment complexes. In some situations, residents do not even have a private room. Services are provided, but they are usually sparse and inadequate. Domiciliary homes have recently come under much public criticism for housing mentally impaired elders who require more care.

The role of the social worker employed in or serving congregate housing and domiciliary facilities hinges on detrimental changes in the elder's adaptation. The study and assessment are a critical feature of the worker's activity, as well as interventions that can help sustain the client's present living arrangement if adequate and prepare for relocation if not. The fear of eviction is a strong component of the frail resident's situation. If his or her condition requires nursing home placement, the relationship with the worker can ease a painful transition. If relocation is not necessary, the relationship enables practical planning to take place.

This chapter has described the various settings in which social work with the frail elderly and their families is practiced. It has attempted to provide a realistic portrayal of the opportunities for and stumbling blocks to the exercise of the auxiliary function model and the differential aspects of each setting. While the practice principles, as spelled out in this book, would apply in any setting serving the frail elderly, it is recognized that emphasis must be given to some functions and de-emphasis to others as indicated by agency auspice. Crosscutting all of these settings is a basic recognition of the depletions that affect the frail elder — physically, emotionally, and socially — calling for a highly individualized approach with opportunities for restitution, compensation, and accommodation.

SECTION II
IMPLEMENTING THE AUXILIARY FUNCTION: THE WORKER-CLIENT RELATIONSHIP

Chapter 4

THE WORKER-CLIENT
RELATIONSHIP: INITIAL CONTACTS

OVERVIEW

The initial contact is the most significant encounter in any social work setting. It is the occasion when much of the information for the study is elicited, when the assessment is shared with client and family, and when the plan is contracted. It is also an opportunity for effectively initiating the auxiliary role of the social worker, be it temporary or ongoing.

For the frail elder, the first experience seeking help often represents the point of entry into the long-term care system. If the initial contact for the worker is but one of a series for the older person, marking a transfer from one agency or worker to another, the occasion is similarly momentous. As first meetings may well shape attitudes toward and use of services offered thereafter, the different worlds of client need and service delivery systems must be understood and addressed.

In Chapter 1, it was noted that the frail older person generally presents a picture of complex interrelated problems arising out of depletions and losses experienced. When attempts at adaptation are unsuccessful, elder and significant others experience a state of crisis. Turning for help to a professional agency, they often choose the setting that is most convenient or visible—not necessarily the one most appropriate. Furthermore, although problems of the population are multiple and continuous, help offered by service providers is usually discrete and time-limited. As a result, the frail elder often does not continue with the agency in which the initial contact takes place. Because the intake worker's role cannot be

limited to screening for agency service, where client and significant others are first encountered is less important than why.

Applications

Agencies serving the aged often process phone or walk-in
applications with the assistance of receptionists or volunteers.
Selection and training of these gatekeepers of service is essential
to insure that the frail elderly reach the stage of the initial contact.
An on-call professional should be available to consult on crisis
situations. Follow-up contacts should be prompt, and placement
on the waiting list should not occur until need is ascertained. The
frail older person may be ambivalent in the search for aid or too
worn out to keep on trying. In either case, a lack of timely
response to his or her effort may well discourage further attempts
and a crucial opportunity to help is lost.

In the initial contacts, the worker's task is to engage the frail
elder and significant others in the helping process, to explore
where help is needed, and to determine agency and client roles in
obtaining that help. As one cannot assume at the outset that the
client is frail and in need of the auxiliary function, appropriateness
of the model is not considered until the conclusion of the interview
when next steps are planned and the contract is discussed.

ENGAGEMENT IN THE HELPING PROCESS

The Client's View

The relationship between client and worker carries role expectations for each participant. Yet the frail older person frequently
enters the initial meeting with little idea of what part he or she is
to play.

If aid has been sought voluntarily, it is usually a request for
information or concrete assistance. Perhaps the elder has not initiated the contact at all but was designated as "a case" by the staff of a
housing project, senior center, acute care hospital, or long-term
care facility that identified a need for social service or case management intervention. In other instances, a client is brought to the
social agency by family or friends with vague promises of help.

Whatever words the social worker uses to explain the purpose of the contact, older persons are generally puzzled by this first experience. Being encouraged to talk about themselves, expose their feelings, and share with a stranger those personal aspects of their lives hardly shared with intimates places them in a position of vulnerability. Over fifty years ago social workers were identified, if at all, with the poor and outcast of society, a class with which the client is not now eager to be associated. The more recent identification of social work with the mental health profession is no more reassuring. The client may fear he or she is now being considered "a mental case," unable to manage his or her own affairs.

The social worker's emphasis on feelings may also seem strange. When the older person was young, self-discipline and control were the appropriate responses to adversity. In a time when choices were limited or nonexistent, negative feelings were often dismissed as irrelevant, for there was little point in complaining about a reality that could not be changed.

The very words the social worker uses have different meanings to one of another generation who may identify emotion in terms of its overt manifestation. "Anger" might translate to yelling or striking and "depression" to crying. Professional jargon is often the specialized use of a popular word causing greater confusion. "Exploring" and "sharing" lend themselves equally to literal interpretations.

The frail elder may be puzzled or angry when access to a concrete service is contingent on cooperating in a counseling process. In the world of the young, it is not necessary to reveal one's inner life to the rental agent in order to secure an apartment. Yet the admission process to senior housing or a long-term care facility usually requires that clients provide much personal information and accept help with "problems" they do not identify as such.

The social worker is often perceived as an authority figure, with the right to grant or withhold services depending on what information is gleaned about the client. The elder who is aware of this may be understandably reluctant to share information that could be prejudicial.

If not seen as a judge, the worker may nonetheless be grouped with other authoritarian figures such as doctors and attorneys who hear the client's dilemma and offer a prescription or solution. The concept of client/worker mutuality in a problem-solving process is new for most older people, more easily understood through experience than explanation.

In whatever authority role the worker is cast, the response of the client will be a characteristic one to those in power. Because most people who are old today were raised in a tradition that respected authority, negative impressions or doubts of the worker's methods or motives may not be overtly expressed but rather manifested indirectly through lack of cooperation or withholding of information.

Elderly clients usually regard themselves as authorities on many matters ranging from politics and social values to the management of everyday life; and so they are. The young worker may thus seem like a child or grandchild who should be receiving guidance rather than offering it.

Even if the frail elder has sought help for her or himself, some embarrassment may be experienced in having to publicly admit to a private problem. Independent older persons may want assistance only on their own terms—terms that are often in contradiction to the realities of service delivery. The more dependent older person may resent having to participate in an active interview process, preferring to be a passive recipient of care.

Whatever the general or idiosyncratic reaction, any doubts the older person may have about accepting help will be secondary to the fear that in so doing he or she is losing control over his or her life. The dilemma of balancing needs for independence and care, a central dynamic in work with the frail elderly, is usually present and must be addressed during the initial contacts.

The View of Significant Others

Adult children may share the elder's feelings or relate to the situation from their own perspective. The older person is an integral part of a family constellation in which the interdependence of all members may predate the initial contact by over half a century. A range of emotions including love, anger, and connection are universally present between the generations. Recognition of the crucial significance of the family of childhood informs us that indifference and disinterest signal a movement away from a disturbing or hurtful relationship more often than a lack of caring.

Many of the accustomed roles, alliances, and communication patterns of earlier family life are recalled when the adult children are reunited around planning for a parent. In the initial contact, the adult children usually find themselves in a crisis situation in which they are overwhelmed either by a sudden deterioration in their parent's condition or the stress of caregiving over an extended period. They may seek to involve the social worker as they would another sibling. Some may view the worker as a surrogate parent, someone who will tell them what to do, to replace the one who is now disabled. They may see the social worker as a judge of their behavior, responsibility, and devotion, someone who will either find fault or approve or place new burdens on them. Family members may bring fears about uncovering the past or, conversely, a desire to reveal and so resolve it; or they may seek in the initial contact an opportunity to discuss personal concerns that are only tangentially related to the care of the older person.

An accompanying spouse will have unique concerns. Perhaps relief is sought, but the desire cannot be openly expressed, or the reverse is true. Often, the caregiving partner is in greater need than the identified client, or both have equally compelling and contradictory needs which dictate compromise.

Unrelated others, such as neighbors and friends, will have a different agenda that is often difficult to discern at the first meeting. Their degree of involvement and continuing commitment to the client now that he or she is in professional hands will have to be ascertained.

Thus, although the initial contact marks the social worker's formal beginning with the frail older person, significant others, and the problem, it is but one step in a process set in motion much earlier. It should also be remembered that the first call for professional help usually follows unsuccessful attempts to handle the problem independently. Fatigue, anger, and skepticism often follow in the wake of these failures and affect professional beginnings.

Very often, the older person's problems are expressed in terms of proposed solutions. Access to services in the areas of housing, legal entitlements, income maintenance, home care help, medical care, and placement in a long-term facility are among the most common. If the frail elder is unable even to imagine a method of adaptation to the depletions experienced, painful feelings of depression, anxiety, or anger will precipitate the call for help.

Whether or not client and significant others express how they wish to be helped, understanding of common experiences and fears at the time of the initial contact hasten understanding of the specific situation.

Specific Demands

The role of the social worker in the initial contact is more focused than in subsequent encounters. While the worker must be directive enough to gain an overview of the client's entire situation, flexibility is necessary to allow for tangential or unanticipated communications that may carry even greater import. Deciding on the spot what is and is not relevant and interpreting this to the older person and family requires an ongoing balance of empathy and skill.

The worker's responsibility in the initial interview is to focus clearly and directly on the older person's problems: exploring, gathering relevant information for the study, partializing and formulating a beginning assessment and case plan including the appropriateness of the auxiliary function model and its application in the specific case. The worker's concentration on this task precludes acting as advocate, judge, or therapist. During the first meeting, a wide range of material must be covered. The client must be helped to present current concerns as well as significant background data. The social worker must interpret the agency and his or her role. A beginning assessment must be formulated, the older person and informal supports engaged in the helping process, and next steps decided.

With such an agenda, the initial contact requires the knowledge and ability of the most skilled interviewer an agency can provide and a period of at least one hour allotted for this purpose. Nursing home intake offices staffed by clerical persons or information and referral services manned by untrained workers cannot meet this challenge. A wife requesting "a list of homes" for herself and her husband is asking for help that a mimeographed sheet or a friendly hello cannot provide. If only the concrete request is heeded, the opportunity for preventive intervention is lost, perhaps never to be regained.

More than emotional benefits are derived from a skilled initial contact. Correctly evaluating a situation is also cost effective and can often avoid erroneous decision-making and expensive sidetracking by client and caregiver. For example, a request for nursing home placement on the part of an anxious older person and family may mask a number of other needs. Intervention measures that are less drastic than placement may provide appropriate solutions. Similarly, repeated visits to a hospital emergency room may conceal loneliness and anxiety that might also be relieved by less drastic measures. On the other hand, a simple request for homemaker service may well obscure a serious, disabling medical condition. The skilled initial interview may suggest intervention measures that in the long run may help ameliorate the medical problem.

It should be remembered and perhaps verbally stated within the initial contact that there is no "right way," no easy answer. If there were, clients would have found it themselves. Nor is there a definitive plan, one that will cover every future contingency. As circumstances change, revisions are to be expected. There are more choices, however, than most clients are aware of as they enter the first meeting. Some are of interim help, others should be considered long-term goals. Whatever course of action is taken, there will be times when one questions if another plan would have been better. Older persons who choose placement often long for return to their own home. Those who remain independent in the community may regret this choice when unable to receive immediate medical attention. Unfortunately, with older frail clients and limitations of services, the choice may have to be the least damaging rather than the most ideal.

Problems in Making the First Contact

Sometimes a severely impaired older person adamantly refuses to meet with a social worker. Troubled family, friends, or involved professionals may wish to be seen alone to seek guidance or consultation in their struggle to provide care. Although such a service is a legitimate component of practice with the frail elderly, the social worker must not forsake the goal of ultimately making personal contact with the older person and in the meantime underscoring the right to participation in any planning that occurs. Frequently others will define a role for the worker, one that the worker cannot assume. For example, families may ask the worker to assume the role of a friend making an impromptu visit, or they may instruct the social worker on how to carry out professional tasks. Physicians might request financial information, feeling competent to arrange all else themselves.

A labelling of such actions as "manipulative" and a defensive response is unhelpful. The first step in responding to conditions is understanding what generates them. Whether motivated by a desperate need for help, lack of trust in the social worker's ability to handle the situation, and/or ambivalence about sharing the care of the older person with someone else, the concerns of referral sources must be explored before any approach to the older person is considered. What do they expect, fear, and wish to happen if the social worker is put in contact with the elder?

A discussion of their thoughts about this meeting may be followed with an explanation by the social worker of the professional approach to an older client. Together, an introduction to the elder must be tailored that is truthful, calming, and suited to the specifics of the situation.

Rejection of Service

Many practitioners speak of the older person's resistance to service when what is meant is that services are being rejected. The difference is more than semantic. The psychoanalytic strategies vis-à-vis resistance do not necessarily apply to working with the frail elder who refuses the help offered. Assuming that it does, or worse applying the term unthinkingly and indiscriminately, precludes the important search for cause.

Paradoxically, it is often the older person who needs service most who rejects it. The old-old who have lived through much material deprivation may experience their later years as relatively comfortable in contrast to objective assessments of their situation. Not socialized to perceiving free or subsidized benefits as "entitlements," they may stigmatize those who avail themselves of them. American values of self-reliance and independence are often internalized, and are overcome only at times of great need (Moen, 1978).

Extremes of depletion and loss may engender incapacitating anxiety or, as defense, denial that a problem exists. The offer of help may be confused, distorted, or otherwise misunderstood. Conditions of service may be onerous, exacting a disproportionate outlay of time and energy for what is eventually achieved or requiring that the client accept a "package" of care when he or she only wants help in one area. Accepting help may have an idiosyncratic meaning for the frail older person based on personality structure and prior life experience. More often, the elder will share with many cohorts the fear that opening the door to outside help is but the first step in a process of losing control over his or her entire life. Often rejection is not expressed overtly at the outset but rather is manifested later in forgotten appointments or failure to follow through on agreed upon tasks.

It is important that the worker identify the specific cause of rejection within the individual client and not globally attribute it to "self-determination" or "organic mental syndrome." Cases should not be closed prematurely, nor should client feelings be disregarded and services force-fed. The severity of the situation and the absence of other supports will determine the extent of the effort. Time and an individualized approach are essential. The client's anxiety level may have to be lowered or raised (through such techniques as structuring and confrontation discussed elsewhere in the text). The offer of help may have to be physically exhibited as well as discussed. Conditions of service may have to be modified. The individual meaning of accepting help may have to be explored, the client's fear of loss of control openly discussed.

If, after all, the client still says no, the parting should be amiable, with the door left open for further contact. This might involve a number left for the client if an emergency arises or a suggestion by the worker that he or she call within a given time period to see how the client is doing. The expression of continuing worker concern, even in the face of rejection, will be "heard" by clients who often can accept service at a later date when they have tested for themselves the amount of control they possess and can exert or who have satisfied themselves that they have no other options.

Hope

Hope is an ephemeral yet crucial determinent to the outcome of the initial contact and an essential component of the auxiliary function. How does one approach the frail elderly client with hope given the often overwhelming nature of problems and limitations of resources to meet them? First, by recognizing what he or she has already survived and the particular strengths it took to do so. The client who is old today has lived through two world wars and a great depression. He or she may have immigrated to this country as a child or youth, left family behind, and learned a new language and culture. Often parents and siblings died prematurely, and early years were fraught with separation and upheaval. Later, he or she may have lost spouses or children. Generally, work was not at an occupation of choice, but rather at whatever was available at low wages. Health care may have been unsophisticated or nonexistent, yet the elder survived epidemics and catastrophes that claimed less hardy cohorts. Homemaking, childbearing, and childrearing were accomplished without the technology of today. Not all clients survived because of positive attributes and endearing personalities. Many survived because of precisely those qualities that antagonize family and caregivers today, but the fact and the way in which they coped is available to the worker as evidence that they can do so again and as clues as to how this may be accomplished.

However limited options may appear, there is always choice. The frail, most depleted client may yet have crucial decisions: perhaps whether or not to undergo surgery, enter an institution, or condone the alternative life-styles of grandchildren. In so doing, he or she still is able, with the auxiliary help of the worker, to act as a functional member of society. The quality of daily life, however onerous the constraints, can generally be improved.

The worker who understands this will have little difficulty conveying hope during the crucial initial contact and will be prepared to go more than halfway in engaging the client. The frail older person who feels at the end of the road may not, at first, believe that anything or anyone can help. An infusion of the worker's spirit and belief is often the auxiliary boost needed to get things rolling.

DETERMINING WHERE HELP IS NEEDED

This stage in the initial interview is crucial to the study and assessment. Information must be elicited about the wide variety of issues discussed in the second chapter. If frailty and impairment appear to be a serious condition for the elder, the worker will be determining the capability of significant others to perform the auxiliary function.

Preparation

Preparation for the initial contact begins with a study of the face sheet data, which contains information from referral sources, or a written application. Sparse though this may be, it offers valuable direction to the knowledgeable social worker. The age, ethnicity, marital status, and living arrangement of the older person will raise questions and hypotheses. Medical and financial information, where available, provides valuable preliminary clues regarding anticipated problem areas and possible alternatives.

The number, relationship, location, and involvement of family members, neighbors, or friends (or the absence of these) is significant. Is there a next of kin or responsible relative? Who is the person to be contacted in an emergency, and does this seem a logical choice in view of existing supports? Who is the referral source, and what is the expectation of service?

Information on client need as it relates to agency service is usually present and warrants close attention, especially when it appears at the outset that there is little congruence. As agency structure and function shape the service offered, the worker whose responsibility is evaluation or the provision of limited service might also give some preliminary thought to transfer and referral possibilities and how a smooth follow-up can be obtained.

With a baseline of factual data, the social worker can construct a framework for study of the frail older person, family, and situation before the first meeting.

Mrs. Cohen, an eighty-four-year-old, European-born Jewish woman was referred by the emergency room doctor to the hospital social service department for placement in a nursing home. Her admitting diagnosis was congestive heart failure and organic mental syndrome. Since admission, accompanied by a neighbor, she had refused solid foods and behaved in a confused and suspicious manner. Background information indicated that Mrs. Cohen had been widowed a month earlier and had one daughter who lived nearby.

The social worker, preparing for initial contact on the basis of this limited information, was struck by many unanswered questions. Familiar with the relationship between congestive heart failure and transient episodes of confusion, the worker wondered if the organic mental syndrome was acute or chronic. Knowledge of the process of grief work raised questions about the client's response to the recent loss of her husband, the possibility of a reactive depression, and the role, if any, this played in the current episode. With cultural sensitivity, the worker noted that the client's refusal to eat could be based on adherence to a kosher diet the hospital did not provide. Awareness of the importance of family relationships raised questions about why a neighbor rather than the daughter was turned to in time of emergency. Last, the fact that the doctor, rather than Mrs. Cohen, had requested placement made her question whether Mrs. Cohen had been informed of the referral and if she agreed with the doctor's opinion.

Even in a center, walk-in clinic, or storefront where the first knowledge of the client is at the moment of meeting, some preliminary preparation is possible. If the ethnic, financial, cultural, and health characteristics of the population served are generally known, the individual problem of the client can be immediately placed within the framework of norms, reasonable expectations and available resources.

Aware of salient issues and unanswered questions, the social worker can move purposively into the initial contact with an idea of the areas to be explored, whether or not they emerge spontaneously.

Openings

Whatever the site or circumstances of the first meeting, the social worker begins the initial contact by introducing him or herself and briefly stating the format of the interview. With a client who is previously known in a congregate setting, the issue of confidentiality must be specifically addressed at the first meeting and fears allayed. Having peers know he or she is receiving help may be an embarrassment for the independent older person. The client who is transferred from another agency or worker can be anticipated to have feelings about it that should also be explored.

When the client is not self-referred, the social worker begins by stating who has involved the elder and why, immediately reaching for client reaction. There is a fine line between outreach and intrusion that must be respected. It should be clear that if at the end of the initial encounter the older person wishes no further service, this desire will be respected. In cases where the social worker is required, through agency mandate, to continue with an involuntary client, this too should be addressed. It is dishonest and destructive to give the elder the illusion of choice if actually there is none. The worker must be continuously alert to nonverbal and veiled cues of anger from the older person and respond to the doubts that frequently arise about the helping process.

In the initial encounter the social worker seeks to understand the problem; the client seeks to know what can be expected in the way of help. Clients are entitled to know the use the worker will make of their communication before they are encouraged to speak. At the outset the worker does not know and can say so. The wish to help and the need to understand more of the situation before venturing what form this help will take can be honestly stated. Beginning "where the client is" assumes literal significance when seen out of the traditional office setting. The client's status either as homebound, a patient in an acute care hospital, or resident of long-term care and the concomitant stresses of each situation must be taken into account whether or not the client presents them as a problem. (Chapters 6 and 8 discuss this at greater length.)

Sometimes the client insists on beginning with questions that the worker cannot answer without further information and understanding of the situation. In such cases, there are usually a few factual questions that can be answered initially that satisfy the client's need for immediate feedback. However, it is unwise to recite agency policy or services offered before understanding the client's need or view of the situation. Services to the frail older person must be individually tailored if they are to be useful. While observing and listening to the client, the social worker must be attuned to ways in which the older person's need and available services can be suitably blended.

For the impaired older person, the very preparation for and participation in the first meeting may involve a considerable expenditure of energy and departure from normal routine, as well as generate considerable anxiety. The social worker's recognition of this is usually appreciated. Talking about such superficialities as the weather or the setting is sometimes a helpful prelude to the first interview. It puts the client at ease while allowing him or her time to size up the setting and the social worker.

Eliciting Information

Observation and Listening

The social worker begins the initial contact by encouraging the frail older client to tell his own story in his own way, even when the case is well documented by the case record or transferring worker. The worker-client relationship is forged in this first sharing.

Wherever it begins, the older person's story is a rich tapestry of interrelated themes from past and present. Tragedy, comedy, and minutiae may be blended in one narrative. Presenting problems can seldom be dichotomized as emotional or concrete. They are interrelated and must be conceptualized and handled as such. Watching and listening to frail older persons can be a difficult experience; there have been so many irrevocable losses, and there is always the threat of future loss and death. Overwhelmed and anxious, the inexperienced worker may unwittingly close off communication or reassure, suggest, and sum up before the older client has a chance to finish speaking.

Most elderly persons know far better than younger workers the limits of bromides and advice. Unsolicited opinions on their condition pour in freely from physicians, adult children, and neighbors. In the first social work contact, many do not expect answers to any but informational questions. They want to be understood and validated as the unique individuals they are. Empathic listening is an active process, whether or not the worker says a word. Understanding will be reflected—a nod or touch may be all that is needed. The greatest service a social worker can offer in the initial contact is to quietly listen, hear, and imaginatively enter into the world of the frail older person. Even for those who have relied all their lives on the advice of others, it is best not to rush in but first to hear what they have to say.

Observation and listening go hand and hand as the worker sifts through the multitude of data presented to identify the salient information needed for the study. What is the client's appearance and overall manner? What is deduced from this about his functional abilities and disabilities? Is it what one would expect given the medical diagnosis and life circumstances? How congruent are the worker's perceptions of the situation with those of the client, family, or other professionals involved?

Sometimes an accompanying person will interrupt, attempting to speak for the older person or introducing contradictory information. The social worker must politely and firmly delay these contributions until the elder is finished, noting that there will be time for all present to speak and listen to each other. Occasionally the older person will be unwilling or unable to present the problem and sit mutely. In the absence of physical or mental impairment to communication, this generally connotes hostility toward the idea of seeking help. In such cases, it is helpful to ask the accompanying family or friends to explain to the older person, in the worker's presence, the reason for the appointment. Their words and manners as they do this and the client's response clearly and quickly illuminate the relationship and problems of reluctance that must be addressed before further exploration into need will be fruitful.

Exploration

After the older person and accompanying collaterals have presented the problem, those areas that may not have come forth spontaneously but that the social worker knows to be essential in assessing the total picture should be explored. How long has there been a problematic situation? How has the client coped until now? How and why have these efforts failed? What events precipitated this appointment? How does the older person handle housekeeping, finances, and self-care? How does he or she spend a typical day?

If it can be arranged, one home visit will provide more information about the client than can be obtained from a series of office contacts. Safety of neighborhood and household environment and management of hygiene and nutrition are easily observed. Client resistance to change, which may appear unrealistic in the office setting, can have validity on the home ground or vice versa; for example, the cane urged by specialists is unnecessary when mobility in one's apartment is assisted by pieces of furniture. The home visit also affords a special opportunity to enter the client's world and view it through his or her eyes. Observations of what has been cherished or discarded through the years and the relative values of comfort and appearances form an important part of any exploration.

Essential information also can be obtained through observation of the client within a group setting. Interactional behavior, which is key to understanding the individual but difficult to obtain within the one-to-one contact, is immediately visible. This is especially valuable when a congregate community or residential setting appears as a possible plan.

Information from family members and other informal supports adds a critical dimension. Weighing of many variables is necessary to arrive at an understanding of the true situation; for example, a daughter seeking placement for a parent may report that her mother is totally dependent in activities of daily living. The mother will turn out to be well-functioning but lonely, and she may be seeking attention through concrete demands for care. Further exploration will be necessary to determine the practical and emotional needs of both parties, as well as the likelihood of a long-term institution to meet them.

Information from other professionals, primarily physicians and other medical personnel, is sometimes contradictory, obscure, or difficult to obtain. Even when this is not the case, the worker must begin with a general store of information about the more common illnesses and treatments of the elderly population in general in order to make sense of the particular. As an obvious example, the chairbound older woman cannot be viewed solely in terms of functional limitations; yet the medical information that she has suffered a hip fracture or stroke or has a degenerative form of arthritis will be of help to the social worker only insofar as these conditions are understood in terms of prognosis and usual emotional concomitants.

Ideally, eliciting information about the frail older person is a multidisciplinary effort, as it requires the knowledge and skills of many professions to understand the variety and interrelatedness of need. In fact, this rarely is the case.

Often the social worker is primarily responsible. This is true not only in a community agency where the client presents with a concrete service need but also in an institutional health care setting where the information each profession notes in the case record generally does not incorporate insights drawn from other disciplines. In the absence of agency sanctioned mechanisms, such as the team meeting for information sharing, the social worker generally has to cull out relevant pieces of information from many sources and thoughtfully order it to reflect the totality of the client experience. The initial contact often involves decision-making as to whether referral or consultation is necessary. Such decisions should not be influenced by an inflexible adherence to agency policy but rather be based on consideration of which aspects of the bio/psycho/social constellation are the most significant for the individual client.

During the initial contact the worker should be alert to two attitudes regarding later life impairments that often are held by elders and families. The first is whether depletions experienced are attributed to "old age." Without a specific diagnosis, prognosis, or knowledge of possible treatments, accommodations may be made while restitution or compensation is still possible. The second is when remedial measures are undertaken they are expected to be totally effective. Medication, surgery, or prosthetic devices that don't "cure" result in frustration and anger, and the client and family are unaccepting of the age-related factors that preclude complete recovery. Thorough exploration is necessary with the client who has not sought medical care or who is dissatisfied with what was received to determine whether expectations were too high, too low, or appropriate.

Exploration of the client's world must extend beyond family to unrelated significant others. The existence and meaning of such relationships are frequently not volunteered by the older person unless specifically asked for by the worker. Often when family is absent or distant, such informal supports are a key to survival of the frail older person. The content of these transactions may offer valuable insights into how to proceed. The worker who can divine what about the elder induces others to help, and how this individual style of seeking and using assistance can be adapted when more formal caregiving is required, will evolve a case plan that includes, builds on, and supports the strengths of the client's personal style of coping.

Particular note should be paid to "deviant" elders who may appear more alone than they are. For example, the single room occupancy alcoholic, whose daily routine—originally rooted in individual pathology—has now become a life-style shared with others, may have a support network unrecognized by the worker and decompensate if moved to a "better" hotel with a different clientele.

Minority clients who are suspicious about the motives of workers of another ethnic background may not be evidencing paranoia but rather culturally conditioned responses to the outsider. When dietary preferences or customs of a culture are in conflict with professional opinion, rational judgment seldom prevails. This does not indicate mental impairment but a value stance that must be respected. Attitudes toward the roles of adult children, medical care, institutionalization, and receiving governmental assistance are but a few additional areas in which client preferences must be explored and considered within their cultural context. Such understanding will often help engage the older person, indicating the best point of entry into a case or the service provider most likely to be accepted by virtue of cultural affinity.

The economic status of the frail older client is second only to health in determining the options available and the chances of success in the helping effort and must be addressed in the initial contact. The worker who is familiar with the regulations and workings of major income providers can quickly ascertain the feasibility of a plan of care, saving clients and families wasted effort.

Knowledge of loopholes or demonstration projects that might accept a particular client can further extend the services available. While there is obviously little point in exploring the client's interest in a service for which he or she is not eligible, the worker should guard against prematurely cutting off potential sources of help to which access is difficult but not impossible.

For those elderly who have savings, attitudes toward money, discussed in Chapter 6, are frequently barriers to service delivery. However the client or worker may feel about the harshness of eligibility requirements, the fact is that older people must spend almost all (the exact amount differing by states) of their own money for care before being entitled to publically supported services. As it stands now, the greatest choice in services are for the extremes of rich (who can afford to purchase whatever is needed in the private sector) and poor (who are eligible for all subsidized services). Those who live even a few dollars over the poverty line are often the worst off, refusing to "spend down" the savings that hold so much more than monetary value for them. They often are deemed ineligible for needed services. Whatever the situation, the older client's feelings about money are as important as the facts and must be equally explored.

Note-taking generally distracts from the smooth flow of an interview and also may inhibit the client. However, in the initial contact, it may be necessary to note such factual data as past addresses, family members, and prior employment. If an agency requirement is to complete the face sheet or intake form, it is often a logical point of departure for obtaining relevant background information. Past history such as the time and circumstances of the aging and death of the older person's parents and siblings are of particular note. The family of childhood remains a point of reference throughout life, in the later years often becoming the yardstick against which older persons measure and predict their own deterioration. The older person who gives the names of his or her children may be asked if there were any others. The death of children may not be raised spontaneously, but it is always significant and usually relevant to the matter at hand. Client reactions to past crises, losses, and separations are worth pursuing. To whom did the elder turn? How did the elder react? What coping mechanisms were used? How long did it take to regain equilibrium?

All of this information may become available to the worker by asking a simple question such as "how was it for you when your husband died?" The answers provide insight into the individual's habitual methods of response and can be incorporated into the assessment and case plan. Although the depletions of age may lessen the adaptive capacities of older persons, they will generally approach problems in the same spirit they did in earlier times.

Reminiscence

Often the initial contact will precipitate the sharing of one or two spontaneous reminiscences from the past. Although exploration with the client is always valuable, lest we assume we understand more than we do, it is not always possible. A close focusing on one reminiscence can lead a first interview far afield from its purpose of uncovering all aspects of the client's situation. The crisis situations that often propel the frail elderly into the social service network do not always permit traditional history taking and psychosocial study or functional assessment before work can begin.

It is in such situations that the following guidelines for reviewing reminiscence are of special value. Although not a substitute for a history taking, they do permit an individualized, workable hypothesis that provides dynamic understanding of the client and a framework within which further information can be added.

There are many levels of communication in each reminiscence: affect, style, content, and theme all command attention. The surface elements of the story often indicate those factors in the present situation that seem to have triggered a particular memory while revealing what element of the situation is most troubling and why; for example, elders being interviewed for placement in long-term care often recall the event of immigration early in their lives, loss of the familiar, and fear of the unknown implicit in the story. The overwhelming mood of the client in relating a reminiscence—nostalgic, fatalistic, bitter, or rueful—may indicate feelings about the present situation too threatening to be shared overtly. Seemingly innocuous memories often serve a similar function.

Also noteworthy is the appropriateness of the affect to the content of the story. Laughter while relating past losses or pervasive

sadness in discussing past good times are a clue to mood disturbances that may not be apparent when discussing current concerns.

What words are used to describe the past event? Are they what
might be expected given the client's native tongue and educational
and social level? When viewed against these norms, sparseness of
language could reflect mental deterioration or depression or a
combination of both. An unexpected richness and accuracy of
description in a client reported as suffering mental depletion can
signal the presence and nature of functioning mental abilities.

The style in which the story is related provides valuable insights into the client's personality type and characteristic methods
of response. Is the story presented in a detailed, orderly fashion
with a beginning, middle, and end, or does it consist of fragments
of memory and hyperbole? Turning to the content of the reminiscence, the client's presence or absence can be noted, as well as age.
The stage of the life cycle, especially if it is the same in several
recollections, can point to a key period in the psychosocial development of the individual—perhaps a developmental stage that
was never mastered or wherein conflicts are reawakened in the
present. The significant others in the described event—family
members, coworkers, or strangers—point to the relational patterns
of the past, intimate or tangential, that might be expected to
continue in the future. Turning to the theme of the reminiscence,
we see if the client assumed an active or passive role and note the
consequences. Of particular significance in view of the frail older
person's increased dependency is the manner of relating to helping and nuturing persons in the past, even as a child.

Reminiscences that do not raise any hypotheses in the initial
contact should be noted nevertheless and reviewed at a later date
when continued contact with the client may reveal their meaning.

SETTING THE HELPING PROCESS IN MOTION

Problem Definition

Throughout the process of the initial contact, the worker is
formulating a bio/psycho/social study and assessment. While this
may be a gross evaluation with many missing pieces that await

further exploration, a beginning understanding of the older person's areas of depletion and loss, adaptive responses, and the auxiliary function that may be required by the worker or others is usually possible. Also included would be knowledge of the life supports available and circumstances and feelings concerning health, money, and receiving care. Most important are prior methods of handling the current problem (and those similar to it), how and why they failed or succeeded, and what the older person and family is seeking now in the social work encounter.

At this point, the worker's definition of the problem is summarized and shared with the clients and reactions requested. This summarization may be quite comforting, signaling that a mass of inchoate difficulties and feelings are communicable, understandable, and thereby open to alleviation. The worker should not couch the summary in euphemisms or sidestep painful issues.

Mrs. Lewis's nieces took her to a family service agency and asked the social worker's help in persuading their aunt to "take life easy" and move to a beautiful place where she could be taken care of. What they were suggesting was a nursing home, because with the sudden death of Mrs. Lewis's caregiving daughter, they had inherited a responsibility they did not wish to assume.

The problem here is presented in a customary way, in terms of a proposed solution. Although not having the whole story, the worker could safely rephrase the problem. It was actually the difficulties experienced by all in adapting to an unanticipated crisis.

Further exploration revealed that Mrs. Lewis had failing vision and diabetes. The loss of her daughter not only left her in a significantly depressed state but also deprived her of the assistance in activities of daily living previously provided.

After the worker's definition of the problem is summarized, the older person and collaterals are invited to comment. Sometimes omitted facts are recalled and additional information is shared. Once agreement is reached on the broad definition of the problem, partializing and setting priorities among multiple needs is usually necessary. *Partializing* refers to the sorting procedure by which various components of the problem are specifically identified and grouped. In fact, it is extremely difficult to differentiate between cause and effect. Health problems, for example, are often both. Yet beginning to separate each one helps identify the point of entry. *Setting priorities* is deciding the order in which the problems are to be tackled. These processes are interrelated and conducted with the client as an active participant.

Any one of a number of factors can influence the setting of priorities. While the most severe problem, or the primary cause, would seem to merit the most prompt attention, it is often the least amenable to immediate intervention. The elder may initially deny problems, or the time available is too short to mobilize necessary resources. Often, a simple expression of empathy or small concrete service will alleviate the acute distress while next steps are planned.

It was established that Mrs. Lewis had several areas of need caused by failing vision, diabetes, and the sudden death of an unmarried daughter who had lived with her. The nieces were able to handle financial and transportation needs (instrumental aspects of the auxiliary role) but unable to supply help with activities of daily living or offer affective support in view of the personality changes that occurred after the death. These were manifested by refusal to keep scheduled medical appointments and neglect of her diet. The worker's offer of a home visit to Mrs. Lewis was gratefully accepted by all. In private, Mrs. Lewis produced a photograph album and cried copiously over each picture of the daughter, sharing memories with the worker. Recognizing that Mrs. Lewis was unable to participate in any plan until the acute stages of grief had passed, the worker deferred discussion of the pressing concrete needs, offering simple empathy and support. The nieces, relieved to share the burden, let up on their insistence on placement, which further relieved Mrs. Lewis. After two individual interviews, the client was able to relate neglect of her own needs to feelings of guilt at having survived her daughter. The refusal of help could then be handled, followed by discussion of possible alternatives of care. Finally decided upon was a communal household with two sisters in another state. Mrs. Lewis herself proposed and carried out the plan given the time and support to do so.

In other cases, the presenting problem is but the "tip of the iceberg," or a relatively minor clerical problem that masks many needs.

The initial contact with Miss Charles, a single woman with no living relatives, was at a home visit. The worker, who was let in by the young neighbor who had made the referral, had been asked to evaluate the need for senior citizen housing, as Miss Charles was unable to meet the rising rental in her present apartment.

The worker observed and explored all salient aspects of the situation. Miss Charles's obesity, swelling of the ankles, and shortness of breath were accepted by both women as "part of the age." Medication prescribed at the local hospital had run out a month earlier. The last clinic appointment had been postponed until the neighbor's car, now in the shop for major repairs, would be available for transportation. Miss Charles was a great favorite of the neighbor's children, who came in daily with delicious (though rich and highly salted) ethnic treats from their table.

The worker quickly ascertained that a move was neither desired by Miss Charles nor warranted by the facts. The neighbor, though overwhelmed, seemed genuinely concerned. Knowledge of entitlements was immediately set to use in exploring eligibility for rent increase exemption. Miss Charles was greatly relieved to learn of this as well as the fact that Medicaid could finance immediate transportation to the clinic. Recognition of the symptoms of a potentially dangerous case of high blood pressure and of poor nutrition was put to work in exploring the health situation and facilitating the next appointment. The informal support of the neighbor's family was recognized as a strength in the situation to be further studied in terms of functional and dysfunctional aspects.

In the cases of Mrs. Lewis and Miss Charles, beginning assessment and intervention based on partialization and setting priorities were begun at the time of the initial contact. However, gaps in the worker's understanding remained to be filled with greater familiarity with the situation.

Next Steps

Consideration is given in the initial contacts to next steps to be taken. These may include gathering more information, interviewing other family members or informal supports, or formulating a plan. Requests for additional information or for contact with additional people that are made initially and matter-of-factly are more easily accepted than if postponed until later.

Needs for agency-provided services must be specific. With what tasks, how often, and for how long? The procurement of home-maker service or other entitlements may require that releases be signed to obtain information from other agencies or physicians. Although this is routine to social workers, it is often a source of anxiety to elders who fear that their weaknesses will be revealed or to those who have been warned against placing their signatures on any document. The social worker, in initial contacts with frail elders, must be prepared to give a step-by-step explanation of all phases of the process. It can never be taken for granted that a client understands or accepts procedures that may be entirely unfamiliar.

When the social worker questions the client and those who accompany him or her about the frequency and quality of contact with those not present, differing information may be received. Often there are many more supports than recognized, prior sources of support having withdrawn as the need for help threatened to overwhelm them. The social worker may decide after reviewing the situation that it is important to involve key people not present. The worker should share this and the reasons why with those assembled. It may be because it is an agency prerequisite to service or because their input is crucial in assessing and intervening in the situation. Sometimes relatives and neighbors who have dropped out of the picture can be reengaged if responsibility for the frail elder is shared and they are assisted by the expertise and backup of the social worker. The social worker might, with the client's acceptance, reach out to these others—perhaps by a nonthreatening letter or phone call—indicating that the worker has been called in on the problem and would welcome any assistance they could provide.

The older person's expectations and pace in accepting new ideas is crucial to future planning. This can be surmised by the client's past history as well as presentation in the initial interview. Some degree of reluctance is to be expected. Whenever ambivalence, rejection, or fear is evidenced, the worker must slow down, back up, and identify the specific cause. Expression of negatives should be encouraged. The frail elder should have an opportunity to sleep on the discussion before commiting her or himself to further action. Dividing initial contacts into two individual sessions or follow-up telephone calls insures time for this process, with the elder person encouraged to make note of concerns or questions that arise in the meantime.

Auxiliary Function Role

When planning next steps and defining roles for worker and client, the appropriateness of the auxiliary function model to the case at hand must be examined. We begin by questioning. Does the older person meet the definitional criterion of frailty? If not, any one of the current models of generic practice may be followed. If so, in what areas of functioning is the frailty manifested? What level of adaptation — restitution, compensation, or accommodation — has been reached? For what functions? Does this appear the best that can be expected given the circumstances? In what way does this affect the elder's participation in the problem-solving process? Who in the surrounding field is currently filling or can be expected to fill the auxiliary role? Finally, what does this leave for the social worker to do? In sum, what level of worker involvement will be indicated?

In many cases, the initial contact functions as a consultation for the frail elder and significant others. Provided with pertinent information, they can carry through on their own. At the other extreme are clients who are totally without support and virtually immobilized by their problems. Among these are the most depleted and hopeless of the frail. Here the worker must extend every effort, going 100 percent of the way, if necessary, to meet the client.

The auxiliary function role will fluctuate in the course of contact with the frail elder as calibrations are sensitively monitored. In the initial phase, a collaborative effort on information gathering will indicate areas of competency and need.

In the aforementioned case of Mrs. Lewis, her nieces were willing and able to handle finances as indicated by their cooperation in making the necessary information available to the worker. However, the worker had to temporarily exercise the auxiliary role of significant other in providing the emotional support formerly provided by the daughter. In the case of Miss Charles, the auxiliary function of the worker was immediately demonstrated in the provision of concrete information about available services and help in access to them. Buttressing the neighbor's flagging energies by the hope of removing one difficult task (providing transportation) and a future plan to share others (food preparation by a homemaker who would also control dietary intake) meant keeping her involved to fill important affective needs.

Contracting

A contract, here defined as an oral agreement about the purpose and goals of the worker-client relationship and a delineation of responsibilities of each, should generally be initiated by the worker in the course of the initial contacts.

For frail elders, whom society or circumstance has prematurely reduced to a state of childlike supplication, the relatively new concept of "contract" has returned a legitimate voice. They control whether or not they see the worker and define work in terms meaningful to them. Clarity of purpose and accountability of the worker are achieved. However, even with the mentally alert elder, the social work contract is more easily defined than implemented. The frail older person's world consists of an interrelated network of problems, of which he or she usually will present only a partial view. While ultimate accountability is to the client, the task of bio/psycho/social study, assessment, and case plan must be informed by the professional judgment of the social worker. It thus may be necessary for client and worker to review and reformulate the contract throughout the relationship until clarity and agreement are reached.

Many involuntary clients are the mentally frail, the helpless, and the hopeless, to whom an offer of service is demonstrated rather than intellectually discussed. Contracting is often impossible until a climate of trust has been established. This is generally achieved through socialization and/or the provision of concrete assistance.

Mr. White, who had not communicated with residents or staff since his admission to the nursing home, was reached through travel pictures. The worker learned that he had spent early years in France, simply sat down with some picture postcards, and began the contact asking for advice on a trip soon to be taken. Food and sights were discussed for the next two sessions. Each time, the worker broached concern about Mr. White's obvious discontent with the placement, but it was shrugged off as inevitable. At the third session, the worker was asked if she could find out how to arrange newspaper delivery. After a month of demonstrating trustworthiness through helping with such small concrete tasks and sharing memories of the past, the auxiliary function of the worker was clarified for the client. He slowly confided his disappointment in the placement and wish to move. It was only at this point that a contract could be negotiated. This involved twice weekly meetings to explore and discuss various alternatives.

The conclusion of the initial contacts is a summation of what has been discussed, what tasks have been assigned to each participant, and the time, place, and agenda of the next contact. The mentally able client who is seeking concrete information should leave the first interview understanding what the social worker can do to alleviate the situation and whether or not the services sought are contingent on engaging in a counselling relationship. The mentally impaired or emotionally depleted client may leave only with a general feeling of being cared for by this new person in his or her life.

Whether the client has sought help or been referred for it, contracting is an ongoing process closely tied to the social work assessment. However concrete, time-limited, or specific in nature, it must be flexible enough to encompass the variety of elder responses to stress and help.

The frail elder's first encounter with the help-giving system is a most important one. It is in this initial contact that the situation is first explored, the assessment formulated, and the case plan used. It is also the time when need for the auxiliary function role is evaluated and often initiated. A highly skilled practitioner and ample time are essential for engaging client and family, determining where help is needed and setting the process in motion.

Chapter 5

THE WORKER–CLIENT
RELATIONSHIP: ONGOING CONTACTS

Whenever initial contacts with the elderly client and his or her family indicate a condition of frailty, exercise of the auxiliary function is in order if the case plan is to be used. Thus, the process set in motion during the initial contacts when an assessment was made and a plan developed is extended into the period of implementation.

Often, change, withdrawal, or transfer of worker and site is required by agency boundaries, i.e. hospital discharge. In other cases, the informal network is sufficiently strong and organized to implement the auxiliary function alone or with supplementation from another type of service provider. Even if the initial agency continues with the case, implementation of the auxiliary function and plan may be transferred to another worker.

Whatever the individual situation, techniques that are appropriate in the initial phases of contact often require modification as time passes. Although the interviewing framework remains constant, middle and termination phases of the social work relationship demand constant adjustments. These are due to the ongoing study, assessment, and changing circumstances of the elder's life, as well as inherent rhythms of the worker–client relationship. The elder may have improved in some areas of functioning as a result of restitution and compensation and/or improved accommodations made by family or other supports.

Facilitating the frail elder's utilization of other services is a central theme in the ongoing contact. For the community client, help in the home encompasses an array of services to maintain self and surroundings, all of which necessitate adjustments on the part of the elder. For the resident in a long-term care facility, adjustment to institutional life and procedures is often difficult. Rehabilitation, medical treatment, and drugs pose problems whatever the setting. Interventions with groups of frail elders are often effective in carrying out individual case plans. This chapter addresses exercise of the auxiliary function in these varying situations and circumstances.

THE MIDDLE PHASE

The middle phase of the worker-client relationship, entered when the work is mutually defined, has particular pitfalls. There are usually several themes present. Planning the concrete task, be it utilizing home care, group, or institutional services, is interspersed with reminiscence of the past, relating of current happenings, or easy sociability between elder and worker. Suddenly something seems amiss, and it is obvious that the work is "stuck." Often this impasse is brought to the worker's attention by repetition on the part of the client. Meetings have a predictable format like a verbal waltz with both partners executing familiar steps and phrases. If the awareness dawns first on the elder, he or she may requestion the purpose for meeting. Help is taking longer than expected or placing too great a burden on the elder. More often, however, the client's expectation of the relationship is less than that of the social worker, as the human aspect may fill a void that is gratifying in itself.

When the worker senses an impasse, doubts about the efficacy of skilled intervention with the elderly may arise. The original plan may be deemed overambitious, and active interest withdrawn from still another long-term "supportive case." Transfer to a lesser trained worker may soon follow suit.

If the impasse is a needed recess from the intensity of work and a regrouping for further efforts, it will spontaneously move within a few interviews. If it does not, the problem often lies more with the professional skill of the worker than with the motivation of the elder. Exploratory and clarifying responses that adhere closely to the older person's verbal productions are essential in beginning understanding and engagement with the client. Carried without modification into the middle phases of intervention, these techniques can place a too heavy burden on the frail older person to find his or her own answers.

With the clearer understanding of both client and situation that has been reached in the middle phase, the social worker can now advantageously utilize such techniques as interpretation, confrontation, education, and anticipation, outlined in Chapter 7. Individualized attention to the decision-making process and the best modality of sharing the work outlined in Chapter 6 may also be useful.

The Shared Review

There is another type of interview pause that sometimes arises in the middle phase of implementation of the case plan. Perhaps the presenting problem has been resolved or found incapable of resolution. Tasks defined in the initial contract have been completed. The question then becomes termination or a recontracting around issues that were of secondary priority or have arisen since the initial contact. At this point, it is useful for elder and worker to participate in a shared review of their activity from their first meeting to this. Such a review would include concrete and emotional issues discussed as well as the changing nature of the relationship. Periodic comparisons of then and now usually highlight greater progress than previously recognized, and, if so, increased hopefulness as steps are planned for future work. If the review yields no such progress but the maintenance function has been helpful, transfer to a paraprofessional may be contemplated. If the work is indeed over and the auxiliary role of the worker no longer needed, termination should be planned.

It is at this point, however, that frail elders may develop new symptoms or problems to hold the worker. Often what they are seeking is insurance that help will be available should further needs arise. For this reason, workers should assure (and agencies provide) that the cold slap of "case closed" not mark the end of the encounter. A more flexible approach, perhaps marked by bimonthly check-up calls, is more responsive to the real needs and security seeking of the elder.

HELPING THE ELDERLY UTILIZE SERVICES

The frail elder will at some time require services from the formal system above and beyond those offered by the social worker. However, the very depletions that necessitate need may serve to limit access to and utilization of resources. Linking this elder to other services and assuring that he or she receives maximum benefit from them thus forms a key component of the auxiliary role.

As barriers exist on both sides of the transaction, the task is not an easy one. The problems of locating appropriate services (and advocating for those needed but unavailable) are well known. Less understood are the barriers posed by the elder. Workers who, through diligent effort, have successfully engaged other providers in a service plan are often surprised and angry at the moment when the elder rejects the help offered. However, earlier indications that services will not be accepted are usually present but unheeded because of the worker's need for accomplishment. Paradoxically, it is the elder who accepts a proposed service plan unquestioningly or is easily reassured who is most likely to balk when the plan becomes a reality. The elder who protests and raises objections is imaginatively trying out the idea and may allay some doubts in the process.

Whoever the elder, whatever the need, the worker's attention to timing and elder preparation is the key ingredient in facilitating utilization of other services. The process through which the frail elder accepts the need for care on the terms offered by service providers is a long one. It cannot be sidestepped or rushed no matter how urgent the situation appears. Premature closure to expression of negatives only insures that they will arise later in stronger form. Educative, anticipatory, and supportive interventions that provide the client opportunity for mastery of an altered life situation before it actually takes place will enhance trust in the worker and service.

While preparing the elder for utilizing service, it is essential that his or her perceptions of the proposed care and caregivers be elicited. These may be quite different than those held by the worker. Sometimes the service has been presented differently to both parties or distortions have occurred in the interim because of the elder's diminished cognitive and sensory abilities or long-standing prejudices. In either case, the elder's perceptions are real to him or her and must be handled. The frail elder who rejects help of someone on the basis of sex or race does not need to be lectured on sexism or racism. No matter how unjust these views are to the worker, providing service to a client in need will precede changing his or her attitudes. If these are the only caregivers available, the client should be informed of the fact, the consequences of spurning their assistance, and finally, helped to verbalize and handle any fears. (Caregivers also should be apprised of what they will be facing and receive the worker's support.) If substitutions are possible and will make the frail elder more comfortable, they should be arranged. While people can change, adopting new ideas and becoming more accepting of those different from themselves, it is unrealistic to expect them to do so when they are ill, afraid, and not in possession of their full capacities. There is little to be gained from winning the point and losing the elder.

Other fears attendant to utilizing service can be better eased by going with the elder's perception than by imposing that of the worker; for example, the elder who fears theft, either at home or in the institution, will be more reassured by having valuables locked up than by a document describing the bonding procedures of the agency.

Our emphasis in this chapter will be on direct interventions with the elder. Chapter 9 will discuss interventions into the service system. Together they describe the two-pronged process that the worker must employ in uniting elder and service.

Home Care

Home care for the frail elderly is an issue of national interest and debate. Development of services and cost effectiveness vis-à-vis institutional care command the attention of legislators and social planners. All too often social work involvement in the area of home care is limited to providing access to the elder. As financial, medical, and bureaucratic barriers to this essential entitlement can be formidable, the social worker has just cause for pride when skilled systems negotiation unites elder and home care provider. However, case service does not end with the arrival of the attendant at the elder's door. This encounter marks a significant juncture in the life of the frail elder that must be understood, prepared for, and monitored if the plan is to succeed.

Home care embraces various levels of assistance ranging from housecleaning through homemaking and personal care services through skilled application of rehabilitative techniques. In the case of the helper who visits regularly, it may overlap with the auxiliary role. In some cases, the home care worker may perform the lion's share of the role.

As the elder is generally more concerned with the presence than the function of the stranger in his or her home, this discussion will refer generically to the "helper." Allowing an outsider to enter one's life and perform those private acts and daily chores that one previously managed on one's own is an open admission of dependence, helplessness, and deterioration. It is also a forcible confrontation with fantasies of being attended to by loving, significant others. It can no longer be denied; someone must be paid to care. In most cases, the elder is unaccustomed to and uncomfortable with the role of employer, erring by being too authoritarian (thus alienating the helper) or too passive (unable to make simple requests). In the culturally diverse United States, the helper is frequently of different ethnic origin than the elder, a member of a group about whom the elder may hold deeply entrenched biases and stereotypes. Above all, the helper intrudes on the daily routine of the elder, which, however dysfunctional, is cherished for its familiarity. The helper brings his or her own regimen of care, as well as idiosyncratic ways of folding a newspaper or shutting the door. Whatever the type or duration of service, the elder must adjust to forced intimacy with a stranger.

The helper may enter the interaction with comparable disincentives to success. He or she seldom receives the training, recognition, or financial remuneration that would accord the position the dignity it deserves. Although experienced in the tasks he or she is expected to perform, the helper often is no more able to individualize the elder from a mass of crochety old people than the elder is to individualize the helper from a feared and foreign ethnic or cultural group. Thus, the best laid plans for home care often flounder on seas of misunderstanding and bitterness.

The social worker's role in facilitating the relationship begins with the individual preparation of elder and helper, before their first meeting. The first step with the elder is a shared examination of the tasks to be performed, leading to acceptance that outside help is needed. This may take a number of interviews. Such acceptance heralds a loss of some autonomy, which, as other losses, must be mourned. There is often the initial shock and disbelief that the age of dependence has dawned, denial that help is needed, and anger at the social worker for directing attention to the depletion.

A period of reminiscence often ensues with rememberance of past days when more demanding tasks of daily living were handled effortlessly. The mourning period is to be expected and encouraged by the social worker. Mourning what has been is a precursor to accepting what is.

Ambivalence about accepting help is not always resolved prior to the event. Sometimes it never is. In the case of severe mental depletion, verbal exploration is inappropriate and the elder must experience the helping relationship to understand its nature. No matter what the situation, however, some preparatory engagement of the elder is possible and necessary before the day of meeting. Trust in the social worker, who was also once a stranger, is often the vehicle by which help is accepted.

Shared attention should be paid to the time frame in which service is offered. Starting with a minimum number of hours and building up as necessary allows the elder a period of acclimation as well as insuring that the helper's care is limited to what the elder is unable to do for him or herself. A full-time helper, in a well-meaning effort to earn wages, may do all for the elder—sapping him or her first of incentive, then of the ability to exercise those faculties still available. The elder's condition may necessitate starting with a maximum number of hours. Care must be taken to reduce these hours if and when restitution and compensation occur or informal caregivers are able to provide more help.

The elder's personal clock and past style of functioning should be adhered to where possible. There is nothing sacrosanct about a bath on arising or dinner at midday. The elder can and should maintain control over these remaining choices in his or her life.

He or she should be apprised of the relevant known characteristics of the helper and encouraged to express whatever feelings this engenders. While unreasoning fear and distrust are seldom dispelled by rational argument, appeals to trust in the worker, a general sense of fairness, or willingness to give things a try are sometimes helpful. Also effective is discussion of points of similarity shared by the elder and the prospective helper. For example, the social worker's knowledge that the elder's early years were marked by hard work for the betterment of his or her children can be related to similar motivations on the part of the helper.

A close social work involvement should follow the initial contact of elder and helper, especially crucial if the elder is a first time consumer of home care services. After individual preparation and some preliminary planning of tasks, the two should be left alone to become acquainted. A follow-up conference to review the service and identify incipient problem areas should be held as soon as feasible. The structure of the conference establishes that elder and helper are to communicate directly rather than waiting for time alone with the social worker to pour out grievances. The problem-solving approach demonstrated by the social worker during the meeting provides a model for the elder and helper as they strive to accommodate to each other's ways.

Any difficulties of the first few days should be brought into the open. A nonjudgmental exploration of the facts is in order. Elder and helper should be encouraged to express their views of the situation to each other, focusing on issues rather than personalities. Whenever possible, a future approach to the problem can be discussed. Increased responsibility and specific tasks on both sides foster a shared ownership of the problem and investment in a satisfactory resolution.

Mrs. Post, age eighty-three, complained of the stupidity and wastefulness of her homemaker, who "threw out half the chicken" before it even got to the table. She compared this with the frugality and skill with which she had prepared meals in earlier days.

The homemaker argued that she knew Mrs. Post's diet excluded certain portions of the poultry and so discarded them before cooking. She complained that Mrs. Post was always "checking up on" her and was angered at the challenge to her competence.

After they shared the facts and their feelings, the social worker pointed out a common theme (neither felt her abilities were appreciated). She also noted that the two had not spoken of the matter when alone together, which had fostered the ill feeling on both sides. Elder and helper were asked for possible solutions. Mrs. Post was reassured to learn that the homemaker was knowledgeable and conscientious about her diet. As the social worker supported this, the homemaker felt less threatened and listened with a new appreciation for the elder. She then suggested several food preparation tips including shopping differently and freezing leftovers to be prepared later for visiting family. The future plan included collaboration on a shopping list, which gave the elder a measure of control while relieving the homemaker from making all the menu decisions.

In cases of unresolvable conflict, quick action to replace the helper is necessary before the ill feeling is generalized to all helpers and the elder refuses further service. The clearer the social worker is as to why the match failed the better able she will be to anticipate and head off future problems. It must be remembered that the helper is primarily accountable to the elder. It does not matter if family or government is paying the salary or if the elder is incompetent to determine his or her best interests. He or she remains the master or mistress in the home, if no where else. This knowledge must inform and guide the worker through all steps of the home care intervention.

Where family or significant others exist, it is important that the social worker reach out as necessary to interpret and clarify the home care worker's role. Sometimes those who were most zealous in pursuit of home care for the elder will react with ambivalence when it is finally available. Perhaps the burdened daughter wanted relief, but did not anticipate her feeling of replacement, rejection, and rivalry when someone else takes over her tasks. The sharing of the auxiliary role with a newcomer may be difficult and social work help needed in redefining roles. Once the frail elder and helper are on a firm footing, the social worker serves an ongoing maintenance function on an as needed basis, unless of course there are other reasons for regular meetings.

The day-to-day proximity, often with no one else present, and the shared storehouse of experience fosters a closeness well beyond what the elder may share with family or social worker. Compensation for lost relationships with significant others is frequently reached. Because helpers get sick, leave (with or without notice), and in other ways have personal crises that will impinge on the functioning of the elder, their fulfillment of the auxiliary role requires that the worker be as sensitive to issues of transfer and termination and as prepared to handle them as he or she is in the professional relationship.

Nursing Home Care

A chief issue addressed in the elder's utilization of home care is the introduction of a stranger into his or her intimate life space. A chief issue to be addressed in nursing home care is introducing the elder into a strange environment.

Separation from a familiar environment must first be considered. It has different meanings for different elders. For some, it may mean giving up a home of many years to which the elder is very attached. To others, the nursing home may represent only the next in a series of displacements in life to which they have become accustomed. The wish not to be separated from familiar surroundings is often a chief reason for the rejection of nursing home placement. However, if disability is severe enough and there are not sufficient supports in the community to maintain an elder, there may be no other choice.

A significant portion of the social worker's tasks in relation to nursing home placement ideally takes place prior to actual entry into the home. If the worker has had an ongoing relationship with the elder, there is opportunity for exploration of the pros and cons of placement and the careful involvement of the elder in the decision-making process.

If placement is an immediate issue because of a catastrophic illness, such as a stroke, then the time available to the worker may be extremely limited, such as a few hospital days. Not only is the worker at a disadvantage in terms of establishing a trusting relationship with the elder and exercising an auxiliary role, but the decision-making process may be abbreviated with little time for appropriately involving the elder. As noted in Chapter 4, involvement is a slow process due to the flagging capacities of the elder, a factor that utilization review requirements do not recognize. The anxiety of relatives and others may put pressure on the worker to abort the process.

Regardless of the time limitations, it is imperative that the worker explore with each elder the real options open to him or her (which may be very limited), help the elder grieve what he or she has and will lose, and begin anticipating what will be faced in the eventual placement. Even the most abbreviated contacts are better than none at all. Decision making, usually with family members, that excludes the older person adds enormously to his or her fears that control is totally slipping away. The grief work that needs to be accomplished may never be realized.

If the social worker is based in a nursing home, the intake process becomes an important time for addressing these issues. The social worker may want to visit the elder in the hospital or his or her home, not only to understand the environment from which the client is coming but to begin to explore issues of separation, anticipation, and the elder's participation in decision making. Aborted intake procedures into nursing homes that are conducted by clerks sidestep the critical need of elders for auxiliary help at this crucial time in their lives.

In anticipation of placement in the home, the worker in an auxiliary role will want to consider a variety of factors that may bridge the home in the community and the nursing home, such as bringing in familiar objects or visiting the nursing home in advance to study the environs and anticipate what physical adaptations will have to be made to them. The accommodation that the elder has to make in terms of nursing home placement can be very stressful, even traumatic: learning to live with less privacy, eating in a communal setting, eating and sleeping at hours dictated by others, interacting with a wide variety of other residents and service providers, etc. The loss of control over one's life, initiated by primary depletions, may be intensified by the secondary depletions often associated with institutional care. These secondary depletions, of course, vary from one nursing home to another and need to be measured in a particular environment in terms of the impact on the individual elder.

The first few months following admission into a nursing home are critical ones for social work intervention. The more intense work that can be accomplished during intake and/or during this period can have important payoffs in terms of the long-term adaptation of the elder. Here, the auxiliary task would involve implementing physical accommodations to the environment, aiding in socializing and meeting other residents, and continuing to help the elder grieve what has been lost in terms of former home and life-style and separation from families. Even though families may visit and be supportive, nursing home placement is often symbolic of a painful abandonment.

The early months of contact also give the social worker an opportunity to complete a full psychosocial study and assessment and map out a plan for the resident's continuing stay in the nursing home. Many new residents, with initial support or even on their own, may respond spontaneously to the overtures of the informal network in nursing homes, such as recreation, nursing and other staff, and make a comfortable niche for themselves in the life of the home. Others may have much more difficulty in this area. Lingering depression, withdrawal, shame over mental and physical dysfunctioning, and a variety of other factors may impede their moving into the social networks of the home.

Many families closely follow their elder into the nursing home and perform critical aspects of the auxiliary role on an ongoing basis. They maintain an important effective link to elders, supervise the care they are getting, and may even provide concrete services and recreational activities. Other families may have a more tenuous connection. But in either situation, families can be as troubled and upset by the nursing home placement as the elder and need a great deal of support and help from the social worker if they are to continue in some aspect of the auxiliary role. Often overlooked is the tremendous drain on families in nursing home placement: the guilt, the stress of visiting, the pain of seeing the elder deteriorate, and the time and burden all of this places on the rest of their lives. Family support groups in nursing homes are an excellent way of addressing these problems.

In some situations, the social worker may wish to involve the family to a greater extent, encouraging them to visit more regularly and in a more supportive fashion. In other instances, the social worker may wish to respect the distance that the family and the elder keep. The equilibrium reached by a family serves an important purpose in terms of maintaining the integrity of individual members, and there is no one standard for proper family behavior in regard to nursing home placement of elder members. The study and assessment, particularly as related to past family patterns of interaction, will provide valuable clues as to future interventions.

Social workers' ongoing interventions with elderly clients in nursing homes relate to changes in the system that may affect the elder's adaptation and changes in the elder, such as further deterioration. New roommates, relocation to another room, and poor care are among the issues with which the elder may have to be helped. When and if they suffer further primary depletion, the social worker must take care that someone is there in an auxiliary role to emotionally support the elder through the time of grieving and anxiety. Needless to say, if these result in transfer to another part of the nursing home or to another facility altogether, the intensive work that accompanies admissions will have to be repeated.

Health Services

For the frail elder, both in community and nursing home, the utilization of health services is an important dimension in his or her ongoing care. The nursing home resident has little choice in this matter, but may still have difficulty in relating to the routines and behaviors of health care personnel. While nursing homes often are the last home for an older person, they are still primarily a health care setting, and the daily routine and activities of elders are often determined by health care exigencies. Interpretation to and education of the elder can be critical here. Careful listening and an empathic response to the fears they express may enable them to better use these services. Communications with health care personnel, discussed in Chapter 9, are also critical. It is for the best when the worker is able to link the elder and health care provider in a discussion of mutual concerns.

For the community client, the auxiliary role may involve direct supervision of health care, depending of course on the condition and needs of the elder. The mentally impaired elder may have difficulty taking drugs, following physicians' and nurses' orders, keeping doctor appointments, and a variety of other duties related to being a "good patient." Education is a vital auxiliary intervention for the social worker or significant other. Participating with the elder in setting up routines and habits that are conducive to good care is often necessary.

Mrs. James had a variety of medications from several different physicians she had visited over the years and was obviously, in the opinion of her most recent physician, not taking drugs properly, exacerbating her confusion and depression. After establishing clearly with the physician what drugs were actually needed by Mrs. James, the worker then spent several visits with the client reviewing what medicines were needed, in what amount, and when they should be taken. Special charts and reminders were laid out and the various pills organized into compartments that could be easily taken by the elder. Knowing that Mrs. James hoarded a great deal of old medication as well as other items in her life in response to the depletion she was suffering, the worker was able to recognize these fears and needs and persuade Mrs. James to dispose of old medications and only have on hand that which she needed.

Often the elder will not wish to "bother the doctor" with new complaints, or the effects of overmedication may be evident to the worker (or homemaker) but not to the elder. Here, the auxiliary role is crucial in directing medical concerns appropriately.

Rehabilitation

While a rehabilitation philosophy permeates the auxiliary function model, i.e. respecting and enhancing competencies remaining to the elder, more direct rehabilitation interventions may be prescribed to which an elder may or may not be receptive. In the nursing home or community, physical therapy may be recommended to improve mobility, occupational therapy to improve self-care, or speech therapy following a stroke.

Motivation and hope on the part of the frail elder are crucial components of a successful rehabilitative experience. This is usually conveyed by the rehabilitation therapist, who can provide an important auxiliary role in relation to the frail elder. However, the problem sometimes facing the social worker is how to involve the elder in this service willingly. The frailty of the elder may discourage family and the elder from thinking in terms of improvement. Often there is poor understanding of the fact that incremental steps can, over time, lead to more independent functioning. However, even if they do not, the psychological boost of regaining mastery over even one small area of self-care should not be underestimated. The confidence thus generated may well stimulate use of unimpaired faculties.

The worker also must believe in these small incremental steps and the fact that restoration of functioning or compensatory activities in some areas is not linear but uneven in progress. The encouragement, hope, and challenge that can be conveyed by a significant other are vital in sustaining rehabilitative efforts. Occasionally, the elder's or family's expectations of rehabilitation are unrealistic, and they persist in seeking service long after professionals deem it productive. If psychologically beneficial and financially feasible, these may be continued. If not, however, the worker must help the elder and family accept the loss and seek a substitute source of hope.

Prosthetic Devices

Prosthetic devices prescribed by physicians, implanted by surgeons, or recommended by rehabilitation specialists can greatly enhance functioning for elders and be an important step to compensation. Yet, there can be fear of these devices or reluctance to use them, often for very good reason. Hearing aids have been notoriously unpopular with elders because of the static they sometimes convey. With improvements in these aids, their use will probably be more widespread. For the depressed elder or the one who wishes to withdraw or control interactions with others, hearing aids may be deliberately not used. A worker's patient efforts to support this use and stimulate social interaction with the worker and others may be an important first step in improvement.

Cataract surgery and hip replacements are, in a sense, other forms of prosthetic aids. Frail elders, like younger persons, can have many different emotional reactions to these interventions in their lives, and care must be taken that they are given individualized support in such efforts.

HELPING THE ELDER IN GROUPS

Group activities can be an invaluable source of support and enrichment for the frail elder as well as for informal supports and, in turn, can provide an excellent framework for mutual exchange. The dyadic relationships that characterize most interactions of the frail elderly, because of caregiving and therapeutic needs, are imbalanced in terms of dependence. This dependence is a legitimate component of frailty and enhancing to most elders if not excessive, but for some elders it must be counterbalanced by activities that promote reciprocity and perceived competence. An important task of the social worker is to seek out, organize, and/or promote these activities.

There are a number of other benefits from organized group activities. Groups can have deliberate psychotherapeutic and rehabilitative agendas: coping with and releasing the anxieties that accompany frailty and dependence, freeing the individual for a more productive investment of his or her emotions. Improvements in functioning can be encouraged through peer support. Mourning and grief situations can be worked to resolution (Hartford, 1972).

Group activity can replenish the social losses experienced in old age brought about by widowhood, death of peers, and institutionalization. New contacts can be made and alternative relationships established. A sense of belonging and self-definition can be promoted (Hartford, 1980). Groups can serve other functions in addition to problem-solving and socialization. They can provide stimulation and recreation and be a vehicle of self-government and social action (Miller and Solomon, 1979). Whatever the format, the individual needs and proclivities of the frail elder are foremost.

Preparation for the group, contracting, and sustaining therapeutic group processes are tasks for the worker, who must "maintain a working balance between a tendency to either overidentify with members' fears and sink into joint despair or to make unrealistic demands for work and court stalemate and struggle" (Miller and Solomon, 1979).

Frail elders with severe hearing and speech difficulties or mental incapacities can be easily overlooked in terms of group activities, since verbal communication skills are diminished. Group interaction takes place on several levels, however, and attention needs to be given to groups organized around activities that tap unimpaired areas of functioning. Art, poetry, and music groups are very successful here (Getzel, 1980).

Even in groups with an emphasis on discussion, the less able client may participate, albeit in a disorganized way. A great deal depends on the contract reached with other group members regarding support and acceptance of such persons.

Initial resistance to participation in group activities is common among elders. The group may be perceived as intrusive of one's privacy, or as an analog of the family, the group may stir up conflicted feelings, particularly old sibling rivalries. It is a pitfall for the worker to assume that this initial resistance will last. While there may be some elders who will steadfastly refuse to participate in group activities, many will with preparation, patience, and attention on the part of the worker.

Residential Groups

Organized groups in the residential setting are a primary social work tool. With all of the elders under one roof, the worker can utilize the group format for implementing and sustaining the auxiliary role.

While not necessarily expecting individual group members to assume the auxiliary role, the worker can tap group resources; and the group, with the worker present, can be a sustaining, dependable significant other for some elders. Others may only be able to relate on a dyadic level and thus form one-to-one relationships within the group.

The worker carried 120 cases, or three floors of the nursing home. The demand on her time by emotionally needy and distressed residents was overwhelming. She organized a weekly group meeting on each floor to which about half the residents attended. Their work together focused on problem-solving everyday "living together" issues, but they also reminisced and shared experiences and feelings.

These floor groups can form the structure of a resident council and be utilized for self-government and planning activities (Silverstone, 1977). Here autonomous functioning on part of the elder is exercised through the group, operationalizing another ingredient of the auxiliary function model.

Many other types of groups can be organized crosscutting geographical boundaries: newcomers' groups, men's groups, oral history groups, special interest groups, therapeutic groups, art groups. Some facilities have a full therapeutic recreation staff to organize such groups. They can be an excellent resource for the social worker.

Groups that make a low demand on members, at least at the beginning, are the best choice for the frail elderly. Refreshments that are satisfying and beyond the usual fare are awaited with expectation and are a great drawing card, especially for older people who can look forward to few such treats. It is usually easier if these can be served rather than presented buffet style (and don't forget those on diabetic or salt-free diets). Eating and side-by-side participation in such spectator activities as listening to a lecture or concert are often preludes to socialization. Arts and crafts groups may fill a similar function, providing members with a reason for the warmth of human contact as well as an excuse to remain apart until they are ready to open themselves to one another. Program and activity groups are especially valuable for the emotionally troubled and mentally impaired who may avoid a more structured experience that would highlight their inadequacies.

The mentally able but physically infirm, on the other hand, are often underchallenged. Workers fearful of precipitating adverse health reactions may avoid controversial subjects for discussion. Conflictual areas are glossed over and consensus prematurely reached with the result that nothing of merit is accomplished, and the members feel infantilized by the process. To be human is to have strong feelings and express them. The older person and his or her peers are generally the best guides as to when enough is enough.

This is not to say that all topics chosen for discussion by a group of frail elderly will be weighty and serious. Discussions of food, which may seem interminable to young workers, are of never-ending interest to long-term care residents (food being the most basic and long lasting common denominator). Nor is it to say that mobilizing for action is the desired outcome of every complaint session. Often the elder, especially in an impersonal long-term care setting, is validating individuality through identifying him or herself as one who hates meat and likes fish. In fact, he or she has no desire to form a committee and take on the chef.

At the same time, there are members who in the course of discussion decide that corrective action should be taken. Sometimes the worker is charged by the group with confronting those in authority with the problems raised. Here, as in work with individuals, assessment must be made of issue content and the capacities of the group, individually or collectively, to act on it independently. This is rarely an all or nothing proposition. Multiple frailties, fears of retribution, and inexperience may inhibit elders from proceeding on their own, even with the preparation of the social worker. Yet there are also discrete pieces of the work that can be handled by members and foster a sense of ownership of problem and solution.

Residents of one floor in a health-related facility were angered that evening medications for residents of the entire facility were distributed in their lounge each evening. This disturbed television viewing as well as created noise and litter. Individuals variously were charged with sounding out nongroup participants about their opinions, documenting the scope of the problem through reporting of their observations, and thinking of solutions (the simplest of these, a giant wastebasket, had been overlooked by staff). Meanwhile, the worker used her knowledge of the system and skills of organizational change to advocate for a more equitable plan.

The discussion of doing for, doing with, and helping the elders do for themselves in Chapter 6 is equally applicable in groups. "Doing with," which provides support to the group as well as modelling behavior for future action, is the plan of choice in many situations.

The new bath schedule on a nursing home floor angered many residents, coming at inopportune times of the day. The group wanted it changed back but was at a loss as to how to proceed. The worker identified the charge nurse as the one responsible and first suggested a committee to approach her. All declined. Next, she suggested that the nurse be invited to a meeting at which they could present their requests for change in the protection of a group and with support of the worker. After this idea was accepted, the worker engaged the group in preparation. This involved role playing the projected scenario and anticipating problems that could arise. Concurrently, the worker prepared the nurse (who was as afraid of the residents en masse as they were of her individually) for the issues to be raised. In this, she was careful to present herself as a mediator who recognized the needs for concession on both sides rather than as a group advocate who blindly ignored institutional realities of care. The result was a compromise solution for baths that was deemed fair on both sides. In fact, the residents, once apprised that the original change was due to union requirements rather than an arbitrary display of power on the part of administration, were far more able to accept the residual inconvenience.

There is often less sharing of personal experiences and feelings in institutional than in community groups with the frail elderly. This is not hard to understand if one remembers that participants cannot retreat to the privacy of their homes between sessions. They must live in close proximity with other members twenty-four hours a day, seven days a week. Maintaining privacy thus becomes important to the integrity of the individual elder, protecting him or her from being totally enveloped in the mass. This need should be respected by the worker, while still encouraging socialization.

Community Groups

Isolation of the frail elder living in the community can be a serious problem. The visits of caregivers, family, and others often do not fill the social void in their lives precipitated by impairment and loss of loved ones. Even the elder living with family members can feel isolated from cohorts. Group activities outside of the home can be an important intervention here as well.

Most of the above examples are drawn from long-term care institutions for good reason. This is where the bulk of group work with the frail elderly takes place. The mobility of the frail homebound is usually limited by weather, infirmity, and lack of transportation. Coming out to see the doctor may be enough of an effort and group meetings therefore would be spurned. However, the provision of appropriate transportation and much patient preparation by the worker often achieves results. Here, as in institutions, the elder may first come to group meetings to please the worker. "I am coming for you, dear," they often say, negating that they have a need the group might fill. It is not helpful to insist, "But this is for *you*." Rather accept the compliment with appreciation and thanks. It is important to recognize that the elder is demonstrating need for affective components of the auxiliary role in meeting a new and frightening situation.

Day programs or day hospitals are excellent settings for a variety of types of group activities, for they serve other needs too. These include health care and rehabilitation needs as well as respite for family. Short of day programs, frail elders can be brought together in weekly or biweekly groups in the worker's own agency, a senior center, or other type of community center. Critical to these groups are staffing and transportation. Groups may be very diverse in membership; however, the worker should encourage equitable participation and contributions from each of its members. Thus, frail elders can easily break out of the dependent role that their condition has forced upon them and that is often reinforced by societal attitudes. They can contribute knowledge, emotional support, and even physical help to their peers, depending on the complementarity of impairments.

The group that met weekly at the center depended on Mr. Levy, who was confined to a wheelchair, to keep attendance, minutes, and track of the time. Mrs. Speer, who was somewhat confused and disoriented, managed the serving of snacks very well. Mrs. Jacob, although quite forgetful, was very expressive emotionally and could be counted on to spark lively discussion on highly charged issues.

The potential for group members to perform auxiliary tasks for one another is guarded. A number of emotional and practical needs of the elder can be met by the group and in no way should be underestimated, but an undue burden is placed upon the group if members are expected to step in for the worker, particularly in crisis situations. The cost-saving and self-enhancing features of such behaviors are negated by the stress they can place on individual members, whose own needs for survival in the community are understandably paramount in their lives. Mutual aid can be promoted on a symbolic level, which is often as supportive as practical help.

When Mrs. Rudd had a minor stroke and could no longer attend group meetings, the worker resumed visits to the home to help Mrs. Rudd cope with the crisis in her life. Group members telephoned and sent messages of support.

In addition to low-demand groups that foster socialization at the client's pace, community recipients of an individual service may be brought together on a time-to-time basis for a specific purpose.

One home care agency had two meetings a year at which clients, homemakers, administrators, and clerical staff mingled informally, enjoying music and refreshments. Polaroid pictures were taken and presented to participants. A specially outfitted van rented for the occasion accommodated even the most physically frail who, though unable to take the excitement and effort on a regular basis, thoroughly enjoyed themselves. A spin-off benefit was the reassurance clients received from seeing the physical plant that housed the service and putting faces to the anonymous voices that handled their queries on the phone. Thus, they saw what words do not always convey: that though an individual homemaker may leave, the agency was still behind them.

In other situations, groups of frail community elders may be recruited for a time-limited group by those planning or promoting a service.

Participants in a day care program were convened by a social worker for a time-limited group of four weeks. The charge, as passed on by the local police precinct, was to discuss in-home protection from crime. This involved providing elders with information about burglar-proofing apartments as well as canvassing them for suggestions as to how the precinct could best meet their needs. At the final meeting, the police representative appeared and a prepared group was able to present an impressive list of observations and suggestions. In fact, some of the innovative tactics shared by the elderly were better than the police could offer. (One widow who lived alone put her late husband's shoes on the mat each evening, to be joined by an umbrella on rainy days, thus broadcasting that there was a man in the house.)

Whatever the setting, groups with the frail elderly rarely resemble those "in the books," and so may pose frustration to beginning workers. Distracting entrances and exits occasioned by bathroom needs may break the mood of a heartfelt interchange. Those with sensory or cognitive deficits may be only intermittently aware of the proceedings, splitting off in twos or threes for side conversations or breaking in with an observation completely off the topic. Group composition will rarely be exactly the same, due to fluctuating conditions of health and weather. For this reason, it is wise to recruit twice the number desired (a group of 16 will typically yield 3 or 4 immediate dropouts, another 4 who are intermittently involved, and 8 solid participants). For all of the above-mentioned reasons, work rarely has an even flow. The members who were revved for action last week may not appear this week or may have forgotten what happened.

The social worker performs an auxiliary role for the group as a whole as well as for its individual members. The worker will be needed to provide necessary structure and reorientation each time the group meets. A brief recap of work up to the present (if possible shared with alert members) is a good beginning, with additions, corrections, and reactions from the group. It should be recognized that the mood of each session will vary and work on agreed upon agendas will proceed very slowly, alternating with digressions, reminiscences, and socialization. The worker's ongoing assessment of the tenor of each individual and the group as a whole will determine when to go with the flow or keep the group to task. Whatever the case, success of a group of frail elderly must not be measured by concrete outcomes, be they the number of knit hats produced or organizational changes accomplished. For many, providing the opportunity to share a warm space for an hour a week with others who expect and welcome them is a service in itself.

The worker who has individual relationships with group members may initially feel torn in many directions as each tries to assert sole possession. This will abate in time as members grow more connected with each other. However, the beginning worker still may be influenced by individual knowledge of the client's depletions, hoping to protect one individual from still another rejection or to protect the group from an overbearing member.

The worker may also carry on individual interviews with each member in turn. Such hidden agendas, or techniques, foster group dissension. For the worker with the frail elderly, dynamics inherent in all groups form a vital part of the knowledge base (see Appendix A for relevant readings).

In groups, as with individuals, the expression of feelings is never an end in itself. Beginning workers often feel that a group session in which members share emotional reactions to topics such as death or sexuality are intrinsically superior to those in which mundane facts of everyday living such as the difficulty finding a good podiatrist are discussed. It is not the content of the communication or even the depth of feeling elicited that matters as much as the opportunity to exchange ideas and opinions in an accepting atmosphere that validates the contribution of each member.

TRANSFER AND TERMINATION

If timing of the social work intervention were determined only by elder need, many of the frail elderly would benefit from an open-ended response to their multiple and cumulative needs for care. Cases would be served by a single, trusted worker, who would offer ongoing support, assessment, and coordination of services. Cases would be transferred rarely and terminated only when the auxiliary role of the worker was no longer needed.

Regrettably such an individualized, integrated approach to service delivery is not often realized. Specific time-limited services are mandated by funding sources and agency policies. Proven programs are phased out and experimental ones take their place. Students leave placements when their field work requirement is satisfied. The turnover of line workers is high. All can result in premature termination or referral to other providers, and it is the degree to which the needs of caregivers prevail over those of the elder that determines the complexity of the termination process.

Transfer and termination pose separate difficulties. In transfer, the elder will combine mourning of the present worker with anticipation of the future one. In termination, the finality may be overwhelming whether or not the need for care still exists. For this reason, assurance of continuing records at the agency and a future open door are important.

The least difficult cases to end are those in which the relationship has been brief, focused on concrete need, and concluded in a manner logical to the client. It is clear from the outset, for example, that the planning function of the hospital social worker will terminate upon discharge of the patient. Although more dependent clients may react to loss of the protective environment poorly and need the opportunity to express their fears to the worker, the relationship itself is rarely a concern.

The client-worker relationship has greatest meaning to the isolated elderly, the homebound and institutionalized, for whom the worker has filled the role of significant other. The elder who has a history of past problematic separations and losses or who is faced with the threat of imminent death is the most vulnerable. Knowledge of the elder's past experience with loss and the coping strategies with which he or she met these is of use throughout the termination process. A reawakening of prior feelings and conflicts, usually experienced as abandonment with attendant feelings of anger and sadness, can be anticipated. If not understood, the elder's response can arouse guilt and defensiveness in the departing worker.

The elder who has been able to integrate past endings into his or her ongoing life most likely will face the worker's leaving with a realistic blend of regret and self-interest. The worker's acceptance of the elder's feelings about termination and willingness to share his or her own with the elder are helpful, especially if expressed as part of a mutual review of the work together. For the elder, the summing up of past combined with a clear formulation of next steps for the elder to take will usually suffice.

The elder who has not come to terms with past losses will most likely face the worker's leaving with residuals of an incompleted mourning process. In this case, the termination process has greatest potential for pain and growth. Perhaps past termination was sudden, leaving the elder with no time to prepare for the blow, or the relationship was so ambivalent and conflictual that it could never be laid to rest. The worker who is prepared for the emergence of material from the past can use the current situation to help the elder separate in a more satisfying way.

Validation of negative feelings and a time frame that allows for detours to the past are essential. Often in the termination process, the elder will share areas of his or her life that are reawakened in the present situation. While some reactions to loss of the worker may follow the linear phases of the mourning process (shock and disbelief, denial, anger, bargaining, depression, acceptance), most vacillate between two or three phases or remain in an early stage.

Certain common behavior reactions indirectly indicate a phase of the mourning process. For example, regression to a lower level of functioning can be an expression of anger (as if to tell the worker that he or she hasn't helped a bit) or of a withdrawn depression. An exaggerated concern about the worker's future is sometimes a form of bargaining (to secure the elder's continued place in the worker's life). Connecting past and present patterns of response to loss to promote insight is sometimes helpful; interpreting current defensive maneuvers rarely so. Most effective is an experiential approach that allows the elder to work through past and present loss simultaneously.

The worker was highly involved in the case of Mr. Peters and concerned about the effect her departure would have on him at this time. His wife had died only three months earlier. He had just begun returning to the center for activities and his crying bouts had lessened. She allowed six weeks to prepare him for her leaving. The first week, she mentioned termination, Mr. Peters responded that he knew such a fine worker would move up in the world. He wished her well and quickly switched the subject, unresponsive to all efforts to focus him on the topic. The second week, he introduced a brand new legal problem involving his wife's will, maintaining that no one but the worker could help him through the lengthy process. She discussed alternatives and then linked the problem to his wish for her to remain. He appeared not to hear her. The third week he cancelled because of illness and did not appear at the center. The fourth week she found him withdrawn, tearful and hopeless about going on without his wife. As she listened, the worker noted and identified a strain of anger toward his children she had not heard before. He lamented their lack of concern with a new vehemence. He asked the worker if she could still visit him sometime. The worker suppressed her desire to comfort him by making that promise. She knew that continued, sporadic

*contact would negatively influence the formation of a relationship with
the new worker. She expressed her own sadness at the finality of separation,
recognized the cataclysmic changes that had taken place in Mr. Peter's life
in the course of their time together, and remembered a few meaningful
moments they had shared. For the first time, Mr. Peters could discuss
termination and reflect on the gap it would leave in his life. Although the
worker had hoped Mr. Peters would move on to beginning acceptance by
the time she left, this was not the case. During the last session he vacillated
between anger and sorrow. However, a six month informal follow-up call
to the transfer worker indicated that Mr. Peters had returned to the center
three weeks after her departure, had settled in to the new relationship
after a brief testing period, and was beginning to reach out to his daughters.*

In this case, the auxiliary role performed by the worker was
transferred, although the relationship itself was terminated. This
is an important point to recognize as the process to be followed
depends upon the future of the case.

A personal bond with the elder may make termination difficult
for the worker as well. Pain over abandoning someone in need
may lead to the promise of future friendly visits, calls, or letters.
Workers must question their own motivation and ability to continue the contact before making a commitment. It is cruel to make
idle promises to assuage a sense of guilt. Similarly, the exchange
of small gifts may be indicated, but never unquestioningly. If these
acts are used to deny the event of termination, they will be ultimately destructive.

Implementation of the auxiliary role forms the core of the
ongoing worker-client relationship and is related to carrying out
the case plan. Concerns specific to middle and termination phases
of the contact speak to the evolving nature of the relationship as
well as to facilitating utilization of other services. Group interventions are an important means of implementing the auxiliary
function model.

Chapter 6

THE WORKER-CLIENT RELATIONSHIP: STRUCTURE AND ISSUES

The auxiliary function model addresses the modifications necessary when translating generic social work principles to practice with the frail elderly. While knowledge and understanding of these principles, as outlined in excellent comprehensive texts (see Appendix A), should inform all practice, differentials in both the content and process of work with the ill or disabled elder dictate variations. Structural and conceptual issues of the auxiliary function model are discussed in this chapter.

INTERVIEW STRUCTURE

Site

The social worker frequently interviews the frail elder outside of the traditional office setting: by a hospital bed, in the corner of a busy clinic, in a nursing home lounge, at a kitchen table.

Interviews that take place in the client's home pose special problems. The elder is often disabled, isolated, and welcoming what is perceived as a friendly visit. Food and drink may be offered, further defining the worker as guest. While simple socialization with the worker may serve a need for the elder and indeed be an integral part of the case plan, care must be taken that the dictates of social etiquette do not preclude any other work taking place. Although indeed a guest on the elder's home ground, the social worker has the right and responsibility to make certain requests. Among these are seating arrangements that facilitate communication, control over intrusions, and the quieting of television and radio. The frail elder who is often unaware that this familiar environment is not conducive to a productive interview can accept the worker's modifications if they are properly explained and in so doing be gently reminded of the business aspects of the visit. At the same time, common courtesies of the guest, such as asking permission to use the phone and bathroom or to smoke, should also be observed.

Institutionalized elders often cannot differentiate among the many staff who provide service. The social worker can identify him or herself from those who "do for" by not only telling but showing that he or she is there to "do with." This may involve finding a space available for private interviewing that affords confidentiality and minimizes distractions, often calling for ingenuity and advocacy with other systems. Benefits are well worth the effort; the message to client and staff is one of respect for the frail elder and affirmation of the right to individualized attention. However brief the contact, the worker should be seated to be at eye level with the elder who is bed or chair bound. Even a visit of five minutes can thus become a meaningful interchange that validates client dignity.

In an office visit, the frail elder should be greeted first, by last name, and seated in a position that clearly indicates that he or she is a primary client. If at all possible, this should not be facing the worker across a desk but in a more informal position. A high straight-backed chair is generally more comfortable than the cushioned variety found in many offices. Noises and interruptions are particularly distracting for those suffering cognitive or sensory impairment and should be avoided whenever possible. Family, friends, or neighbors who may be present should also be greeted by name, their relationship clearly established, and seated in such a way that all can be seen and heard. While it is wise to allow some time alone for the elder in case he or she wishes to share private information, it may diminish the elder's sense of security to be separated immediately from others who accompany him or her as well as deny the worker the important opportunity to observe and understand the interaction between them.

Appointment Time

Needless to say, the social worker should be punctual for all interviews. The altered time sense and sparseness of events in the frail elder's life may arouse great anxiety and fears of being forgotten at even a few minutes delay. Unavoidable tardiness should be explained and the elder given the opportunity to express feelings about it. Length and frequency should be planned with the particular needs of the individual elder in mind (this may involve skills outlined in Chapter 8).

Appointment times should be as scrupulously adhered to in inpatient settings. The "captive" elder in a hospital bed should not be subjected to an unexpected interview while preparing for a bath. The nursing home resident should not be tracked down at bingo to discuss a roommate problem. While such commonly employed practices may fit neatly into the worker's schedule, they are inconvenient and demeaning to the elder.

The worker may be constantly visible in nursing homes and senior centers, fostering a tendency for some elders to nab him or her on the spot for questions, complaints, or simple attention. Unless the *study, assessment, and plan* for an individual elder indicates this as the intervention of choice, it is far more satisfying for client and worker if these contacts are structured into scheduled appointments, perhaps a few short ones each week. Office visits are usually by appointment but a drop-in policy may exist in certain settings. The elder should be told at the outset how much time is set aside for the interview so he or she can pace accordingly.

The elder is rarely as occupied as the social worker and may contribute to impromptu appearances, invidiously comparing his or her passive status to that of the social worker. "You are busy but I have plenty of time." The social worker's unquestioning acceptance of this formulation defines the elder as a powerless recipient who should be grateful for the worker's kindness at a time when an atmosphere of mutuality and respect should prevail. Setting a specific time, issuing an appointment slip, and cancelling of appointments with due notice and apology are essential. When this procedure is omitted with forgetful, confused elders, a self-fulfilling prophecy results in which the elder has no reason to make note of time. Memory loss is all the more reason why calendars, clocks, and reminders should be used.

The social worker has many clients; the frail elder has one social worker. The more limited the elder's life, the greater the significance of the social work interview. The elder needs to prepare physically, mentally, and emotionally for the encounter, which insofar as possible should take place at a time of day when the elder is at his or her best. Clients who are disabled and/or depressed generally do better in the afternoon, requiring the morning hours to marshal their forces. Their insistence on a specific hour may seem arbitrary and rigid to an overburdened worker, but when viewed as adaptive behavior makes good sense and should be honored whenever possible.

Appointments with the frail elder must be timed flexibly for maximum benefit. The fifty-minute hour is rarely the rule. Time may range from five minutes to several hours, depending on the elder's condition and the purpose of the meeting. Clients may be seen daily, weekly, or monthly.

The Telephone

The telephone is a useful, underused adjunct to in-person interviews with the frail elder and family—maintaining continuity, offering tangible support, alerting the social worker to potential emergencies, and supplementing or substituting for regular appointments when health or transportation difficulties cause cancellations. A daily five-minute talk with the worker during a time of crisis may be of greater value than a standard hour appointment when both are free to meet together. Telephone confirmation to the homebound on the day of an appointment will serve as a reminder for the confused and prepare the functionally impaired to be near the door at arrival time. If possible, a "phone hour," when the worker is available to family members or attendants who are primary caregivers of the frail elder, is a valuable service.

Providing the elder and those involved in his or her care with the name and number of a backup person at the agency for emergencies is reassuring. The homebound elder may have trouble understanding agency purpose and function if the only contact is with the worker who comes to visit. Emphasizing the client-worker relationship while minimizing the agency role deprives the elder of the security of a significant support system, especially important at the time of worker termination and transfer.

Fees

Today's elders are not accustomed to receiving something for nothing. Questions about fee are usually uppermost in their minds, whether or not openly expressed. Most social service agencies operate on a sliding-fee scale or free basis, receiving supplemental funding from third-party vendors, governmental grants, or private philanthropies. These programs are frequently confusing to the frail elder and may have to be explained at length.

Although the attitudes elders have toward money vary, certain patterns prevail. In most cases, they have worked long and hard for their money and saved at great sacrifice, sometimes continuing to put aside for a rainy day when most observers would agree that the time had come to spend for care. Often, elders have no savings and are dependent on the monthly arrival of Social Security and supplemental benefit checks to meet their basic needs.

While some elders are open to discussing financial issues, many are reluctant to divulge this information because of embarrassment, suspicion, or the etiquette of an earlier time that branded the public discussion of money as bad form. In these cases, the social worker must be sensitive to the meaning of fee to the individual and interpret the arrangement with flexibility and sensitivity. Thus, the reticent elder, with savings, may rather pay a flat fee rather than disclose full financial information and undergo a means test.

All elders feel greater investment, pride, and autonomy in a professional situation in which they exchange fee for service. It is essential that those financed by other sources be told that they are not receiving charity but rather an entitlement due them by virtue of paying taxes and/or making contributions to various causes over the years. The concept of entitlement is particularly important to reinforce with the institutionalized elderly, who are often reluctant to make service demands because they erroneously believe they are being given free care and should be grateful.

They are consumers with the same rights as private pay residents.

Dilemmas sometimes arise when an elder wishes to pay even if clearly unable to afford it. This may be an appreciative gesture or may be an attempt to tip the social worker in an effort to achieve a coveted spot in senior citizen housing or long-term care. In the latter case, the elder, not understanding the professional role, may simply be following society's customs. If, after interpreting fee and service policy of the nonprofit institution, the elder or family still persists, the worker may suggest a contribution to the sponsoring organization. If the gesture is offered as a personal tribute, a letter of appreciation to agency administration might be posed as an alternative. Such suggestions honor the elder's wish to contribute and express appreciation without compromising the integrity of the social worker, agency, or other staff.

Form of Address

In the initial contacts the elder should be addressed as Mr., Mrs., or Miss. If use of first names are a group norm (frequently the case in senior centers) or a growing bond between worker and elder make the use of first names more appropriate, this should be mutual. Appellations of "Dad" or "Mother" or the unilateral use of the first name of an elder are an abridgement of cultural customs and signs of respect and have an insidious infantilizing effect. Social workers should not only avoid this themselves but bring it to the attention of allied professionals.

Preparation

Preparation for the initial contact, covered in Chapter 4, is generally recognized as essential. Less recognized is the need for worker preparation before each interview, no matter how long, or well, the elder is known. This is especially crucial when caseloads are large and elders seen less frequently. Notes for the worker's own use, whether or not included in the written record, are then used to record nuances or themes that could be lost if left to memory.

The elder can also be encouraged to prepare for meetings. This might include making note of questions or thoughts that arise between sessions or gathering together papers needed for entitlement applications. This, as an additional benefit, makes tangible the elder's active role in the process.

Past activity should be continuously reviewed in terms of content, style, and movement toward the original goals. Recent information must be integrated into the ongoing assessment. Perhaps the elder has shared additional material that puts a different focus on his or her need, collaterals have become newly involved, or an exploration of outside resources and entitlements has yielded new alternatives that must be discussed.

The social worker enters each meeting with some expectation of what is to be discussed and accomplished. Preparation is not, as some beginners fear, tantamount to forcing one's own agenda on the client, nor does it preclude responding flexibly to the unforeseen—the emergence of new material or shift in emotional content that characterizes all worker-client relationships of any duration. To the contrary, having, as one student put it, "something in your pocket," lets the worker take advantage of such surprises at the moment when they can be most helpful. Much might have happened in the frail elder's life between interviews. Even in a week, changes in health and functioning are common. Attitudes may have shifted as a result of intervening experience or consideration of what was previously discussed. As the elder cannot be expected to be in the same place, each interview begins with the elder's communication of his or her current state, at his or her own pace, and in his or her own way.

Mr. Olds started out excitedly and confusedly to report on a call from his sister in California. The sister who had not been involved since the initial contact six months earlier had all but been forgotten by the worker. Taken unaware, she was not able to make sense of the situation until she returned to the office and reviewed the record. She then called Mr. Olds back, by which time he had forgotten the answers to her questions.

In this case, as in others where the elder is not seen frequently or regularly, minutes spent on preparation are amply repaid in efficiency.

Focus

Focus is often difficult to maintain in contacts with the frail elder. The blend of socialization and work on tasks, various communication impairments, and the anxiety or personal style of the elder may career the interview from one direction to another. Interruption, limit setting, and reminders of the contract may be misunderstood by the elder causing further confusion. After starting "where the elder is," active listening, paying particular note to transitions from subject to subject, is essential. Even if content or theme at first seems totally unrelated to the purpose of the meeting, there is usually a connection. Focus does not necessarily have to pertain to content. It may, just as productively, relate to theme.

Mrs. Peck and the worker had contracted to work on getting needed medical attention. An essential appointment with the eye doctor (cancelled several times previously) was to be discussed, but Mrs. Peck kept avoiding the subject, speaking instead about items stolen from her during her last hospital visit, crime in the neighborhood, and her sister's last painful illness. The worker abandoned efforts to keep Mrs. Peck on one topic and instead limited her responses to the dominant theme she had identified. The hostile and frightening feelings left from each experience, underscored and legitimatized by the worker, then became more acceptable for Mrs. Peck to express in terms of medical care.

If, after careful examination, the digression is unrelated and yet another digression leads the elder further afield, it is best to listen to, but not explore, any topic until the elder runs down and looks to the worker for a response. At this point, the worker can pick up one theme from the content that bears on the work at hand and begin exploration and discussion.

The auxiliary role may include cuing the elder into the reason and time frame of the meeting at various points. This is especially true of the elder with memory or sensory impairment; for example, "In the half hour we have left, we should get that clinic appointment straightened out for next week," may be all that is needed to get back on track.

Closure

Care must be taken to insure that the frail elder is not left at interview's end with an overflow of painful feelings or in a state of anxious concern. Unlike the less isolated and more able client who leaves the interview to face the distractions and demands of everyday life, the frail elder often has no outlet for the emotions aroused. Left alone in a passive state, the elder may continue to dwell on unsettling issues with unfortunate consequences. A lighter, more social tone in ending is often in order.

Mrs. Childs began the interview by lamenting her daughter's future vacation, expressed fears about an upcoming doctor's appointment, shared an amusing anecdote about her grandson, and concluded by commenting on a television special of the night before. Finally pausing, she asked the worker if she had seen the program. The worker, understanding that medical care and fear about her daughter's departure were both important work areas, decided to begin on the doctor's appointment as she had important new information to share with the elder and the vacation was a way off. She briefly shared her reaction to the television show, then suggested they talk more about the doctor. After discussion, it was mutually decided that the worker would arrange transportation and call the doctor to arrange a referral to VNS. Mrs. Childs would expect a VNS visit shortly thereafter to evaluate her need for home care. With ten minutes left, the worker decided not to pick up on the emotion-laden theme of the daughter but to defer until next time. Mrs. Child's energy for the day was spent. As it was important not to stir up troubled feelings and leave the elder alone to deal with them, the worker decided to ask more about the adored grandson. In this nonconflictual area, Mrs. Child's mood lightened and they shared a few laughs about his exploits before reviewing the plan and saying goodbye.

INTERVIEWING ISSUES

Personal Use of Self

The social worker is often the most significant figure in the frail elder's life—a reality attributable to many factors. The peopled world of the very old is steadily shrinking. There may be no other elders who can serve as confidants. Spouses, siblings, old friends, and coworkers may have died, be ill, or too far flung to provide support. Relationships with younger, more able people, including adult children, may be nonexistent or conflictual, further reducing opportunities for warmth when they are most needed.

The auxiliary role with the impaired elder is of a personal and active nature. With the mentally frail, the worker must introduce thoughts and perceptions as a supplement to those waning in the elder. With the physically frail, information and linkage to resources must occasionally be augmented by the actual performance of concrete tasks.

To the homebound or institutionalized elder, the social worker is an emissary of the outside world. The worker's selective introduction of what is happening in that world and a shared reflection on it can extend a limited horizon of thought and feeling, for it is in the personal encounter that the elder is returned to the self he or she was once.

The social worker must be open to personal involvement with the frail elderly and prepared to be touched and changed in some way by the work with each new client. The worker cannot be cloaked in professional anonymity; there must be a conscious use of a variety of roles—the most essential often being as a significant other in the elder's life. The worker will be seen as parent and child and as friend and advisor—frequently by the same elder.

Sometimes the worker has a minor problem with which the elder, by virtue of past experience or special skills, can assist: the fitting of a dress, the decision of where to vacation. Elders are a storehouse of unsought knowledge and ungiven gifts. Appreciating and using what they have to offer is crediting their abilities and providing them with a continuing involvement in life. Being able to give makes it far easier to receive.

To the aged who have sustained irreplacable losses of significant others, the social work relationship will fill symbolic and real needs for human attachment. The use of touch is particularly important with the frail elderly who may have outlived their sources of human warmth or who, for various reasons, cannot fully participate in a verbal interchange. The touch of a comforting hand, a kiss of greeting, or a reassuring hug may well be appropriate and indicated within the interview, depending on self-awareness and acute tuning into the elder's cues. Of course, there are elders who would be frightened or offended by a worker's use of touch, which may be viewed as an aggressive or a sexual approach. The study, assessment, and plan, combined with the worker's empathic moment to moment understanding, will assist the worker in knowing if, when, and how to physically reach out.

The elder takes in many nonverbal messages from the worker's appearance and manner. Colorful, attractive dress is an uplift to the spirits of workers and elders. Some elders are tolerant of casual fashions, hairstyles, and a breezy manner, but others question the capability of a professional who does not look or act the part as they envision it. Protecting the sensibilities of such a client may require some adjustment on the part of the younger worker in presentation of self.

The young worker's pace of thinking, moving, and speaking is generally faster than that of the elderly client. Sensory losses and physical and mental impairments often necessitate new approaches to communication. The worker must be able to modify personal mannerisms—voice, touch, manner—and pay increased attention to nonverbal methods of relating (see chapter 8).

In contacts with the frail elderly, the worker must walk the difficult line between hiding behind professional anonymity and dismissing the professional role as irrelevant and becoming a friendly visitor. A social exchange may be as valuable an intervention as goal-directed work on tasks. As such, it is equally subject to the worker's professional use of self and skill.

Mrs. Bond returned from the hospital to find that the heat was turned off and her window sill of plants had died and called her social worker. The heat was restored by a phone call, but the worker, remembering how the plants (grown from fruit seeds in soup cans) were very important to Mrs. Bond, suggested a "welcome home" visit. She thought of, and rejected, stopping at a florist for replacements. It was not Mrs. Bond's style. She did, however, buy some grapefruits and oranges. She made and shared a fruit salad with Mrs. Bond, after which they prepared the seeds for planting. In the process, Mrs. Bond tearfully recalled her husband who always liked growing things, then proceeded to show her own expertise. This intervention was structured and conducted according to the worker's assessment and case plan.

Mobilizing Strengths

The pulls between dependence and independence that exist throughout life are heightened at a time of depletion and loss for the frail elderly. Latent conflicts may be reactivated and characterological responses intensified. At one extreme are those clients who are all too willing to place their burdens in the social worker's lap with the magical expectation that someone at last can meet all their needs. At the other extreme are those who steadfastly maintain that they can manage everything themselves despite severe health and functional limitations. The majority of elderly fluctuate between these two poles as time and circumstance dictate their needs and shape their attitudes.

Dependence on others for the meeting of basic needs is reminiscent of childhood and, as such, may be accompanied by regressive behavior in totally unrelated areas of life. Social workers in nursing homes are often called in to settle minor disputes between residents, much as a mother is appealed to for justice in sibling contests. Community practitioners are aware of elders who demand help in activities of daily living long after self-care is possible and indicated. While the study of some of these elders will yield a lifetime pattern of dependent behavior, more often it will point to years of self-actualizing independent functioning that ceased as they entered the world of the frail.

Frailty is not a total or even chronic condition. While all definitions of this population speak to the vulnerability, multiple needs, and at risk aspects of their condition, few address the significant strengths and coping capacities that may remain in even the most severely depleted. The auxiliary role of the worker, to help the elder reach the highest level of adaptation possible, is frequently realized through the mobilization of strengths. Understanding that every situation, however new, has in it elements of the past, a past that the frail elder has survived, in some way gives important clues as to the strengths to be called on to meet the problems of today.

Mobilizing elder strengths requires three separate processes. The worker must first identify strengths, those exhibited at present and those that existed at some time in the past as revealed in the study. The worker must then determine how they can be transferred or adapted to meet the problem at hand. The last crucial task is to put the elder in touch with these strengths so they are once again his or hers to own and use.

Mrs. Lane, a nursing home resident, appealed to the social worker to make her roommate stop hanging her clothes to dry all over the room. The worker did not reply directly, but instead recalled what Mrs. Lane had previously told her of the ingenious way in which she had engineered travel arrangements for the disabled husband she nursed until his death. Mrs. Lane, proud and pleased the worker remembered, added to the story by giving another instance of her resourcefulness. The worker then said, "and you can't think of how to handle this?" Sheepishly, Mrs. Lane admitted she could and came up with a solution of her own.

If there are not current or past indications of strength, the worker must question how the frail elder survived throughout life. Often, it was through dependence on other people manipulated by "the tyranny of the weak." In such cases, it may be appropriate for the worker to be the first to freely feed the dependency need, legitimized at last by the frailty of old age.

When the VNS determined that their LPN was no longer needed for medical reasons, Mrs. Nator complained that no one understood how sick she really was. Her constant demand for attention from the daughter who lived nearby was causing tension in the daughter's family. Recognizing that Mrs. Nator was now using her daughter as she had her late husband — and that she had never developed the skills to cope independently — the social worker applied to another agency for homemaker service. A psychiatric validation of the elder's agitated depressive state was necessary and obtained. With someone in the house to lean on, Mrs. Nator's pressure on her daughter lessened. The daughter, who had all but withdrawn, was now able, with the worker's help, to respond only to the mother's appropriate requests for care.

Strengths are often labeled weaknesses in the frail elderly, making it imperative that the worker look beneath surface manifestations. The elder who bosses everyone around has not yet lost interest in or opinions about the world and can be helped to find a more appropriate outlet. Similarly, personality characteristics that were dysfunctional in earlier years may prove functional as needs change. The elder who was a clinging vine may do very well in the protective care of an institutional setting.

Knowledge of past reactions to life crises and stress is, as mentioned throughout the text, essential.

Miss Jabot was seen by the rehabilitation worker three weeks after her stroke. She was withdrawn and depressed—appearing quite helpless to cope on her own. However, in response to questioning about Miss Jabot's past reactions to loss, the niece provided information as to the recent one of the job that had been her "life" and the loss of her closest sister many years earlier. After both occurrences, Miss Jabot had retreated for a time but came "back to herself" with the demand of new responsibilities. The worker was able to share this information with the treatment team, who had been tentative about "pressuring" the elder into greater efforts on her own behalf.

The Decision-Making Process

Compare the sheer number of daily decisions made by the frail elder with those of his or her younger days. Small decisions such as what to eat or wear or how to travel may no longer be called for as restrictions curtail choice. Large decisions such as the purchase of a home or car have not been faced for decades. In the past, some decisions may have been made reflexively while others may have been the result of comparison shopping or information gathered from cohorts. Whatever the case, decision-making capacities were continuously exercised, the consequences of these decisions forming the basis for future judgment. In contrast, the frail elder lives a predictable life. It is small wonder that when approached with a major decision, he or she often defers to those in power or flatly refuses to consider a projected plan. Deciding whether to have an operation or to enter a long-term care facility is just too much to handle when the frail elder is out of practice in making decisions. As opportunities for choice and the information necessary to make intelligent choices are lessened, confidence and capacity diminish.

The auxiliary role of the worker in enhancing the decision-making process thus includes both increasing options and supplying the information with which to exercise them. There are those elders who for all their lives deferred to others in most decisions. They also may wish to defer totally to the worker, and this may be the only course of action possible. It also may be preferable in terms of allaying the elder's anxiety. The potential for some decision-making, however, should be tentatively explored.

The angry and depressed frail elder is often one who is living out the consequences of a decision made for, but not by, him or her. A lack of mourning for what has been lost may freeze adaptation at an uneasy accommodation when a higher level of functioning is possible. In these cases, retrospective decision making may be useful. The auxiliary role of the worker is in providing the information and emotional support necessary.

Mrs. Small was referred to the nursing home social worker because of difficulties with floor staff since admission six months earlier. The study data indicated that Mrs. Small had been managing well in a retirement community in Florida until eight months earlier when she traveled north to attend a nephew's wedding. At her daughter's home she fell and was hospitalized for a hip fracture. Complications led to pneumonia and Mrs. Small, in her weakened state, agreed to enter a nursing home where she could receive care in a setting close to family.

The worker was the first person who took Mrs. Small's expressed wish to return to Florida seriously. Together, they explored all aspects of the proposed move, resisting pressures of home staff and family who opposed this approach as unrealistic and arousing false hopes. In the process of discussing the move, Mrs. Small mourned all she had left behind, recognizing that she was a "different person" now and it would not be the same. Having made the decision to stay on her own, she was able to better use the resources offered by the nursing home.

Of course, coping mechanisms and strengths cannot be exercised in a static situation. Without choice, or the possibility of improvement, talk of autonomy is meaningless. When depletion is accompanied by a lessening of options, the worker is usually attuned to the necessity of garnering resources. Too often, however, once these are obtained they are presented as a *fait accompli* to the elder, obscuring the fact that he or she actually has a choice.

Miss Victor's prehospital nutrition was poor, and the worker planning

*discharge was urged by the attending physician to make a better arrange-
ment. After much time and work, she found two services for which Miss
Victor was eligible — a meals-on-wheels program and transportation to a
senior center lunch program.*

*Understanding that a long hospitalization following a heart attack,
during which everything was decided for the patient, had encouraged a
passive, dependent role, the worker did not begin by presenting the two
choices. Miss Victor would have rapidly selected one or the other — or
asked the worker her opinion — in neither case recognizing the complications or accepting the responsibility for her decision. The worker, preparing the elder to take control of her life again, began instead by focusing
the interview on the physician's concern that Miss Victor continue the
healthier diet of the hospital and asking her opinion. When Miss Victor
concurred, the worker suggested that there were community services
available to be decided upon by Miss Victor after they looked together at
her needs and preferences. Through exploration, the fact that Miss Victor
ate little when she was alone indicated the communal program. But, as
her persisting weakness made ambulation difficult, socialization at meal-
time had to be weighed against the investment in energy involved in
going outside. The major portion of two interviews were devoted to
discussing both alternatives. At the beginning of the third interview, Miss
Victor asked if she could begin meals-on-wheels and switch to the center as
she grew stronger, evidence that she was now "owning" the decision-
making process.*

Sometimes a frail elder will present the social worker with a
predecided plan and ask only for help in implementing it, or the
elder will turn down a suggestion of the worker without consideration. Perhaps this elder is unable to articulate questions or is
accustomed to denying all difficulties because facing them is
frightening and painful. It is important that the worker not negate
the choice, but rather ask the elder how the decision was made.
The response, which illustrates problem-solving capacities and
style, can then be used to determine if further consideration is
needed. As a rule of thumb, if the elder is overly positive, it helps
to point out possible difficulties, and if negative, to suggest
advantages. In either case, the worker is helping the elder exercise
and strengthen the decision-making capacity.

Sharing the Work

Assessing for, helping utilize, or monitoring the delivery of a service, giving support over a period of stress, and helping resolve interpersonal problems are a few of the common reasons for social work intervention with the frail elder. All are accomplished through the work of the relationship, in which the auxiliary role is exercised to maximize the level of elder participation.

The work, which forms the major focus of the social work interview, is usually broken down into tasks shared by elder and worker, as well as tasks each must perform on his own.

Mr. Hall was unable to use the medical services of the V.A. Hospital OPD clinic, although follow-up on the ulcerated condition of his leg was necessary to prevent possible amputation. Work between Mr. Hall and the worker was to identify the reasons for the breakdown to better fit his need and the hospital service. The shared task of problem identification yielded that Mr. Hall could not tolerate the wait for service for more than ten minutes before becoming abusive to staff and storming out. The worker accompanied the elder to one appointment to better understand and convey her investment in this problem. The worker's task then became to advocate for appointments at less busy times, interpreting the elder's low level of tolerance for any frustration as being the barrier to his using service. The elder's task was to give the resulting appointment plan "a chance," and if he became upset, to contact the supervising nurse (who was clued in to the situation) before he "blew his top." Together, elder and worker monitored the ongoing success of the plan.

There are three ways of sharing the work with the elder: doing for, doing with, and enabling the elder to do for himself or herself. Sometimes used in progression, more often in a fluid zig-zag as circumstances and frailty fluctuate, these methods should be understood and carefully selected by the worker in accordance with the assessment and case plan.

Doing for is the obvious choice when physical or mental impairment renders the elder incapable of the task. It is useful with the suspicious elder who requires tangible proof of the worker's investment before there is any trust. The hands-on intervention of the worker can provide the nurturant environment in which the chronically dependent elder can function optimally, as well as legitimize the dependency needs of the staunchly self-reliant. Doing for can be a valid method in itself or the first step in a process geared toward greater elder autonomy.

Doing with the elder may involve specific tasks for client and worker, or the two may participate in a common task. Following through on a specific task helps the overwhelmed frail elder experience mastery over one aspect of life while letting the worker handle more arduous tasks. In time, the elder's share of the work may increase.

In cases where elder and worker participate in a common task, the worker is modeling appropriate ways of handling problematic situations. This is particularly effective in contact with authority figures such as physicians or landlords with whom the frail elder may have difficulty communicating.

While enabling the elder to do for himself or herself should be the goal wherever possible, those who work with the frail elderly must not assume the most independent mode of functioning to be the best until the consequences for overall adaptation are clear. Value judgments that negate the elder's entitlement to concrete as well as emotional support from the worker as appropriate to need are to be avoided.

The auxiliary function model requires that attention be paid to certain structural and conceptual issues in the dynamic interplay between worker and frail elder. These include such concrete issues as the site and time of the interview and interpersonal issues as the worker's use of self and sharing the work with the elder. Consideration of these issues is a prerequisite for effectively utilizing the variety of interviewing techniques discussed in the next chapter.

Chapter 7

THE WORKER-CLIENT RELATIONSHIP: TECHNIQUES AND THEMES

INTERVIEWING TECHNIQUES

Interviewing skill is far more than selecting the appropriate response to an elder's production or artfully phrasing an inquiry or suggestion. With the frail elder, it is predicated upon an understanding of the individual's areas of depletion and loss, the adaptive process in motion, and the auxiliary role that will best supplement it. The commonly employed techniques discussed here are thus accompanied by an explanation of the worker's purpose and choice. The worker is also directed toward comprehensive texts from social work and other mental health disciplines that address interviewing techniques at length and are the foundation on which the following discussion is based (see Appendix A).

Active Listening

To listen actively is to hear the underlying conflicts, fears, and hopes, note significant omissions, and continuously inform the original assessment with the additional knowledge gleaned from acquaintance over time with the elder and his or her situation. Active listening communicates far better than words that the elder is unique and important to the worker.

Active listening is the core of all social work interventions with the frail elder. While the necessity is clear in initial encounters, ongoing contact offers a special challenge. The basic problem is known, as are its antecedents. A few reminiscences may have been repeated time and again. The words and style of the elder are familiar. All may lull the social worker into a passive form of

151

listening—nodding attentively while inwardly noting that the story has been heard before and biding time until the elder runs down and real work can begin.

The auxiliary role, to provide an opportunity for the elder to hear himself or herself think, may be a service in itself. Deprivation of other listeners to whom the elder can speak thoughts and feelings makes the worker important as a sounding board against which ideas can be tested and examined and coping strategies exercised.

Exploration of Fact and Feeling

In order to be helpful, more information than the elder spontaneously presents is usually necessary. The social worker questions that which is unclear and relevant to the matter at hand. This, rather than the length of contact or strength of relationship or intimacy of subject matter, determines the areas for exploration. For example, a disclosure of financial assets of family and elder could be relevant during the first interview if the presenting problem is a decision between home care or long-term placement and if the elder is first made aware of the necessity for the worker having this information before planning can begin. On the other hand, questions of idle curiosity such as a son-in-law's means of employment, though perfectly acceptable in a social context, are inappropriate within the helping relationship. The fact that elders frequently share personal information with the worker they regard as a friend (much of which does not bear on the problem contracted for) requires that the worker exercise self-discipline in such explorations.

Some inexperienced workers find exploration with the frail elder difficult. In everyday life, they hesitate to seek information that could be considered prying. They may skirt about areas of sadness in an attempt to spare others the pain of relating their sorrows (and themselves the pain of listening). Many concerns of the aged are denied by society in general: sexuality as inappropriate, death and dying as morbid. Older clients may remind the worker of parents and grandparents whose word could not be questioned. Each worker must recognize within himself or herself those areas of elder experience that tend to be avoided. As inhibitions to exploration are understood and overcome, the social worker is faced with a number of decisions as to why, when, and how to question. Often the elder will use a shorthand in communications, leading the worker to think a situation is understood before it actually is. A more detailed inquiry is usually in order.

Mrs. Evans used one sentence to sum up an entire experience or relationship. The interaction of multiple physical and emotional ailments was expressed as "feeling weak all over." Fifty years of marriage were encapsulated in a single phrase, "My husband never made a living." She could not live with her son because her daughter-in-law was "a cold person." As she listened to the elder, the worker had innumerable questions. What constituted "a living" for her? What alternate methods of support were found? Was this fact accepted with resignation or a source of never ending discord? Why did the elder present this fact now to the exclusion of all others? Is it an example of her suffering or strength or is there quite another reason? The social worker does not know the elder's definition of "a cold person" and must not assume that it matches her own. She still has no idea of how the living arrangement originated or why it failed—and must if she is to be helpful in formulating an alternative plan.

Beginning exploration should be as unstructured as possible, allowing the elder to expand further along whatever aspect of the situation has meaning. This may result in the sharing of a particular incident.

Asked what it was like living with and raising a family with a husband who did not make a living, Mrs. Evans recalled a specific incident of their married life that illuminated her longstanding feelings of martyrdom in the relationship and its importance to her today.

Asked what lead her to the conclusion that her daughter-in-law was a cold person, Mrs. Evans described an interaction between them that alerted the worker to the fact that Mrs. Evan's permissive stance with the grandchildren was the major source of friction.

An exploratory question should not beg an answer or carry within it an expected response. Labels that reduce the complexity of human experience to jargon must also be avoided. "Do you and your son have a good relationship?" thus fails as a question on all three counts. "What was it like when you last saw your son" will yield facts and feelings of greater import. "What" questions are generally better than "why" ones. "What bothers you about this plan?" will yield more information than "why are you afraid?"

Beginning with open-ended general questions and moving toward the specific is a fruitful method of exploration for most elders. However, it is not as useful with the mentally frail. Less able to conceptualize, they may associate freely on the general subject and require greater direction and structure from the worker.

Mrs. Barnes was asked how she handled her financial affairs. She responded by lamenting the high cost of everything. Asked again, she recalled that her son knew about those things. The worker then asked how she gets the rent to the landlord.

At these specific words Mrs. Barnes started to cry. She would be put out, she feared, because she couldn't find the rent bill. Specific questions revealed that the rent had not been paid since the son's death. Continuing to use concrete words and short sentences, the worker was able to keep Mrs. Barnes focused with a minimum of digressions. By the end of the interview, she had a clear idea of the extent and type of trouble Mrs. Barnes had handling money.

Sometimes a mentally impaired elder becomes flustered when asked direct questions. These are perceived as a test of capacities and as such are met with anger or denial. In such instances, the worker must forgo direct questioning and go with the elder's flow. This, of course, will require greater worker effort in piecing together a coherent view of what is happening and the elder's perceptions of it.

Back to back questions ("Would you rather do this or that?") require the elder to weigh several factors before answering. The auxiliary role of the worker dictates that many elders due to primary or secondary depletion need support in sorting out the issues, obtaining the necessary information about various alternatives, and in the actual decision-making process.

Miss Gregory knew she needed help in the home to care for herself after hospitalization for cataract surgery. Charged with finding out how many hours were needed, the worker utilized a series of open-ended exploratory questions each addressing the elder's preceding answer. Beginning with "What do you see as your needs for care" and then estimating the time for each task, the elder was helped to realistically determine the help necessary. When the worker then provided information about the kinds of service available, Miss Gregory could intelligently make her own decision.

Often the frail elder will ask the worker, "What would you do if you were me?" The reasons for such a question vary. It could be a testing, a transferential reaction to the worker as if he or she were the client's parent or good child, or a simple wish to know how another would respond to the same situation. Whatever the meaning, or the way it is handled, it should not be assumed that the elder who asks has no ideas of his or her own. Most elders have a plan or a hope that their problems will be resolved in a certain manner. Exploring these expectations is always important.

Exploration is often helpful in the case of the repetitive elder. The meaning of the same story (from past or present) told over and over may be revealed through questioning that moves forward and back in time from the repeated event.

Mrs. Stone began every interview with a recitation of her disappointment in her two daughters' lack of attention. In the same words, she described their daily calls and weekly visits, concluding that they were not interested in her. The social worker wondered at the elder's repetition of this theme and the conclusion that did not seem to jibe with the facts. Moving backward in time she asked Mrs. Stone about her own mother. She learned that Mrs. Stone's mother had spent the last ten years of her life, and died, in Mrs. Stone's home. The social worker then asked what Mrs. Stone had expected from her own children in her old age. Mrs. Stone replied that she had not expected to be taken in. What she had planned on, however, was a three-family house in which all generations could live together. Using the elder's repetitive phrase as a point of departure and imaginatively moving backward and forward in time the elder's meaning was revealed.

It is important in using this technique that the elder be apprised that the new line of questioning is to better understand the situation. Otherwise, it may be perceived as changing the subject. Parenthetically, one should not jump to conclusions on the basis of limited information; for example, in this case, the fact that mother and daughter spoke together daily did not in itself indicate that the interaction was warm or supportive. Such frequent contact may be more acrimonious than a weekly or monthly meeting. Who places the call and what is said and not said during the conversation is more to the point.

In all cases, the selection of a general question versus a specific one is a function of the worker's understanding of the elder in any point in time. A heavy reliance on general exploration makes for a diffuse unfocused interview with many areas touched on and none handled. Too close an adherence to detailed questioning lends the interview the feeling of an interrogation.

The frail elder can be expected to have many feelings about the depletions and losses experienced, whether and how these are expressed or acted upon determining, to a large extent, the level of adaptation. Feelings that are not self-evident should never be explored merely for ventilation or intellectual identification. Knowing that one feels "guilty" or "angry" offers the elder no relief unless that knowledge can be put to some use. Elder feeling is explicitly explored when it is expressed inappropriately or unexpressed, in either case impeding the adaptive process.

Mrs. Adams displaced her anger at her husband for dying and at her children for placing her onto one roommate after another at the nursing home. Empathizing with the feelings of abandonment and anger expressed by the elder and reattaching it to the determining event of placement was a necessary step before Mrs. Adams could invest in her new life situation with any chance of a successful adjustment.

The long-term care worker thus encouraged an expression of anger, a feeling that may not have been indicated with other residents. She knew that most elders placed by their children harbor some degree of bad feeling, whatever their expressed view. Yet they also love their children, need to think well of them, and rationalize the placement by claiming that their children could do nothing else. If they are otherwise doing well, such defenses serve a useful purpose and are better left untouched by the worker.

After suffering a hip fracture, Miss Drew stopped attending her senior center lunch program, embarrassed to be seen using a walker. Miss Drew settled into a homebound status, a premature dysfunctional accommodation since compensation was still possible. The worker recognized that mourning for her former mobility had never taken place. After Miss Drew was helped to express some feelings about the loss, she was better able to handle the reactions of others.

With the frail elder it is seldom fruitful to ask the ubiquitous "how do you feel about that?" Unaccustomed to introspection, he or she will generally answer by repeating the reasons given or with a fatalistic response, "that's what happens when you get old." It is better to elicit feeling from the facts. Thus, the worker did not ask Miss Drew how she felt about the loss of mobility, but rather what changes it had meant in her life. In the telling, Miss Drew's feelings of sorrow and anxiety were clearly evidenced, to be identified, empathized with, and worked through. Thus the feelings were structured for the client.

The social worker knows that there has been sufficient exploration when he or she sees the outer as well as feels the inner reality. He or she has a picture of the marriage, living situation, adult-child relationship—what in it is idiosyncratic, what common, and if, how, and in what ways it differs from norms of personality and behavior. He or she will then choose from among the repertoire of other interviewing skills those that will best advance the goal-directed case plan, always alert to the opening up of new areas that will require further exploration.

Clarification

Sometimes it is difficult to understand what the frail elder is trying to say. He or she may move from major themes to minutiae and from past to present so quickly that the point is obscured. A premature attempt to cut off such a narrative bespeaks a lack of interest; yet letting it continue too long will tire the elder without bringing any relief or assurance that the message has been heard. In such cases, it is helpful for the worker to briefly rephrase what he or she perceives as the essence of the thought, referring it back to the elder for verification. Here the auxiliary role is one of integrating and extracting relevances from the detail.

Mr. Drake spoke of loneliness since his wife's death, of the increase of crime, and then of his need for household help; then told a joke, the theme of which was that no one could be trusted. The worker ventured, "it sounds as if you're wondering if it is worth the risk to let a stranger in your home to provide the care you need."

Such a response often has the effect of a profound discovery to the elder. The elder is reassured that he or she is understood, or the elder may see that the worker has not grasped the intended message and volunteer new information to illuminate the situation. Such clarification techniques, with opportunities for elder feedback, used at many stages, insure that elder and worker remain apace in their perceptions and expectations of work together.

Support

In a broad sense, all exercise of the auxiliary role is support. But just what is being supported and why is often unclear. To support the elder is first of all to affirm his or her life view and feelings. This does not necessarily mean that the social worker shares all perceptions—only that their meaning to the elder is appreciated. Supporting the frail elder's independent functioning is risky until one understands its cost.

Miss Green neglected her own deteriorating heart condition for many months in order to care for her disabled sister. If the worker had entered supporting the elder's devotion and care to her sibling, Miss Green would be unlikely to later admit her own need for care. Instead of supporting the elder's actions, "It's wonderful how much you are able to do for your sister even though you are ill yourself", the worker supported the elder's intention, "You worry about your sister and want to do all you can for her although it is an effort when you are feeling so ill yourself."

This leads easily into a consideration of other ways of meeting the problem without the elder losing face. Similarly, the fears of the paranoid elder are real to the elder, and support in the difficult time he or she is facing precedes all other interventions.

Workers with the frail elderly must often support the elder's legitimate dependency needs in a society where independence is highly prized. In so doing, the worker is not using authority, as some would arrogantly assume, to grant permission. One does not give permission to elders, but rather helps them give permission to themselves through a closer view of the current reality and helping them make connections between their perceived responsibilities and their capacities to meet them.

Support is often interpreted as reassurance and inappropriately offered in a variety of situations. The use of false reassurance with the elderly is such a common response in our culture that a social worker may unthinkingly transfer its use into the professional relationship. The frail elder does indeed have much to worry about. Minimizing difficulties closes off communication and isolates the elder further as well as being confusing. The ailing individual who is told he or she is "doing fine" will soon distrust either himself or herself or the informant. Realistic reassurance is putting the elder in touch with the supports that exist, including personal strengths and those of the people who care.

The verbal and nonverbal expression of empathy is frequently used as a supportive intervention, the auxiliary role being validation of the elder's feeling. The best responses flow naturally from the work at hand, based on active listening and the worker's continuous effort to put himself or herself in the elder's shoes. Compassion, admiration, and apprehension are but a few of the worker's emotions aroused. Instead of telling the elder that the worker knows "just how it feels" (which no one can), the worker can use his or her own reactions "that sounds frightening" or "what an amazing experience that was!" to express empathy. The use of touch is also very useful in conveying understanding.

The worker's empathy with the elder's view does not preclude sharing his or her own view when it differs. Especially with the depressed elder, the worker's belief that things can be better, if based on realistic evidence, can be very supportive.

Silence

Silence, a valid though ambiguous means of communication, is a common aspect of the social work interview with the frail elder. The causes are many: impediments attributable to physical processes such as aphasia are common as are a variety of emotional determinants. The depressed elder may manifest a slowing down of all functions, speech among them. A slower processing of information due to the aging process and/or sensory impairments may also contribute to silence. Confusion and memory loss can render one mute. Silence can be the sign of resistance to ongoing inquiry or the time when a thoughtful assimilation of previously discussed issues is taking place. Often, as in the period immediately following a death, there *is* nothing to say; the enormous impact of the events may render one speechless. For the understanding of why silence is occurring with a particular elder at a particular time, the social worker is guided by knowledge of the elder's style, what is happening in the elder's life in general, and what is happening in the interview in particular that triggered this response.

Accepting the silence, through a comfortable participation in it, is the worker's first step—often the only step necessary. The acceptance of the elder's silence comforts the aphasic and bereaved, gives the scattered elder time to pull thoughts together, and affirms autonomy in the angry or resistant elder. (It might also be remembered that not every elder communication requires a response from the worker. Or a response may seem called for but the right one does not come to mind. It is then better to reserve comment than to offer one that is inappropriate.)

In the absence of organic impairment, silence is generally self-limiting. Waiting patiently for it to be broken by the elder often yields a significant reward; the content and affect of communication immediately following a silence is usually significant. However, the worker sometimes finds it necessary to be the one to break the silence; for example, if there is a palpable feeling of unexpressed discomfort on the part of the elder that begs release. A beginning comment on the silence that legitimizes it for the elder, such as the observation that "it's hard to talk," may open the way for the elder to tell why.

When the elder is physically or emotionally immobilized for speech, the worker may feel he or she has to take a therapeutic gamble and verbalize concern. This is the riskiest approach. Assuming and presuming are interventions of last resort, and infinite care must be taken to select a minimum of words that convey preliminary understanding and the wish to understand more. An honest expression of the worker's own feelings is one way to avoid overstepping.

At their first interview after Mrs. Walsh's death, Mr. Walsh only nodded at the worker's expression of sympathy and concern. They sat in silence for some time. The worker then began, "What a shock your wife's death was to me when I heard of it. It's hard for me to imagine she's no longer here." She avoided comments that told the elder what he was or should be thinking or feeling. Such expressions as "You miss your wife" or "This is a lonely time for you" could have widely missed the mark.

Education

The frail elder usually has little exposure to the problems of aging or the resources available to meet them before he or she needs help. Typically, understanding is based on a grab bag of information obtained from many sources: medical explanations, experiences of neighbors or friends, articles in the popular press. Misconceptions and lack of knowledge can be assumed to exist in everyone new to the experience of aging. The auxiliary role of the worker is never more obvious than in marshaling the information necessary for understanding and responsible decision making.

As the problem-solving efforts of the frail elder are based on a thorough understanding of the circumstances involved, it is usually the task of the social worker to share, explain, and interpret information from a variety of sources. Then a decision must be reached as to what information the elder and family need to make an appropriate plan.

Mr. Murray and his daughters met with the hospital social worker to evolve a discharge plan. The options under consideration were return to his own home, a short stay at one daughter's, or temporary placement in a rehabilitation center. Before the interview, the worker identified several sources from which information would be required. The medical diagnosis, treatment plan, and prognosis had to be obtained from the attending physician, the availability of beds at the center was needed from their intake office, home care possibilities had to be negotiated through a third-party vendor, and the daughters' ability and willingness to offer care had to be explored with them. At the time of the meeting, the worker had obtained the medical information. Before sharing this, however, she asked the family and elder their understanding of Mr. Murray's present condition and needs for care. She listened carefully to the content and manner of their presentation to determine what additional knowledge they would

need from her and how she could integrate it with what they already knew.

Education of the frail elder and his or her family is a collaborative effort involving input from many disciplines. Social workers should be aware of the public information material disseminated by the major associations devoted to research and care of chronic impairments as well as those distributed by public and voluntary agencies that offer entitlements (see Appendix A). Such handouts are informative, useful guides that elders can take home and study at their leisure. When functioning as case manager, the social worker must either gather and coordinate information from all significant service providers or enable the elder and service providers to communicate directly with each other.

Advice Giving

Many practitioners who reject the advice-giving role fail to recognize that they are expressing an opinion in the content and manner of their presentations. The worker's knowledge base is far greater than will be needed for each elder, and the bio/psycho/social assessment of the individual will narrow possibilities still further. In determining the information to be shared, the worker should continually monitor his or her own investment in the elder's choice; for example, the worker with an anti-institutional bias may, by brief mention and nonverbal disapproval of long-term care facilities, indeed be giving advice without intending to do so.

The perspective of the auxiliary function model sheds a different light on advice giving than that which holds in traditional practice. The worker cannot always reject the expert role in which he or she is often placed by the frail elder. In the following case, advice giving was indicated given the individualized study, assessment, and case plan.

The worker had known Mrs. Fuller, a legally blind woman with a severe heart condition, for six months, during which time she had coordinated health care and homemaker services for her. At a point where Mrs. Fuller was functioning better than she had in years, her only son, an alcoholic with a history of psychiatric hospitalizations, surfaced after a long absence. He proposed that his mother give up her apartment to live with him and his family in a distant state. Although Mrs. Fuller recognized that she was wanted primarily for her pension checks and did not wish to be uprooted she felt she could not say no to her child in trouble. The worker pointed out the elder's very real needs for care and the unlikelihood of her receiving it in that situation. She also involved the doctor who underscored this view. Mrs. Fuller was relieved to cede the responsibility for the decision, telling her son that "doctor's orders" prevented her move. In this case, the worker saw and met the elder's need for a way out.

Of course, there are other instances where the worker's advice is not heeded. Often the elder and family must live out the consequences of an ill considered plan, or a precarious level of adaptation will be clung to tenaciously and any service, however needed, will be rejected.

The worker whose advice is spurned must accredit the self-determination exercised by these elders and leave the door open for them to return when and if they wish. Better yet, the worker can remain in touch over the transition period to consult on problems as they arise. In any case, irrevocable decisions should be cautioned against, and time-limited trial periods suggested. This face-saving strategy allows elder and family the opportunity to experience a plan without feeling bound to it. If, for example, Mrs. Fuller decided she wished to move to her son's home, the social worker could have reached out to him to explore the possible consequences. Because no one could predict how the plan would work, a visit of a month, with Mrs. Fuller maintaining her apartment, would be suggested before a permanent move.

Anticipation

Concentration and conceptualization are often difficult for the frail elder owing to the nature of the depletions experienced. The worker's auxiliary role is thus to help the elder anticipate the steps that lie ahead. In so doing, the worker is augmenting existing capacities to plan and imagine with the timely insertion of concrete information and role playing exercises. Instead of being a passive recipient of explanations, the elder is engaged in the process of intellectually and experientially trying out new situations or methods of relating before they actually occur. Because anticipation is a technique that requires active participation of the frail elder in obtaining mastery over his or her life situation, it is applicable in many settings and situations.

Although Mrs. Kane had been interviewed and had toured the nursing home, she could not clearly recall it, confusing the memory with that of the hospital. Reviewing the past history, the social worker saw that Mrs. Kane decompensated with every recent change in her life and posited that placement in the nursing home would pose similar problems. She thus set preparing Mrs. Kane for the move as a major priority of their work together.

Mrs. Kane could not relate to abstract explanations of how living in the home would differ from her present arrangement. Therefore, it was the worker's task to relate what she knew of the home's routine to Mrs. Kane's day-to-day concerns. When Mrs. Kane spoke of preparing food, the worker described how food would be served "like a restaurant." When Mrs. Kane spoke of self-care, the worker described how baths are given and about the laundry. Together, they went over Mrs. Kane's belongings and clothing to determine what to take. All had to be repeated each visit for several weeks until Mrs. Kane could internalize the fact that she was moving and begin to voice her concerns about it. (If possible, more visits to the home and participation with residents in some of their activities would have been helpful.)

Anticipation is also valuable with more able elders. Asking "what would you most like to happen?" or "what is the worst thing that could happen?" may yield important insight into the elder's hopes and fears that can then be discussed. Occasionally workers are so tuned in to the intrapsychic meanings of life events to the elder that they miss the concrete concerns with which anticipation could be useful. For example, placement in an institution may on one level mean "the waiting room for death" as an elder phrased it. On the other hand, it also means that the elder has to learn anew how to get the laundry done. Preparation for the latter problem may increase a sense of control, which in time will make the existential issue easier to bear.

If the elder is experiencing communication problems intimately with family and caretakers or generally with the larger bureaucracies that affect his or her life, role play may be helpfully incorporated into the interview. Elder and worker may feel silly the first time they try this. A shared laugh is a good beginning to trying on and sorting out the actual words that invite or discourage aid.

Role playing past or anticipated transactions with others is also a useful way to try out new ways of relating and to increase self awareness.

Mr. Farris had difficulty seeing cause and effect and little understanding of the role he played in his problems at the OPD clinic. The social worker first empathized with his problems of service at the clinic, then asked him to pretend she was the supervising nurse and to tell her what was wrong. The exercise allowed for much ventilation of rage as well as revealing that Mr. Farris had one constructive idea as to how service could be improved. The worker gave him positive acknowledgement of his idea, noting it was hard for her to hear it while he was yelling so. As the intervention plan was for him to bring future problems to the supervising nurse before storming out, they role played again how he could approach her. The social worker also anticipated the possibility that the supervising nurse would be unavailable at the moment needed and helped Mr. Farris prepare for that contingency.

A doctor's visit is a difficult time for everyone, particularly the elder, who is more often ill and has greater reason for apprehension. The elder may feel too rushed, intimidated, or fearful to obtain the answers he or she wants. Before the appointment, the social worker can help the client compose a list of questions. If the elder invites the worker to attend, and this is possible, the worker can help the elder articulate concerns or ask for clarification when it appears the elder does not understand and has trouble questioning. This intervention not only has the advantage of securing needed information for the elder but serves as a role model for the elder when in a similar situation and unaccompanied.

Universalizing

For the frail elder who is isolated from peers, it is often helpful to know that the experience is not unusual and that his or her reactions are understandable. Very often, people fall far short of their own expectations for functioning, often based on erroneous assumptions about others. The worker's familiarity with a large number of the elder's cohorts in similar situations can be used effectively. The frequently overused response "This must be very difficult for you" implies that the situation would be less difficult for someone else. It is better for the worker to make a more specific empathic response and then universalize so the elder can place this problem in perspective.

Mr. Gale spoke of how hard it was for him to sit down to his solitary supper after fifty years of dining with his wife. The worker responded, "It's hard to get used to eating alone." She then added that this feeling is common to many people who have lost the partner of a long marriage, that it takes some time for everyone to adjust, and that the crying bouts he had at these moments were part of a normal process. This information was reassuring to Mr. Gale, who felt it was unmanly to cry.

Confrontation

Confrontation is a lesser used interviewing technique with the frail elder. There is obviously no need for its use if a more gentle intervention is possible. However, there are times when it is the only appropriate response. Perhaps the elder courts self-destruction in a denial of a life threatening situation, or impairments of cognition and judgment prevent the elder from recognizing certain problems.

The worker's realistic view of the situation must be used as an auxiliary to the elder's limited view before entry to offer service can even be effected. Confrontation is a blow to self-esteem, and care must be given to support the elder's strengths throughout the intervention. A comment on the situation, rather than on the elder's perception or handling of it, is a good beginning. This can be followed by an alliance with the elder's striving for health through a consideration of ways in which the situation can be improved.

When Mrs. Doolittle was first visited by the social worker, she maintained that she was perfectly able to care for herself. She was obviously malnourished and there was no evidence of food in the apartment. The worker asked what she had for breakfast. Mrs. Doolittle responded as if by rote, "I always eat a good breakfast. It is the most important meal of the day." Contradicting her, "You are surely not eating because you're so thin and weak" would result in anger and defensiveness. Asking to see what was in the pantry would have been demeaning. Instead the worker empathized with Mrs. Doolittle's intention, "I can see that you understand the importance of eating properly but there isn't any way you can, now that it is so hard for you to shop and cook." Mrs. Doolittle was able to own this interpretation of the problem and begin to listen to suggestions for improvement.

Sensory and mental impairments combined with a paucity of socialization opportunities may prevent the frail elder from recognizing how his or her behavior is perceived by others. The worker's confrontation may be necessary to alert the elder to the feelings and possible recourses of those who may have been offended. Exercises in empathy that appeal to the elder's self-interest are often helpful. Remonstrances and moralistic pleadings that make the elder feel like a naughty child are not.

Mr. Moss described to the worker how he had "told off" the reception-ist at the food stamp center. The worker remarked that if she were the receptionist she probably wouldn't rush to get Mr. Moss's forms approved but would work harder for the people who were nice to her. The worker's linking of cause and effect in a gentle confrontation helped Mr. Moss to look at and modify his behavior.

When Affect and Content Differ

The frail elder may nonverbally express a message contrary to his or her spoken words. Some illnesses are characterized by disturbances of affect. Lability of affect is commonly associated with post-stroke elders, chronic inappropriateness or deadening of affect with psychotic disorders. In such cases where the nonverbal communication is a less reliable indicator of elder feeling than the verbal, the worker response is best directed to the spoken word.

Mrs. Ross habitually spoke in a depressed monotone. Interviews always began on a note of complaint against those who did not recognize how sick she was. One day she added a new symptom to her litany and repeated it a few times within the hour. As her affect remained unchanged, it took some time for the worker to "hear" and respond. Further explora-tion and medical follow-up yielded early detection of a potentially serious medical condition.

With elders who customarily employ a wide range of affect, the worker should respond to the nonverbal emotion rather than the spoken word.

Mr. Wiley spoke objectively about his wife's impending hospitalization — matter of factly listing the procedures she would undergo and praising the wonders of modern science. The worker noticed a slight tremor of voice and clenching of fist she had never seen before. She agreed that there had been many advances in medical care but added that facing surgery was still very frightening for patient and family. Mr. Wiley was then able to specify some of his concerns.

Interpretation

The interpretative response, aimed at promoting elder insight, is of specific and limited usefulness with the frail elder. Beginning workers who detect patterns of behavior and response in their clients are often eager to point them out. Their interpretations may be denied, objected to, or unheard by the elderly, who are unaccustomed to making such connections and see little relevance in doing so. On the other hand, elders who seek counseling for intrapsychic or interpersonal problems and understand the role of self-awareness in resolving their difficulties can benefit as greatly as those of any other age.

If, when, and how one uses interpretation are dependent not only on the elder's capacity for insight but also on the nature of the work contracted to be done and the degree to which unexamined issues impede it. Transference reactions toward the worker are a primary example, and one that can be understandably communicated.

Physically and mentally depleted, Mrs. Earl agreed to the plan for home care worked out between her husband and the worker. Yet on the day the practical nurse arrived, she lifted herself screaming from the bed and ordered her out, shouting racial epithets distressing to all. Shaken, but the wiser for her oversight, the worker spent a session alone with Mrs. Earl. In this discussion the elder clung to her and kissed her, begging her to stay and do the caregiving herself. Remembering Mrs. Earl had lost her only child, an attentive daughter, the worker who could accept the elder's rage and sorrow at now being cared for by a stranger said "I know you wish I were your daughter and could come every day — but I am not and I can only come once a week to talk with you and Mr. Earl about your plans." (Had Mrs. Earl been more actively involved earlier, much hardship would have been avoided.)

Summary

A summary, or review, of what has occurred between elder and worker can be used at many places in the contact. Mutuality, with emphasis on client participation, is the key to the success of this technique. It can be utilized at the end of an emotional session with an isolated elder, helping reestablish controls. In another instance, shared review of tasks completed and the next steps to be taken can provide the elder with a sense of accomplishment and continuity over time in a problem-solving venture. Summing up the major points of the activity to date is also useful at those times when elder and worker seem to have reached an impasse in their work together; it is then used to identify the point at which things began to fall apart.

SPECIAL THEMES

As performance of the auxiliary role draws worker and elder ever closer, themes of importance to the frail elder usually arise. Often intertwined with concrete work on tasks, such content may form a secondary, but nonetheless important, part of the overall contact with the elder, as well as requiring an interpretative or mediating approach with others.

Sexuality

Most people thrive on human touch and shrivel without it. Deprived of it by their depletions and subsequent isolation, the frail elderly are prone to reach out for it to their workers. Individual as well as cultural factors play a great part in how this need will be expressed.

Young workers who are comfortable with the hand holding or parting hug of an elder are frequently dismayed when the nature of the touch or the accompanying verbalization have a sexual connotation. Unexpected, the elder's expression of sexuality is often met by reflex responses of panic, anger, or judgment. The worker who accepts the centrality of sexuality throughout life is ready for its explicit or implicit emergence in work with elders of all ages and anticipates that the frail elderly are more likely than most to express these feelings in socially inappropriate ways. The mentally or sensory impaired may not be fully aware of time, place, or person. Self-control and censorship may have become lax. Regressive behavior in such basic areas of functioning as eating and elimination can be accompanied by sexual expression appropriate to that phase of development. The frail but alert elderly may have all energies sapped by pain and the struggle merely to survive, with sexuality, dormant for long periods, erupting in sudden, unexpected ways as strength returns. Frailty often leads to isolation. Opportunities for appropriate expressions of sexuality, whether at home or in an institution, are diminished.

Response to sexual touch is, as response to all other elder communications, dependent on an individualized assessment of the elder and situation at that point in time. The worker must first be sure that he or she has not inadvertently stimulated the elder through the setting or conduct of sessions; for example, the home-bound elder who is not bedridden should be encouraged to dress and meet the worker in a living area—a procedure that fosters a productive working relationship whether or not inappropriate expressions of sexuality are an issue. Seductive clothing or a flirtatious manner that are habitual to the worker's generation may be interpreted as an invitation by the elder.

Even a rudimentary knowledge of the elder's past methods of relating sexually is helpful in understanding the significance of the current situation. The man who prided himself on being a playboy or the woman whose self-image depended on male attention may be reacting as they always did to members of the opposite sex. A light handling of the incident that validates the elder as a still sexual person, while restating the nature of the relationship, may be all that is necessary. The elder who has been withdrawn since the loss of a beloved mate may be manifesting a return of feeling that should be affirmed and directed more appropriately. This may require a more thorough exploration and discussion. Homosexual feelings, either active or latent through life, may emerge through proximity with the younger worker who represents a more accepting generation. The handling of such material is dependent on the elder's level of awareness and its influence on the work and tasks at hand.

The elder who does not act out sex-related concerns may also wish to air them, but he or she may be restrained in discussion because of delicacy or embarrassment. One young worker interpreted an elder's refusal to speak about upcoming prostate surgery as denial; actually, the elderly gentleman felt the topic unsuitable for discussion with an unmarried woman.

Testing of the worker is often practiced by elders fearful of being met with ridicule if their interests are expressed openly. Reflections on the changing sexual mores of society or comments on May–December marriages may be the elder's way of introducing his or her concerns and should be explored.

Mrs. Taylor, a widowed foster home resident, complained to her social worker about the attentions of a newly admitted male. The worker, who heard the ambivalence in her tone, commented that he was an attractive looking man in whom many women would be interested. Mrs. Taylor then spoke of loneliness since the death of her husband and fears that she no longer knew how to behave with a man, issues never before raised in the contact.

Specific information about sexuality in the later years, which forms an integral part of the worker's knowledge base, can be extremely useful. The worker's assessment will determine how this can be best employed. Written material, to be pursued in private, is helpful to some. Others, like the aforementioned Mrs. Taylor, may need to role play anticipated social situations about which they feel insecure. Films and group discussions have also been useful in congregate settings. Recognition of the elder's sexual needs is troubling to family or other helpers and may require interpretation from the worker. A consistent nonpunitive response combined with an effort to provide a realistic outlet for normal human feelings will remove the secrecy that breeds stigma and shame.

Reminiscence/Life Review

As anyone who speaks to elders knows, memories from the past are practically ubiquitous. In fact, their absence may be an early indication of emotional problems. Reminiscence generally accompanies concrete work on tasks, although in counseling cases it may constitute a major portion of the work. It includes the spontaneous grab-bag of memories, freely associated from past to present, which can arise in the first meeting and persist throughout the ongoing contact with the frail elder as well as the ordered evaluation of a life.

Sharing the past with the younger worker can have many meanings to the frail elder. Memories can be used as denial of present losses and the threat of future loss. Recalling past pleasures can be a comfort in a time when there are few. Unpleasant memories can serve to document that trouble is no stranger or that life has always been unfair. Repeated stories from the past often indicate areas of continued concern; also, they may be a way of informing the worker that he or she did not appear to listen the last time. Reminiscence is sometimes the attempt to narrow a fifty or sixty year life span between worker and elder. "I was not always what I am today. I was once young, as you are young," is the message of such recollections. Finally, reminiscence can be the elder's gift to the worker — the passing on of what has been learned in a long life is often with the hope that the worker will learn from the life experience of the elder. The elder is bearing witness to what he or she has known.

One auxiliary role of the worker in reminiscence is as both individual and generational representative, a recipient of the elder's sum total of experience and wisdom, a link in the chain of life. Another auxiliary role is as coevaluator, helping the elder place individual experience within a wider context; for example, the failure to financially provide for one's family when linked with economic realities of the Great Depression can help the elder accept, in Eriksonian terms, his or her "one and only life", accorded extra worth in the lessons it holds for following generations (Erickson, 1959). Finally, the auxiliary role helps recycle the experience of the past for the elder's present use.

While recall of one's life is therapeutic when the conclusions reached lead to satisfaction, it is less so when the sum total of life experiences leads to disappointment and bitterness. A group experience in sharing nonconflictual, nonpersonal past experiences may still be helpful. At one day-care center for geriatric mental patients recently deinstitutionalized after many years in hospitals, a successful group took place, centered on individual recollections of universally shared experiences. Sharing of these memories affirmed for each member that, despite the limitations of each individual life, a role was played in the collective history. Oral history groups serve a similar function and can be facilitated in many settings. The homebound elder will usually need little encouragement to talk about mementos and photographs. The worker's unfeigned interest girded by the conviction that the content to be shared is as important as anything else encountered in an interview may be all that is needed.

Often, in the process of sharing the past, still viable strengths or interests emerge that can enhance current functioning. The popularity of adult education classes in long-term care facilities speaks to the needs of many elders to expand intellectual horizons. Caution should be exercised, however, toward a hasty or literal transfer of concrete skills of the past. The older woman who spent a lifetime sewing for her family does not necessarily wish to continue this in an occupational therapy class. In addition to changed interests, depletion of the later years may render the work product less competent than that performed in the elder's prime, underlining the losses endured. Less painful is a new activity, related enough to be familiar yet different enough to preclude unfavorable comparisons.

Death and Dying

Death and dying, once a taboo topic, in recent years has assumed professional and lay attention. Many newcomers to social work with the elderly assume that, in fact, the frail elder is the dying elder and that the personality dynamics observed and theoretical constructs developed in experience with younger clients are directly and universally applicable.

Despite obvious parallels, this is not the case, empirically or

clinically. The elder who has today reached the age of sixty-five has an excellent chance of living much longer. Even the very old and very impaired elder may survive five or more years beyond the first social work contact. The new enthusiasm about death and dying on the part of workers has had unfortunate consequences for those frail elderly who are more concerned with mundane matters of life and living. Sensitivity to the fluctuating nature of elder needs is nowhere more important than in concurrently handling the concrete problem of the moment and the contemplation of eternity that characterizes so many interviews with elderly people.

The diagnosis of cancer springs to mind when we think of dying; yet in the elderly, the illness often develops slowly, so that the individual may be asymptomatic, unconcerned, and eventually die of another cause. A functional disability such as severe arthritis can cause far greater physical and emotional distress. Similarly, the elder who has experienced frightening episodes of congestive heart failure may recognize and fear an imminent death, although he or she appears to be active and well to the untrained eye. Some guidelines, however arbitrary, must therefore be drawn for this discussion. A grave and limiting medical prognosis with an elder struggling with the concrete and emotional demands of coping would appear to be necessary conditions.

This is not to say that the subject of death is rarely raised among the frail elderly population as a whole. Those who have personally cared for dying relatives (such as surviving spouses) or are surrounded by the ill and dying (as in long-term care facilities) are prone to reflect on their own dying long before they personally experience signs of its being near.

Unlike the younger client, the elder has usually experienced the death of many people close to him or her, and through the years, has reached intuitive, as well as intellectual, awareness of the life-cycle and of mortality. While this may not insure acceptance or comfort in facing death, it does mean that the shock, disbelief, and sense of unfairness at being singled out to die while others live, which permeates the reactions of many younger clients, is not observed generally in the old.

In some cases, the fact of death will reactivate or stimulate anxiety and depression in the elder. This occurs in the case of people who believe in a hereafter, who may seek and fear being reunited with loved ones who have died previously or who anticipate a judgment day. Such situations, of course, deserve social work attention. However, in most cases, it is the method of their dying that concerns elders.

Indications that the elder is preoccupied with dying vary from individual to individual, usually in keeping with the general personality type. The intellectualized elder who handles anxiety through control and planning will possibly devote attention to the preparation of a will and anticipate funeral arrangements. The more dependent or hysterical elder may develop the dying symptoms of a close relative or dwell excessively on deaths that appear on the news.

In the fear of a long, painful dying, themes of deterioration, dependence, and loss of control are universal. The social worker must be able to listen without false reassurance or attempts to turn the elder away from "morbid" material. In fact, a specific exploration of the fear of dying is crucial. What is it specifically that the elder fears—pain, dying in a hospital, being in a helpless position with no one to hear the call for aid? Information, clarification of procedures, and concrete assistance in assuring that the most dreaded occurrence will not materialize are as helpful here as empathic understanding of the feelings expressed.

In addition to work with allied professionals and family, one can help the elder handle fears by reinforcing his or her habitual defenses; for example, helping the controlling elder plan the funeral or demonstrating to the fearful client how help will come when the call bell is used.

In every situation, the social worker follows the elder's lead. If the elder is healthy but preoccupied with death or dying, that is the area of work. If the elder is in fact dying but preoccupied with matters of living, then help is directed to that.

Kastenbaum cautions against a "set," in which the worker, prepared to help the dying client through the now well known stages delineated by Kubler-Ross (denial, anger, bargaining, depression, acceptance), is unable to individualize the elder or his or her situation. He notes that this scheme does not account for such differentials as illness, mode of treatment, environmental context, ethnicity, or life-style of the client (Kastenbaum, 1978).

The auxiliary role of the worker with the dying elder recognizes the importance of all of these considerations. The worker often must be more than a sounding board and help in a variety of concrete ways.

The nursing home worker assigned to Miss Kase, after her third surgical procedure in six months, carefully studied chart notations that indicated widespread metastasis and a grave prognosis. She expected to meet a woman preoccupied by death and dying, but found instead that Miss Kase did not wish to discuss the subject. Her need for the worker's help was in expediting the delivery of a pair of orthopedic shoes on order for three months. These shoes were needed to take Miss Kase, albeit with great difficulty, to activities and meals in the ambulatory section of the home. After this was accomplished, the worker was assigned other concrete tasks such as arranging the disposition of belongings. During the contact, which lasted four months, until Miss Kase's death, the worker's attempts to elicit feelings were repeatedly rebuffed. Miss Kase, who had never shared her emotions with others, wished to die as she had lived. These wishes were respected in the exercise of the auxiliary role.

Interviewing techniques with the frail elder are ones commonly employed with any age client. The unique circumstances of the frail elder call for the special approaches explored in this chapter. The special themes of sexuality and death and dying and the relevance of the life review have been underscored. The challenge presented by particular problems and behaviors is next discussed.

Chapter 8

THE WORKER-CLIENT RELATIONSHIP:
MANAGEMENT OF SPECIAL PROBLEMS

This chapter addresses some of the problematic conditions and behaviors that can hinder communication between the social worker and frail elder and interfere with the client's utilization of needed services. The frail elder's ability to communicate and relate to others may be handicapped by basic depletions, such as hearing and sight loss, and by troublesome conditions, such as depression and suspicion. Most often in later life, the latter represent dysfunctional accommodations to depletion. These may originate in old age or extend from earlier life patterns.

Elderly clients with such problems may at first alarm the social worker who feels inadequate to deal with what appears to be a serious psychopathological or organic condition. In our combined clinical experience, however, a significant number of these elders can be helped by immediate implementation of the auxiliary function model. Such a step can diminish or even prevent the need for more highly specialized interventions, or at the very least insure that psychosocial factors are addressed. It is often the social worker who, through advocating and mediating with medical personnel and using the anticipatory and problem-solving techniques outlined in Chapters 4 and 9, facilitates provision and acceptance of needed care. For such reasons, the worker must not hesitate to engage these frail elders, yet with a differential application of intervention skills. Much has been written elsewhere about diagnostic and psychopathological considerations in working with the elderly and the reader is referred to these resources for further study (see Appendix A).

Our discussion is three-fold: in relation to each category, we shall describe the general nature of the problem and some common styles of adaptation to the problem and offer practical suggestions for the worker in engaging and helping the elder. These suggestions may serve as a model for others who fill the auxiliary role.

PRIMARY DEPLETIONS

A number of primary depletions directly affect the elder's ability to communicate and interact with the environment. Three general categories must be considered: sensory loss, speech-motor loss, and mental impairment. The first, sensory loss, is a common attribute of aging. In varying degrees, sensory thresholds are heightened as one ages, requiring greater or adjusted amounts of external input in order to register stimuli. Sight, hearing, taste, smell, touch, and kinesthetic sensitivity can be affected. These losses and changes, the compensations and accommodations made to them, and the residual abilities remaining affect all aspects of the frail elder's life. Here we shall focus exclusively on the loss of hearing and sight, both of which dramatically affect communication.

Hearing Loss

At least half of the population over sixty suffers some degree of hearing loss. It is an invisible impairment, easy to overlook or deny, especially in the early stages. The elder who complains that everyone mumbles, is inattentive or uncooperative, engages in long monologues, answers inappropriately, or has begun to avoid gatherings of more than a few people may be suffering a hearing impairment.

Hearing impairment in old age can be the normal result of the physiological effects of aging itself or the result of pathological changes. Functional impairments associated with the aging auditory system usually affect the higher frequencies first. They include a distortion of loudness perception, difficulty in sound localization, a decline in discrimination especially of speech, and a decrease in time-related processing abilities. Auditory dysfunction in the aged is affected by a number of interacting factors. In addition to local sensorineural loss and other impairments in the auditory system, hearing loss may be related to systemic diseases such as diabetes, kidney disease, or arteriosclerosis (Fisch, 1978).

The manifestations of hearing loss in any one individual can be contradictory and vary from time to time. This does not mean necessarily that the elder is malingering or hearing selectively for psychological reasons. Unamplified speech can sometimes be heard on the phone but not in person, or certain individuals may be understood better than others. The variable nature of hearing loss is dependent upon such factors as the slowness with which it may develop, the situations in which it occurs, the type of stimuli, and fluctuations with the general state of health and well-being. Sound may be heard but misunderstood, leading to fears of mental deterioration. The primary reason why hearing impairment is ignored is that it is considered either incorrectible or less serious than other somatic problems the elder may be experiencing.

Adaptation on the part of elders to hearing loss is often problematic. As noted, it is an invisible impairment, easy to overlook or deny. Elders may withdraw from normal social intercourse in order to avoid confronting the problem. Aside from the stigma attached (deaf and dumb, an appellation many elders remember from childhood), admission of this handicap does not result in much sympathy from others. Contrast the common feelings experienced when helping the visually impaired individual cross the street with those that occur when repeatedly giving directions to the hard of hearing. In the first instance, the helper's reaction is usually one of self-satisfaction at having done a good deed; in the second, it is one of irritation at having been detained.

Total restitution in the case of most hearing loss is not possible, even with the use of hearing aids. Their use requires much accommodation on the part of the elder, necessitating a period of trial and error. Elders who expect hearing aids to be a cure-all for normal hearing are invariably disappointed. An aid is an amplifier that makes everything louder, including distracting and distorting background noises. Resonance of tone is lost. For improved hearing, the elder must learn how to listen all over again and be prepared for disappointment and adjustment during the initial period.

Devices that can be used with or without hearing aids include telephone and doorbell amplifiers and adapters, radio and television coils and headsets, and lights that go on when the phone or bell rings. The local telephone company business office is a good source of information on resources available, as are appliance manufacturers.

Many elders are not troubled by the reduced volume but rather by the diminished clarity of the sound they hear. Training and speech reading (a somewhat broader form of lip reading) can help them utilize nonverbal clues in following a conversation that is incompletely heard. Auditory training teaches the elder listening skills to maximize whatever hearing may remain, as well as the ability to make sense out of distorted sound. Such compensatory adaptations are of greatest helpfulness to the alert, motivated elder; however, the reluctant or denying elder should still be made aware of the possibilities available. If even one device is accepted and works, the effort is well worth it.

Psychologically, the impairment can be devastating: the isolation resulting from even partial loss of hearing can lead from loneliness and lowered self-esteem to paranoid symptoms or severe depressive reactions. While specific problems attendant to hearing loss are safety, lack of socialization, and deprivation of prior sources of pleasure such as music, no area of functioning remains unaffected.

Whether or not prosthetic devices or other rehabilitative aids are used, the following considerations and techniques are useful within the interview situation. A distraction free, well lit environment is necessary. The worker should get the attention of the elder before beginning to speak, positioning himself or herself before the elder, facing the light to facilitate lip reading. Smoking, gum chewing, eating, or hand gestures that cover the mouth are to be avoided. Care must be taken to speak clearly, but emphasizing words or raising one's voice is usually not helpful and perceived as patronizing as well. Speaking a little slower than usual can help the elder who needs time to sort out sound.

It is good to rephrase rather than repeat a question, as the elder may have less trouble with some sounds than with others; for example, "Where do you live?" substituted for "What is your address?" may communicate the intent of the question to the elder even if only one word is understood. The worker must be selective in both questions and responses, getting a message across in as few words as possible and listening harder to pull out needed information from long monologues. Nonverbal responses, such as touch, head nodding, and facial expressions, are useful in conveying a whole range of messages to the hard of hearing.

A supply of scrap paper at hand is also useful. Many hard of hearing elders who tend to wander in their speech react well to a structured interview and respond more appropriately to questions and comments written by the worker. (Large print and a felt-tip pen would be appreciated by all). Flexibility and common sense suggests having the elder do some writing as well. Filling out his or her application form for a service, although this is customarily done by a worker as part of the intake process, may be indicated.

The elder should be asked as often as seems necessary how the communication is going—and suitable adjustments made. The worker should also be alert for signs of fatigue on the part of the elder (straining to hear may be an unaccustomed activity) and be prepared to terminate interviews when they become unproductive.

It is particularly difficult for the hard of hearing to benefit from group services. A large room, distracting stimuli (chairs scraping, coughing, etc.), many people (often unclearly seen), speech of differing pitches, and speakers often overlapping one another are the worst possible conditions for hearing. Workers at congregate settings often overlook this and repeatedly urge their hard of hearing elders to attend group meetings anyway, stressing the benefits of socialization. If the elder wishes to attend and can fit in with the group, he or she should be encouraged to do so; however, benefits to the individual member must be weighed against the cost to the group as a whole. Frequent delays while things are repeated and interruptions from the hearing impaired, who do not recognize that others are speaking, can be disruptive.

In one long-term care facility, the problem of three hearing impaired members of a floor group of thirty was discussed by the group as a whole. One resident volunteered to meet with the members individually to update them on matters of importance that had been discussed. The idea of written minutes was suggested and adopted. Mutual aid was fostered through involving the group as well as the concerned individuals in the problem-solving process. One of the visually impaired members who always denied disability was seen later asking a neighbor to help her read a letter.

Assembling small, homogenous groups of the hearing impaired under optimum hearing conditions can be valuable to the elders. As with other groups of people with a common disability, it is unwise to push too quickly for the sharing of experiences and feelings. Beginning on an educative note, i.e. instructions on hearing aid maintenance, provides useful information while giving elders the chance to relate first in a low demand setting.

Visual Loss

Visual acuity declines significantly in old age, particularly in situations of poor lighting and contrasts. Tolerance of glare diminishes as well as the range of the effective visual field. In extreme old age these changes are exacerbated often by degenerative changes in the retina resulting in severe difficulty in seeing (Welford, 1980). Two commonly encountered causes of visual impairment in the elderly are glaucoma and cataracts. Cataracts, opaque spots that form in the lens of the eye and interfere with the passage of light rays, result in such symptoms as blurring and dimming of vision. Glaucoma, a disease characterized by increased pressure in the eyeball, is a major cause of blindness that can be arrested if caught early. Routine examinations are essential to detection, as the disease develops slowly and painlessly (Leighton, 1978).

Eyedrops and drugs are the most commonly used treatments for glaucoma. Recent surgical advances have made operations for removal of cataracts a comparatively safe and easy process, and the success rate is quite high, even for the very old and frail. However, some elderly refuse such surgery when offered. Others are waiting for their cataracts to "ripen" (or reach an optimum state for surgery), a time during which doubts and fears are commonly expressed. Misconceptions abound regarding both problems, specifically cataracts. Some are due to the differing levels of training and competence of the professionals consulted, others to memories of past times when eye surgery was a riskier and more complicated procedure. As with other impairments, the level of adaptation achieved is often below that which is possible.

Eyeglasses, the most accepted and easy to use of all compensatory devices, are nonetheless underutilized in many cases where they would be helpful. It is not uncommon to find an elder with a drawerful of glasses, confusing old and new prescriptions, or with glasses that were broken and not replaced because of cost or inconvenience, or who last had a checkup five years ago and needs a change of prescription (also running the risk of undetected glaucoma). In these situations, the auxiliary role of the worker first is used to facilitate the necessary care and second to lend his or her sight where it is needed.

Whether or not the elderly client's vision is assisted by corrective lenses, he or she may be helped by a variety of low vision aids, such as hand and stand magnifiers and telescopes. Nonoptical aids, such as talking books, braille, large print publications, telephone dials, and playing cards, marking pens, and reading guides, may be unknown to the elder until brought to his or her attention by the social worker. Rehabilitation training can provide restitution to the visually impaired through help in the use of canes and guide dogs. Activities of daily living such as food preparation, clothes selection and dressing, and travel can be mastered through the acquisitions of new techniques. Adequate lighting and the appropriate use of colors are important (see Appendix B).

The elder with a sight loss requires ongoing verbal cues if he or she is to participate optimally in life. Within the interview situation, this involves accompanying the worker's entrances, exits, or movements with descriptive commentary. Frequent verbal feedback, as a substitute for nodding or facial expression, will also be necessary. Descriptions—be they of the layout of a room or the way that snow looks on the sidewalk—aid in orientation as well as enriching elder experience. Inexplicably, people often raise their voices or adopt an overly simple vocabulary when speaking with the visually impaired. In the absence of other deficits, a normal conversational attitude is appropriate.

The visually impaired elder should be asked if he or she would like assistance before it is provided. Often, the elder has devised his or her own methods of adaptation to the environment, which can be buttressed by those around the elder. If help in walking is desired, the offer of an elbow will be appreciated and the movements of the partner's body will indicate when and where to step, stop, and start.

Touch is another sense that can be employed as a method of orientation. When helping the elder to be seated, the elder's hand can be guided to the back of the chair. Placing a ruler, or otherwise indicating the place for a signature on forms, is also helpful. The use of touch such as holding hands or a physical gesture when meeting or parting is important to the visually impaired, who may not pick up emotion from the voice alone. Reading to the elder or arranging for others to do so is a primary way of sharing necessary information as well as enhancing the quality of life.

Because sight deficits can arouse uncomfortable feelings in the worker, the subject may be avoided within the interview, so denying the elder the opportunity to discuss it. One brave social work student took the plunge by freely admitting her own reaction to her elderly client.

"I closed my eyes and tried to imagine what it would be like to sit in the dark with a stranger; it is scary. I have such admiration for all that you have been able to do since losing your sight." To which the elder replied, "Yes, especially as everything I did I needed my eyes," and went on to review positive aspects of her life as well as mourn the loss of her vision. This elder was ultimately helped to dictate her reminiscences to the worker for inclusion in an oral history project of the long-term care facility in which she lived.

Group services are especially valuable for the visually impaired, and they can be integrated fairly comfortably into any situation. To all the above techniques should be added the worker's recognition by name of all speakers, especially the one with sight loss, who may not recognize when he or she is being called upon. Seating this elder by the worker and utilizing a gentle restraining touch on the arm may be helpful to the elder who, unable to see the reactions of others, may talk on after interest in what he or she has to say has flagged.

Speech-Motor Loss

The coexistence of speech and motor depletion is the severest of losses to the elder, most often the result of cerebral vascular disease producing a stroke. Strokes clearly number among the common neurological disorders of the elderly. They may be due to inadequate flow of blood to the brain with deprivation of oxygen and nutrients or to forceful leakages of blood into the brain, causing damage to surrounding tissue (Drachman, 1980).

Spatial and perceptual deficiencies are common results of strokes when there is damage to the right hemisphere of the brain. They may or may not be accompanied by paralysis of the left side and speech impairment. When speech is unimpaired, problems evidenced by elders who suffer spatial and perceptual deficiencies may not be attributed to the stroke. Subtle depletions that go undetected could include confusion in carrying out activities of daily living resulting from an inability to estimate distances, or the elder may exude confidence and act impulsively out of proportion to abilities. Generalization, or the ability to carry over skills from one situation to another, may be absent. The post-stroke elder may find it difficult to recapture former capabilities.

Lability, or sudden mood shifts evidenced by laughter and tears, is characteristic of stroke victims. The post-stroke elder may manifest a lack of appropriateness or inconsistency in expression of feelings. Although by-products of a stroke, lability may be viewed by others as a sign of mental illness.

Aphasia, or difficulty with speech, can be manifest in a receptive or expressive problem, or both. The elder usually can understand more than he or she can say. The aphasic elder is often hesitant, cautious, and anxious in communicating with others.

Physical, speech, and occupational therapies can be very effective with stroke victims, restoring at least some of their functioning. Unfortunately, stroke victims and their caregivers often accommodate to the losses inflicted by a stroke at a lower level of functioning than is necessary. The elder may be infantilized and denied prerogatives that still can be exercised. The elder then may be presented for concrete services when the burden of care becomes too great, or the fact that the elder may understand the complex and fail with the simple is interpreted as an emotional difficulty.

If the elder is seen in the hospital immediately after an occurrence, the social worker often has a range of resources available to aid in assessment, communication, and work with prospective caregivers and elder. Physical and speech therapists can offer consultation on prognosis and the possibilities of restitution and compensation. The family, mobilized by the crisis, is more likely to be open to professional assistance. In short, depletions have not yet become a given in the elder's life, and an openness to mourning as well as rehabilitation exists.

The family and other caregivers of the post-stroke elder should be asked their understanding of the impact the condition has on the life of the elder. Misconceptions can be corrected through the use of educative discussion (with worker or physician), and written materials specifically prepared for the layman (see Appendix B). Although the discrepency that exists between the elder's actual need for care and those perceived by the family may be due to idiosyncratic dynamics within the family, the more obvious explanation, that they lack sufficient information, should be explored first.

In the interview situation with aphasic clients, it is important to use simple short phrases in a normal tone of voice and nonverbal methods, such as demonstration and pantomime. The elder can benefit from cueing information and positive feedback. Reassurance on attempted speech should be frequent and follow the occurrence immediately. Negative feedback is not helpful. Because old learning is better recalled, linking a new piece of information with something remembered from the past can aid the elder in recall. It is best to keep the new learning briefly keyed to essentials and not confuse the elder with a mass of detail. As noted before, the ability to carry over skills from one situation to another may be missing. Again, keeping to a routine and associating the new with the old could be tried; for instance, rearranging the place setting at a nutrition site to conform with what is experienced at home may prod memory of feeding skills.

It is common and unfair to aphasic elders to overestimate their ability to understand, leading to the labeling "uncooperative," when they simply do not know what is expected of them. Sometimes the elder who cannot speak gives evidence of understanding with a facial expression. This can be misleading, however. Response could be to the "music" of the worker's speech and attitude rather than to the words. This can be tested by the worker saying one thing while gesturing the opposite. The elder who does not understand speech will not evidence any confusion and respond only to the gesture.

The worker must be careful not to show any signs of impatience, as stress has a pronounced negative effect on functioning. Since it becomes increasingly difficult for the aphasic client to speak when he or she tires, it is wise to terminate interviews when fatigue is evidenced. Appreciation of the elder's isolation and a relaxed ability to express empathy in nonverbal ways is always an asset. Although the elder may not be able to respond to the worker, it should not be assumed that he or she receives no benefits from the contact. The presence of a person who can sit understandingly and patiently for a time may be reassuring. Used as an adjunct to work with the family, a brief visiting period with the most severely impaired demonstrates to all that the aphasic elder remains a human being deserving respect.

Sudden mood shifts, or lability, evidenced by inappropriate laughter and tears pose problems for the interviewer and are frightening for the elder. The worker who openly identifies lability as a by-product of the stroke, one that often improves over time, will calm the elder who may fear he or she is going crazy. After the issue is once discussed, the interview should proceed geared to content, the inappropriate affect disregarded. Physical touch, to acknowledge the strain that the lability is imposing on the elder while continuing the interview, is a better technique than calling further attention to it.

The anger often exhibited by post-stroke elders to social workers should not be personalized or stifled but rather encouraged. Extreme dependence on those who provide physical care may suppress expressions of the negative feelings expected under the circumstances. Providing an outlet for these is a service in itself.

With stroke patients suffering spatial and perceptual deficiencies, the auxiliary role may involve encouragement of both elder and caregiver to verbally anticipate each step of a proposed physical task. A clutter-free environment with necessary objects close at hand will go a long way toward promoting more effective functioning. Sometimes this client will neglect the paralyzed part of the body; for example, an elderly man shaving only one side of his face. Calling his attention to the neglect is a matter of discretion, timing, and relationship. Seating oneself on the unimpaired side of the elder is a must.

Group services for post-stroke patients are often conducted in rehabilitation and outpatient settings. Whether these are clubs existing mainly for socialization purposes or are directed toward facilitating ongoing functioning, they have been found most effective in helping the newly disabled recognize that an active life, though difficult, is not yet over. Anyone who has watched the post-stroke rehabilitative efforts of the old and frail must be impressed by the enormous degree of motivation and energy required to make even minimal progress. The advice and support of others who have been there bolster whatever motivation and energy exist for maximizing adaptation.

Integrating the post-stroke elder into heterogeneous groups with elderly people who have not undergone a similar experience will be more challenging and worth the effort of a skilled worker. The sight of a paralyzed and/or aphasic cohort awakens fear in the minds of the more able, as it is the worst fate most imagine for themselves. The impulse of the elderly, as for the rest of us, is to sweep unpleasantness under the rug or, in the case of an institutional or day program setting, argue that "those people" would be more comfortable meeting with their own kind. The worker who lectures on acceptance will not be heard, and the worker who seeks to protect the more disabled elder from anticipated rejection by segregation is contributing to the elder's lessened self-esteem. The integration of at least two higher functioning post-stroke elders into a larger task-related group is a good beginning. Resident councils or oral history groups, where participants can discover common interests in areas unaffected by the disability, help not only the impaired but the more able elderly.

An often overlooked aspect of speech impairments in the elderly is due to ill fitting or absent dentures. Elders who use these only to eat or who have discarded them completely because of discomfort or lack of access to service often do not realize that teeth are necessary for clear speech. Also, embarrassment over an empty mouth can lead to a gesture of muffling it with a hand, which further complicates communication. Linking the elder to needed services and/or encouraging him or her to use dentures, at least within the interview, may be necessary.

Mental Impairment

Mental impairment in the elderly can be caused by a variety of diseases and conditions, including strokes. Of all the depletions suffered by the elderly, it is the most difficult to assess and handle and arouses greatest feelings on the part of caregivers. It also has the most pervasive effects on overall functioning.

Typical symptoms occurring together that result in impaired mental performance of the elder are disorientation to time, place, and person, memory loss, confusion, and deficits in judgment and perception. The social worker first might be alerted to the presence of mental impairment by an overall sense of vagueness, evasiveness, a repetitive perseverating quality, or lack of coherence that pervades the client's communication.

Most crucial in understanding mental impairment is knowing whether the depletion is acute (reversible), chronic (irreversible), or the secondary manifestation of anxiety or depression. An acute state of brain depletion that results in a temporary loss of mental functioning is more common than recognized. Such conditions as congestive heart failure, stroke, drug or alcohol mismanagement, infection, and malnutrition may be contributing factors. States of anxiety or depression may produce similar symptoms and so be misdiagnosed. When the primary source is identified and treated promptly, the acute condition is cured. The longer the elder goes untreated, the less likely he or she is to totally recover. Suddenness of onset, depression, memory loss, impaired judgment, and marked confusion are indications that expert medical consultation be sought at once (Busse & Pfeiffer, 1973).

There are several types of chronic mental depletions commonly found in the elderly. The most often encountered, senile dementia, progresses evenly over time and is characterized by impaired orientation, perception, judgment, and memory loss. "The hallmark of (senile) dementia is a deterioration of previously acquired intellectual abilities of sufficient severity to interfere with social or occupational functioning" (Raskind & Storrie, 1980). Impairment of memory, abstract thinking, use of symbolic logic, and judgment and the loss of impulse control and personality changes are the most prominent features. Senile dementia of the Alzheimer's type is a common cause of mental impairment in later life, associated with degeneration and atrophy of the brain cells. The elder may continue to relate to others as he or she did in the past, although increasing impairment usually leads to more dependent and regressive behavior.

Whether the loss of mental functioning is acute or chronic, the elder's current life situation, temperament, and past history will greatly influence the manifestation, adaptation chosen, and auxiliary role adopted by the worker. In approaching this elder, it must be remembered that while perceptions may be faulty and conclusions erroneous emotions are always valid. There is no cell death of the feelings or spirit. The most vague or bizarre presentation often conveys a message to be heard and answered.

Accepting and exploring such frequently metaphoric expressions of feelings is different from accepting them as facts. Premature reality orientation efforts seeking to orient the elder to the worker's reality, before the worker becomes oriented to the elder's reality, impede the elder's attempts at communication. An exchange that took place in a class on social work practice with the aged illustrates this point.

One student was struggling with the proper approach to a nursing home resident who refused to participate in a recreational activity, claiming that she had to wait and speak with her mother (who had been dead over fifty years). When the question was posed to the class, the first response was that the communication should be ignored and the elder gently, but firmly, encouraged to come along. A second student disagreed. She believed that the elder should be reminded that her mother had been dead many years and that her present home was in the institution and then encouraged to join the activity. This approach was widely approved by the class, until a third student spoke up. She was curious as to what the elder wanted to speak with her mother about and thought she might explore that theme before trying either of the above approaches.

This suggestion sounded so right that everyone wondered why it was not thought of earlier. Perhaps because of the assumption that an elder so confused had nothing of worth to contribute. Yet, using the elder as the primary source of information is a necessary step in maximizing adaptation. The elder's inner reality, used as a bridge to the external reality, is the point of departure. In addition, to decoding puzzling communications as the one above, this could involve starting with an interest that the elder once had (as shared by elder or other informants).

In one case, collecting wild flowers had been a cherished hobby. The worker brought in a bouquet and an illustrated book on the subject and was rewarded by seeing the elder's eyes light up as memory traces were stirred. Touching, smelling, and exclaiming on the color of the flowers was followed by a walk on the lawn to identify dandelions. Thus one aspect of the outer reality became familiar and welcoming.

In all but the most severe cases of mental impairment, the elder will exhibit some degree of awareness and anxiety about the problem, although this may only be visible to the discerning worker. Even a mild memory loss can be equated by the elder as being "crazy" or "senile" and a great cause of concern. The ways in which the elder will cope are generally in keeping with his or her general personality structure and habitually used mechanisms of defense. Denial, or minimizing the importance of what is forgotten, is a frequent response. The confused elder is not helped by the worker who reassures that "everyone forgets sometimes." The elder needs acknowledgment and an opportunity to share what, when, and how forgetting affects his or her life. The auxiliary role is then offered as help in compensating for this loss.

Knowledge of the individual elder is invaluable in helping him or her compensate for mental depletion. The elder with a more organized approach to life is able to use such aids as date-books, lists, calendars, and clocks. The more globally dependent elder who never exercised such discipline is not about to begin now, but may respond to a structured routine or direct concrete assistance from a caring protective worker who accepts a parental type of auxiliary role.

Mrs. Cooper was prone to greet her social worker on her monthly visit with a statement such as "I am cursed." The worker's previous explorations had revealed Mrs. Cooper's distress that she could no longer manage her financial affairs because of her confusion and forgetfulness. "My husband always took care of these things." Reassuring Mrs. Cooper that she was not cursed but rather in need of help, the worker assisted her in sorting out her monthly bills and paying them and attending to other business matters.

Security comes with a sense of control over one's self and the environment, increasingly difficult for the elder who has trouble assimilating and processing information. The hyperactive and anxious state of severely mentally impaired community elders, may relax almost immediately upon institutional placement, illustrating their inner awareness of this lack of mastery and appreciation for being looked after. However, care must be taken not to remove all opportunities for decision making lest remaining abilities atrophy from disuse. The goal is to allow the elder the maximum degree of choice possible commensurate with his or her capacities.

PROBLEM BEHAVIORS

Frail elders characterized as behavior problems frequently are encountered by the social worker. Such behaviors cannot be viewed in a vacuum. They are part and parcel of transactions with the environment that can result in a lack of person-environment fit. Yet, the behavior of the elder must be treated differentially by the worker if the auxiliary role is to be implemented. While separated for the sake of the following discussion, they rarely exist singly. The most salient factors may act as a guide for the worker's approach.

Depression

Depression, as a common reaction to the depletions of age, is present to some extent in many elders. As an affect, it extends on a continuum from mild cases of the blues to a pathological state. It may describe a subjective feeling tone of short duration or one that is sustained over a period of time. The term depression is a confusing one because it is used to describe the normal feelings of sadness and mourning that people of all ages experience and a clinical disorder that may range from a lack of zest for life to complete despondency. Symptoms of a clinical depression may also include insomnia, loss of appetite, fatigue, constipation or diarrhea, agitation or withdrawal, hypochondriacal preoccupation, and loss of self-esteem.

In the frail elderly, frequent allusions to death are not, by themselves, indicative of a depressive state. The elder who is planning the disposition of belongings or wants to insure that there are sufficient funds for his or her funeral may be adapting optimally to his or her life situation. Physiological and psychological symptoms of depression must be present with some regularity to warrant a designation of clinical depression.

Depression is often masked in the aged. While some depressed elders exhibit the fearfulness, monosyllabic responsiveness, and negative outlook commonly associated with the state, others may conceal the mood behind a philosophical or angry manner. Still others may become preoccupied with somatic complaints, often the case in long-term care facilities where the sick role receives positive reinforcement. Presumed signs of mental impairment may appear, obscuring the depressive state and thwarting diagnostic accuracy.

Depressive states are viewed by some as either organic in origin or reactive to external influences such as loss. This dichotomy is a troublesome one, particularly in the case of the elderly where biological and social depletions frequently coexist, each possibly contributing to a depressive state. The social worker's task is to insure that both avenues are explored. Medical care and, in some cases, psychiatric intervention are essential and may ameliorate the effects of primary depletion (Busse & Blazer, 1980).

Talk or gestures of suicide must be taken with the utmost seriousness, as elders are high suicide risks. Psychiatric consultation must be sought at once. Hospitalization may be necessary, as talking is often not possible or may take too long to achieve results, leaving the elder a suicide risk in the meantime. Elders who feel better with the structured routine of a hospital, however, may not maintain their gains when they are returned to the original situation that precipitated the stress unless additional supports are built into the environment. Sometimes suicidal intention or a severe depression are cries for help, indicating that the community elder may be ready for placement in a more protected supportive setting or at least be ready for more service at home.

Suicidal behavior should not be confused with the commonly voiced readiness of the very old to die. These expressions arouse conflict and concern in most health care professionals. The subject of dying, however, should never be avoided by the worker, who may be the only person the elder can confide in at this loneliest of human hours.

When depression is presented clearly in terms of mood by an elder, family members can be alarmed and threatened. Depression can evoke guilt and hostility on the part of significant others, which in turn may only further exacerbate the condition. The social worker's interventions should be directed to helping family members understand and manage their feelings and address problems associated with the depression.

When the cause of depression in the frail elder is commonly reactive to secondary depletions, a symbolic or real replacement of the loss may be helpful and in keeping with the auxiliary role of the worker. Identification of the loss and its particular meaning for the individual elder is an important prerequisite. Secondary depletions can range from the loss of caring figures to the loss of feelings of mastery and control over the environment. What is missed by one elder might not necessarily be missed by another. Replenishment might involve concrete services or the use of self as a compensation for the irremediable loss of significant others. The first instance is self-explanatory, the second less so.

The personal use of self by the worker is nowhere more important than in work with those depressed elders whose losses are interpersonal. Loneliness, or the unhappy awareness of being separated from satisfying interaction with others, can be a precipitant of depression in the elderly. Strangely, this is as common in institutional settings where the elder is surrounded by peers and helpers as in the community where he or she is virtually isolated from human contact. In either case, the auxiliary role serves as a bridge to increased participation in the mainstream of life.

Through selective sharing of parts of the worker's life with the elder, subjects such as vacation plans or family activities may become the basis for discussion. Reciprocity can be encouraged, with the elder sharing his or her experiences and opinions. Small gifts of flowers or home baked treats may be exchanged. The auxiliary role thus serves to reawaken socialization skills long dormant for lack of opportunity. Monitored and orchestrated by the worker to insure that the elder understands the limits of the relationship, this role satisfies many needs.

The elder who meets with a positive response from the worker may be then more prone to seek such gratification from others. Used as role playing or an anticipatory prelude to new relationships, rusty communication abilities are improved, and conflicts about past friendships can be expressed and resolved. Premature efforts to involve the depressed elder in peer group activity or hobbies often fail because this preliminary step is overlooked (Busse & Pfeiffer, 1973).

A complementary approach is for the worker to foster the parental, authority role often ascribed to him or her by the dependent and depressed elder. Inspiring the elder to trust the worker through "doing for," the worker feeds the need for nurturing that underlies many depressive states, allowing the elder to feel in control of the worker, if of nothing else in his or her environment (Goldfarb, 1969).

When depression is rooted in feelings of powerlessness, efforts should be made to increase opportunities for mastery on the part of the elder. The auxiliary role of the worker would thus be directed toward "doing with" or "helping the elder do for himself." Methods of sharing the work in tasks in which the elder can be expected to succeed are assigned. This bolstering confidence and stimulation of further efforts may be helpful in combating the "learned helplessness" observed in some frail elderly (Hooker, 1976).

Finally, workers should be aware of significant anniversaries and holidays for their clients, for these occasions can trigger depressive reactions. Being more available at these times is an important aspect of the auxiliary role.

Anxiety States

Anxiety states are not uncommon among frail elders. They may accompany mental impairment, depression, and paranoidal or hypochondriacal preoccupations. Anxiety is a distressing affect, subjectively experienced as nervousness, similar to fear of a real danger or the anticipation of danger. The affect may be a response to a flooding of external or internal stimuli and/or the anticipation of loss. It may also be related to feelings of guilt and shame or anticipation of punishment, it and may be a warning signal in response to unacceptable impulses or fantasies. For the old, anxiety in relation to loss is prominent. It is referred to as depletion anxiety, which is closely akin to separation anxiety (Verwoerdt, 1980).

Anxiety can be unconscious or openly expressed in agitated behavior. The diminished energies of old age make the repression of anxiety and the thoughts and feelings that provoke it more difficult and ego defense mechanisms less effective. Coupling the depletion in ego functions, both defensive and executive, with the increased stresses of frailty, it is not surprising that agitation is often present. The agitated elder is here defined as one who exhibits such overt behavior as nonstop talking or questioning, jumping speech from topic to topic, and continuous body movements such as pacing or repetitive hand motions. Impulsivity and problems of control are evident in most areas of life. With the agitated client, toxic reactions may be a contributing cause.

As with depression, the worker's tasks with the anxious client are to insure physical care and take those measures that can help ameliorate the condition. Environmental interventions and the worker's direct interventions may be effective.

With the agitated client, the worker must carefully monitor his or her responses. The overall frenetic quality of the client's behavior, whether or not accompanied by urgent demands for help, is invariably distressing to family members, who may respond by mirroring the anxiety or moving into precipitous interventive action. The social worker is no less susceptible to these pressures and first must seek to establish meaningful communication with the agitated elder. The worker who can respond with a calm caring approach has effectively initiated the auxiliary role.

The monologuist may have cognitive or sensory impairment, be irate over a real or perceived injustice, wish to control the interview, or simply be lonely with a pent up need to speak to someone. It is essential to establish a climate of trust with the agitated elder before attempting to break in. Listening quietly for major themes will yield a beginning direction for the intervention as well as convey a willingness to hear the elder out. Often such filibusters are holding devices adopted in desperation by home-bound or institutionalized elderly who experience constant rejection as caregivers terminate contact when they, not the elder, are through. Sometimes the elder fears he or she has not made his or her point as listeners just nod and move away without comment. The overlong discourse quite literally may be a cry for help.

The worker who patiently waits for the elder to finish and has established a beginning relationship may begin by summing up for the elder the essence of what the elder has said or recalling with the elder elements of the story remembered from the last visit; for example, a helpful response to one limitless series of complaints from an elderly man was, "You have suffered a lot since moving to this home. The food, your roommates, the clinic. Life here has been very hard for you." This worker, who provided structure for the elder, identified the core problem, and helped place it in perspective, was rewarded by a shorter monologue at the next meeting. The elder, calmed that he had been heard, was ready to move on to considering problem resolution only after several such sessions of ventilation and understanding response.

Mrs. Krouss, an eighty-four-year-old divorced resident of a health-related facility, was medically diagnosed as having moderately severe organic mental syndrome and self-diagnosed as "a good time girl." Her ongoing monologue to anyone who would listen consisted of recollections of the past as a singer, punctuated by excerpts of French songs, and a lamentation about the high cost of keeping up a good appearance. Actually, her clothing was generally soiled, mismatched, or inappropriate, a fact attributed to her waning mental faculties and so dismissed by the staff until Mrs. Krouss began resisting needed assistance in hygiene. The social worker, called in to help, listened to Mrs. Krouss for a long while, sympathized with the problems of looking nice on a limited budget, and asked about the clothes Mrs. Krouss used to wear on stage. After sharing these reminiscences, Mrs. Krouss invited her to see her wardrobe, a chaotic jumble she had forbidden anyone to touch. It became evident that Mrs. Krouss was aware of her inability to maintain her dramatic self but could not relinquish control. The worker spent the interview hours helping Mrs. Krouss as she reminisced and sorted through and ordered her belongings, relegating those most extreme to storage for "special occasions." With fewer choices to make each morning and a few new items purchased with her allowance, Mrs. Krouss could maintain control, receive necessary positive feedback from staff, and many manifestations of agitation abated.

The worker helped by defining the task to be done together and providing structure to the contact based on the elder's ability to comply. Positive reinforcement was given at the moment for efforts at self-control, as in the decision to pack away her dressiest clothes. Finally, staff was engaged in understanding and supporting the case plan.

The agitated elder will often disturb family by frequent phone calls, annoy the hospital staff by constant rings on the emergency buzzer, and exasperate everyone by repeating the same question moments after he or she has received an answer. The elder is thus caught in an endless cycle of fear, impulsive reaching out, and rejection. To break into this cycle, structure and reassurance are needed. Families and caregivers often need direction here.

The elder should receive positive consistent reinforcement for efforts at self-control: receiving a warm response if he or she calls at specified hours, being asked to call again when it is more convenient. The elder's time should be ordered as much as possible to provide distraction from the preoccupations that produce the anxiety. The elder who paces may have to be accompanied on a walk for a bit and then encouraged to sit, if even for five minutes, and his or her efforts at control acknowledged.

The underlying message of communication that must be heard and responded to is of greatest importance. Factual answers or explanations to "Where is my doctor?" do not speak to the fears of being abandoned and ill. The elder who is told that the doctor comes in only on Wednesday mornings will ask again and again. Reassurance that there is always someone on duty who understands the problem and a "hands on" gesture of caring are often more helpful.

The agitated elder may often voice the same somatic complaints over and over. Often these are irremediable and take time away from more productive work. Yet any attempts by the worker to change the subject will result in greater perseveration. It is better to go along, perhaps persisting until the elder tires of the subject. In the process, of course, the worker will confirm that all necessary medical measures are being taken for the elder. Attention then should be directed toward eliciting the fears underlying the expressions and helping the elder master them through some positive action. If the constant back pain doctors attribute to arthritis is feared to be cancer, a discussion of another medical opinion may convince the elder of the worker's genuine investment in helping him or her feel better. Often, having gained the attention sought, the elder will then minimize the complaint and discuss other concerns.

The client who masks anxiety is no less responsive to the structure and positive reinforcements offered by the social worker. Direct confrontation regarding the client's unfounded fears will miss the mark and frighten the client further. Clinical experience has taught us that whatever the unconscious meanings of such symptoms, a simple exploration of what the elder fears to lose is often sufficient to motivate him or her to try out a feared activity. The worker is often in a position of being able to accompany the aging client through a terrifying experience. The prosthetic boost of the auxiliary role can go far in ameliorating anxiety.

Mr. Furgesson refused to take the elevator to activities on the main floor. His isolation increased, he became depressed, but he continued to make up numerous excuses for remaining in his room. The worker, through patient listening, discerned a fear that he would be trapped in his wheelchair on the elevator. She offered to personally accompany him until his fears abated. After several weeks he allowed a volunteer to transport him.

Suspiciousness and Paranoid Disorders

Suspiciousness or paranoid behavior, just as depression and anxiety, can arise from a variety of physical, psychological, or environmental causes. Often both are related to vague complaints on the part of the elder about external forces controlling his or her life. The personality pattern may be lifelong or may have manifested itself for the first time in old age. If these characteristics have been evidenced in earlier years, they are less likely to be causing acute distress at present. This is in contrast to the frail elder who has recently begun to think that he or she is threatened or in danger from the ill will of others.

Such suspicions, often accompanied by overt manifestations of fear and wariness, may involve individuals close to the elder and be an exaggerated response to a real situation; for example, the facts that caregivers are unkind and adult children are waiting for an inheritance may be true. Abetted by isolation and impaired cognitive or sensory abilities, such thoughts can add up to ideas of deliberate persecution. Situations of suspiciousness may be precipitated by a loss of control over one's environment and major environmental change. The subject of money, which is usually in finite supply for the elder, can provoke much distrust. Corrective measures that address these precipitants may help ameliorate suspiciousness (Eisdorfer, 1980).

Paranoid behavior can also be provoked by real situations. As with depression and anxiety, it can range from a mild condition to a pathological state. A paranoid psychosis and its accompanying delusions may require psychiatric intervention. Paranoid behavior, as differentiated from suspiciousness, is usually exhibited by attacking others. The condition often reflects a lifelong history of disavowing the need for tenderness and intimacy. The effect of paranoid behavior on interpersonal relations can be devastating since significant others (family, staff, neighbors) may be implicated and alienated. The auxiliary role of the worker in interpreting the client's behavior is critical here.

Suspiciousness and paranoid behavior are commonly found in protective service situations. Being unable to trust others or fearing dependency, these elders have become isolated at a time when their interpersonal needs are great. The sensitive and patient approach of the worker can result, in time, in their utilization of services.

Suspicious Mrs. Collins was reported to the Protective Service office by neighbors since she was locked in her house refusing to open the door, but she was obviously in distress. The worker visited several times, knocking quietly, and leaving notes offering help. After several refusals by Mrs. Collins to grant admission, the worker left a box of Christmas cookies on the doorstep the week before the holiday (neighbors had told the worker of her love of sweets). The next week, Mrs. Collins, although wary, invited her in and eventually was able to accept medical help and home care.

In the interview situation, the first step for the social worker is to differentiate between suspiciousness and paranoid behaviors. The wariness and fear exhibited by the suspicious elder calls for gentleness and encouragement to take a risk in trusting. The feelings expressed should be recognized, while simultaneously checking the reality situation. Perhaps the suspicious thought is a partial or metaphoric representation of a true event that can be addressed.

One nursing home elder complained of fumes that surrounded old ladies in their beds at night. A check revealed no such problem. After exploration, it was found that she was actually pointing to a callous aide on the 11:00 to 7:00 shift. The social worker who investigated this problem was able then to remedy the situation.

In contrast to the suspicious elder, the social worker's approach to a paranoid client should be more business-like than personal. Demonstrations of empathy, warmth, and personal interest may be regarded as invasive by the paranoid elder and only heighten mistrust. Situations should be avoided that would make the paranoid person feel need and weakness or experience humiliation. Before referring a nursing home resident for medication, it might be better to move him or her out of a double room.

Mr. First became increasingly belligerent with staff, seemingly in relation to changes in the floor routine. It became apparent that the intimacy imposed by having to room with another man was exacerbating a paranoid reaction, and he was moved to a single room.

Life in a congregate setting is particularly difficult for the suspicious or paranoid elder, who will interpret inconsistencies in approach and explanations among staff members as evidence that they are lying. For this reason, it is crucial that the elder's concerns be channeled to the member of the interdisciplinary team who will perform the auxiliary role. Professional identification is less important than that the elder and staff person can communicate clearly and consistently.

Sometimes paranoid thoughts are face-saving to the frail elder. Projection, a primitive defense and one commonly observed in the elderly, may reinforce denial of depletion. In so doing, it protects the elder from recognition of weakness or provides an excuse for inability to perform as before. Thus, he or she is no longer employable because of an arbitrary retirement rule, no longer able to continue a hobby because others withhold the necessary materials. While there is often some truth in these assertions, it is not the total truth. However, for the elder who needs to save face, it need not be challenged.

The level of distress and the degree to which the paranoid ideas are functional or dysfunctional will determine if the worker intervenes. The use of the auxiliary role in positing an alternative meaning of events, filling in missing pieces of information, and a rational approach may help when paranoid ideas are freed from cognitive deficits. The elder with cognitive impairment may be unable to comprehend or forget explanations, often becoming more fixated on the delusion and upset at attempts to rid him or her of it.

The elder whose suspicious nature is of lifelong duration has developed, no doubt, some adaptive strategies that a close look at his or her past will reveal. The fact that a frail elder may have a history of psychiatric hospitalizations does not mean, in itself, that he or she will pose special problems for the social worker. Often, persecution delusions of many year's duration can coexist with a fairly high level of functioning and require no intervention whatsoever. The elder whose energies are addressed in preparing a case against the city, army, or other authoritative organization for unfair treatment decades earlier is often encountered in practice. The elder may attempt to involve the social worker in these struggles. The "case" thus becomes a *raison d'etre*, which in old age may serve a preservative function. The worker can accredit the elder's feelings and ability to work independently while offering the auxiliary role in more appropriate areas. Challenging or exploration of the paranoid belief will not be helpful.

Deviance

The deviant elder is defined here as the frail elder who fails to act as others wish or who acts in ways unacceptable to others, placing the definition clearly in the eye of the beholder. Sexual deviancy can be a problem for frail elders. Noncompliance may be a lifelong pattern or new in old age, its causes ranging from mental impairment to angry defiance. Its significance depends on the consequences: that is to say the extent to which the well-being of the elder or others is endangered by the deviant behavior. Even if there are not many such elders in any one caseload, it will seem that there are. A disproportionate amount of time and energy is usually extended to deviant clients as well as to collaterals and service providers involved in their care.

The difficult task of engaging and helping the deviant elder utilize needed services is frequently complicated by pressure from other sources to make the elder conform. These pressures are particularly hard to withstand when they emanate, as they often do, from the worker's own agency.

The auxiliary function model, which is activated only by the individual depletions and preferences of the elder, precludes coercive behavior on the part of the worker. In other words, pressures toward conformity exercised by family, service providers, or agency directives are important only insofar as they constitute the reality faced by the elder, a reality of which the elder must be made cognitively and emotionally aware.

Eighty-year-old Mr. Redford was a disruptive new member of a senior center, who interrupted planned activities with outspoken voicing of his own concerns, on two occasions provoking physical fights with other participants. The center director and nurse asked the worker to either curb his activity or have him transferred elsewhere. The worker's first task was to openly address the issue with Mr. Redford. She voiced her concern that he was experiencing difficulty, specified what behaviors were troublesome and why, and asked for his reaction. When Mr. Redford protested that he couldn't care less what others thought of him, the worker responded

that center by-laws gave them the right to discharge a member on these
grounds and wondered what Mr. Redford would do if this happened.
Hurt and angry, Mr. Redford maintained he didn't care, he'd just go to
another center. When reminded that this had happened before, Mr.
Redford replied that he would not "sit and rock like an old woman" for
anyone. This led to a discussion of what the passive role forced on him at
retirement meant and his inability to find a place for himself since.
Succeeding interviews directed toward mourning the past and finding
compensatory activities in the present were helpful in controlling, if not
totally preventing, his outbursts.

In situations where deviant behavior is the consequence of
mental impairment, the auxiliary role dictates that the worker
supply the judgment that is lacking. An example would be
suggesting more clothing and reminders about the temperature
on a cold day when the elder goes outdoors inappropriately clad.
The confused elder who does not reject such advice and care has
been helped, whether he or she is capable of a contract or even of
recognizing the worker as a helping figure.

In all cases of deviance, a weighing must occur between the
social work value of self-determination and the demands of society.
Advocacy on behalf of the elder who, after all, has earned the
right to a little nonconformity may be chosen when the upset of
bureaucratic procedure is all that is at stake. Mediation between
elder and those who are communicating and working at cross
purposes is helpful when the deviance places excessive burdens
on caregivers or is preventing the elder from reaching adaptive
potential. Direct persuasion of the deviant elder is a course of last
resort not to be used unilaterally. Consultation with allied professionals should be sought. The elder who refuses medical care in
the face of grave need is a frequently cited example of deviance,
and the necessity for interdisciplinary collaboration in planning a
helpful approach is clear.

In cases of sexual deviancy, the worker must define what is
meant. If it is merely masturbation, such acts must not be criticized.
Masturbation occurs at all ages and may be far preferable in the
old than depression. When sexual behavior impinges on someone
else's rights, it must be explored, but not in a blaming manner. It

simply may be the result of mental impairment or the accidental consequence of misunderstanding.

Mr. Williams, who suffered from mental impairment, wandered a great deal in the halls and once was found crawling in to the bed of a female resident, whom he terrified. He later told the worker that he thought she was his wife. The worker helped him understand the reality of the situation.

Sometimes frail elders may make sexual approaches to the worker. Here also, the worker can nonpunitively set limits, explaining the boundaries of the relationship. For the sexually deviant client, activities should be found that are more socially acceptable but that meet a like need. Mr. Williams, for example, was encouraged to participate more in group activities with women.

The Manipulative Client

Workers with the frail elderly often use the term "manipulative" to describe those elders or families whose actions or words seem deliberately designed to elicit a desired response from the worker or other service provider usually for greater attention or more help. These efforts are looked on with disfavor, often resulting in case closing so time can be freed for those who "really" need it. No one likes to be used. Yet, manipulation may well be a strength in disguise, one that needs to be understood and redirected. The elder who manipulates has not laid down before his or her losses but rather is fighting to adapt to them. The elder, in fact, is seeking actively the auxiliary role to extend power and mastery. The elder may be trying to control others as he or she loses control. On the other hand, manipulation may be a defense against depression. Focusing on how to get others to help precludes experiencing the pain of recognizing dependency, or perhaps the elder may have always related in a manipulative manner with others and knows no other way of communicating.

It is thus necessary to look behind surface manifestations and ascertain their cause before the case is written off. The elder with still functioning managerial or persuasive skills may be helped to find a more appropriate outlet. Political or congregate groups for older people, in community and institution, frequently are able to utilize such expertise. If manipulation is a useful defense, or is all the elder knows, it may have to be endured or even encouraged. While realistic limits must be stated, restated, and upheld, the punitive manner in which this is often done should be eliminated.

In management of such a case, a nonpunitive, but highly structured, stance must be maintained, with regular appointments and timetables for service clearly stated and followed. Here, as always, the frail elder's right to the auxiliary role is related first and foremost to the depletions experienced. Undesirable personality characteristics will pose additional burdens on the worker, but they should not act as a barrier to provision of services.

Alcoholism

Alcoholism can be a form of deviant behavior. It refers to a dependence upon alcohol that has reached a degree such that it interferes with health, interpersonal relationships, and social adjustment. Studies of alcoholism among the old are few, but experience to date suggests that increasing numbers of elderly are becoming alcoholic in their later years, perhaps in relation to the stresses of aging, and that increasing numbers of lifelong alcoholics are surviving into the later years. If diagnosed properly, late-life alcoholics have been found to be amenable to treatment (Busse & Blazer, 1980).

Our experience suggests that alcoholics of long standing become frailer at a younger age than the average elder. They appear to exhibit the same personality characteristics of younger alcoholics: neuroticism, egocentricity, and deviant behavior (Rosin & Glatt, 1971). Current or recovering alcoholics increasingly comprise the case loads of frail elderly, although relatively young. Their condition of frailty generally forces them to give up drinking, which in itself can lead to other problems because of the loss suffered. Alcoholism may have also masked other psychological problems, now uncovered.

Sixty-nine-year-old Mr. Harris was recently discharged from the hospital, where he was treated for an acute psychotic episode. It was originally thought that his condition was due to advanced brain disease, but it may have been a reaction to his having stopped drinking only a few months earlier. His history revealed a lifelong habit of alcoholism, which he gave up one day when "he saw the light." A further loss to Mr. Harris was the companionship of his drinking buddies at the local bar. Isolated from family and friends for years, his only support in his life was the social worker who visited him regularly.

The fact that frail alcoholics tend to be socially isolated necessitates ongoing auxiliary role activity by the social worker. There may be no one left in the environment able to offer the support needed. Their own personality difficulties tend to alienate the potential for involving family, friends, and neighbors in support and care. As in earlier life, frail alcoholics tend to be evasive and are controlling and manipulative with others.

Mr. Harris made a great many demands on his social worker, calling her frequently at the agency and requesting a variety of types of concrete services, which she later discovered he was asking others for also. In her visits, he tended to be quite aggressive and hostile and then guiltily apologized and became ingratiating in manner.

The provision of a consistent, structured relationship is most important in providing auxiliary care to such an elder. The worker must be on guard not to be drawn into the elder's manipulations, keeping carefully to the contract, and not taking personally the elder's hostile behavior. While the behavior of such a person has resulted in alienation from others all his or her life, a different response is now required from the environment, owing to the frailty and very concrete dependence of the elder alcoholic. The social worker may be the only nonexploitive and supportive person to whom these isolated frail elderly can turn.

We have attempted to describe a number of primary depletions and behaviors commonly encountered in working with frail elders, yet are hindrances to the client's adaptation. We have argued that problem behaviors also double as ego resources for the elder and thus should be approached with caution within the context of implementing the auxiliary function model. Finally, we have suggested some time-proven strategies for dealing with these conditions and problems. Understanding the thinking behind these strategies, the seasoned and resourceful worker will formulate plans adapted to the particular situation of individual elders.

IMPLEMENTING THE AUXILIARY FUNCTION: ENVIRONMENTAL INTERVENTIONS

Chapter 9

ENVIRONMENTAL INTERVENTIONS

Frailty signals a life transition that "requires new responses from the environment" (Germain, 1979). These responses are closely related to the multiple depletions suffered by the frail and their need for different and greater inputs from the environment.

The auxiliary function model of social work is inextricably linked with interventions that affect these environmental responses. It seeks to identify and/or strengthen the part of significant others in filling the auxiliary role and ameliorate noxious environmental influences, including those that frustrate dependency needs or diminish the frail elder's competence. These interventions can be made on behalf of one or more frail elders.

For the single elder, the "case management" component of the auxiliary role calls for an array of environmental interventions, particularly the location, enlistment, coordination, and monitoring of services and collaboration with other care providers. For groups or communities of frail elders, other important social work interventions come into play, including community organization, organizational and policy change, and planning.

We begin by asking whether or not the environment is now, or can in the future responding, supportively to the elder as frailty takes its toll. The depletions, impairments, and losses accompanying frailty call for replenishment and adjustments that enhance adaptation on the part of the elder. Must the physical environment be modified or changed to encourage restitution or compensation? Are there one or more persons in the social environment who can provide an emotional and cognitive link to the elder and to some degree serve as advocate and case manager? Can the family, friends, neighbors, and larger informal networks respond emotionally and

211

practically to the needs of the frail elder? If these are not sufficient, what formal supports can be mobilized and in what ways can the formal and informal systems best work together? How can the health and social service system environments respond responsibly to the frail elder and family in a life enhancing manner? At the interface of client and environment, how can interaction be encouraged that promotes the competency and autonomy of the elder?

Each of these components of the elder's life space is critical to adaptation. The auxiliary function model calls for unceasing efforts to adjust the fit between frail elders and their environment, a fit that comprises affective and instrumental elements. The following discussion is broken down into the arbitrary divisions of the physical, social, and service environments, although each overlaps and is dependent on the other. Where in Chapter 5 we outlined strategies for helping the frail elder utilize a responsive environment, here we shall examine environmental interventions that can enhance this responsiveness. Required are a wide variety of intervention skills that this text does not address in detail. The reader is referred to recommended texts and articles in Appendix A.

THE PHYSICAL ENVIRONMENT

"The physical environment comprises the natural world and the physical world" (Germain, 1979). It takes on different dimensions for frail elders whose sensory, motor, and/or cognitive impairments can impede autonomous functioning and control over their surroundings. Different aspects of the physical environment will have meaning for frail elders depending on their impairments as well as their state of health. Very often, they themselves and/or their families may not be clear as to the exact problem. Thus, the assessment process spelled out in Chapter 2 is critically important.

In Chapter 8, we stressed the importance of employing prosthetic devices and/or engaging medical interventions that can promote restitution or compensation to the frail elder and with it control over some aspects of the physical environment. Advances in cataract surgery have certainly been significant, and other such surgical interventions as hip joint replacements and pacemakers have enhanced the functioning of many. Short of severe impairments, however, the very state of frailty suggests that sensory thresholds are heightened, motor abilities slowed down, and energy diminished, rendering even the most minor physical obstacles overwhelming. Thus, the notion of barrier-free, supportive, and accessible physical environments has gained much attention in recent years (Costa & Sweet, 1976).

Barrier-Free and Access Issues

A supportive, barrier-free, and accessible physical environment is so important to the elderly that many in their late middle age and early old age begin making preparations on their own for such surroundings. Migration to southern states upon retirement or moving to a retirement community or apartment from a multi-storied house—all of these are preparations for a physical environment where elders can either compensate for the impairments they may incur or accommodate to with the least amount of stress.

Undoubtedly, an attractive feature of some modern long-term care facilities is that they are designed with the frail elder in mind: providing ramps rather than stairs, hand rails and wide doors for wheelchairs, and color schemes appropriate for the aged eye. In a well-designed retirement village, skilled nursing facility, or housing project, the frail elder does not have to climb stairs, travel many miles to the doctor, be concerned about whether or not food can be purchased, be confused or distracted by clutter, noise, and spatial complexity, or even be made uncomfortable by adverse weather conditions.

Improvements in the physical environment are probably cost-effective in the long run, for they help sustain autonomous functioning and decrease dependence. Problems in social isolation and the increased need for human support services to bridge environmental obstacles can be mitigated with such improvements (Lawton, 1970).

The most severe problems for the elderly outside of the home are safety and travel. There is fear of abuse by other persons, but also fear of obstacles, inclement weather, traffic, and the unknown. Some of these problems can be directly attacked.

The worker had two clients living in the housing project who had difficulty crossing the road to the supermarket since there was no traffic light. Although cars were supposed to stop at the crosswalk for pedestrians, the elders felt vulnerable there. After surveying the building and finding this was a problem for many tenants, the worker organized a tenants' group to successfully petition for lights.

Whenever more than one client is affected by a potentially remediable problem in the physical environment, the intervention should be on a group and organizational level. By the same token, idiosyncratic situations can occur that demand individualized attention. In the above described situation, one client, fearful about crossing streets because of her poor sight, required escort service.

Transportation is a severe problem for the frail and often becomes a major task for the family. A lack of transportation can result in social isolation, poor medical care, or improper nutrition. Dramatic efforts have been made to improve public transportation, and many public and private agencies provide special services (Bell, 1974).

Mrs. Zane could shop for herself if only she could get to the supermarket. The worker considered enlisting a volunteer to shop for her, but knew it would deprive the elder of an important self-enhancing activity. After talking with other staff, it became apparent that a number of elders in the neighborhood needed transportation to the shopping center, and the local school bus was enlisted twice a week to transport the twenty elders.

Attention must also be paid to a variety of less obvious environmental obstacles that impede mobility and access for wheelchair-bound elders. Actions on the part of younger disabled persons in the past two decades have done much to remove these impediments, such as sidewalk curbs and steps into public buildings. Architects are taking a much sharper look at building design that enhances functioning (Elderly Housing, 1981). Still, constant alterations in the physical environment are needed to accommodate the wheelchair-bound elder.

Mrs. Charney's severe arthritis required almost constant use of the wheelchair. For chapel services and social functions, she was placed in the back of the auditorium where there was room for wheelchair-bound residents. In view of her poor hearing, however, she refused to attend any more functions. The worker alerted the recreation staff to this problem, and the seating arrangement in the auditorium was altered so that Mrs. Charney and other wheelchair-bound residents with sensory deficits could sit nearer the front.

The reader is directed to Appendix A for resources that will broaden the worker's knowledge of the physical environment. Physical and occupational therapists, of course, are experts in assessing, correcting, and helping the client adapt to the physical environment. If available, they should be enlisted by the worker to address this important environmental issue.

Policy issues related to the physical environment have been addressed over the past few decades. Subsidized housing for the handicapped elderly has been an active program of the federal government. Retirement villages have flourished under proprietary and voluntary auspices. As noted, laws benefiting the handicapped, particularly in regard to barrier-free access and transportation, have had meaning for the frail elderly.

For many however, particularly those without financial resources or living in rural areas, problems in the physical life space can be overwhelming. Wherever such impediments can be removed or the physical environment enhanced, direct social work interventions are required. An important caveat, however, is in order. The benefits of a safe, accessible, and barrier-free environment must always be balanced with the social and service components of the environment and the capacity of the elder to adapt to new surroundings. A physically desirable nursing home may be socially oppressive or isolated. A relatively barrier-free housing complex may lack necessary personal services. A severely depleted elder may not be able to adapt successfully to even the most desirable of environmental relocations (Lieberman, 1974). The substitution of mechanical communication systems for personal contact may take away a needed social contact.

A cadre of "visiting" residents had been organized in the senior apartment house to check up on the frailer residents who might need help. An alarm system was installed, which negated the practical need for the cadre. Some residents welcomed the additional privacy; however, most missed the regular visits of their neighbors.

Inside The Home

"Home" is usually accorded highest value by the elder. The home and its familiar objects may represent continuity with the past and be all that is remaining of an earlier life if spouse and peers have died. Most elders, as well as younger persons, can be powerfully attached to their homes and physical possessions. To many, continuing to "keep house" may symbolize the one role remaining in old age.

The strong feelings that many elders have for their homes, when coupled with a desire for privacy, independence, and continuity, explain the tenacity with which they hold on to their dwellings. This aspect of the physical environment can also contribute to a sense of well-being and quality of life. Any efforts that can be made to retain an elder's home—if this is his or her choice—seem more than justified.

A variety of measures have been enacted to help elders financially to retain their homes: reverse mortgages, rent and heating subsidies, and repair and chore services. The battle is often an uphill one, particularly when a house is old, which it often is. Size alone and the endless need for repair can be financially draining.

If the elder is to remain at home, the following issues need to be addressed. The issues also would apply to the homes of family members who have a frail elder living with them. Basic categories to be considered are those related to climate and temperature control, lighting, safety, and access to important areas within the house as well as to the outside.

The mental and sensory functioning of the elder will determine to some extent the breadth of interventions to be considered. If judgment is impaired, the elder may overlook or instigate a number of situations that can create discomfort or be hazardous: improper clothing, poor ventilation and lighting, garbage accumulation, and misuse of appliances.

Mentally alert but frail elders and their families may be unaware of devices such as handrails on the bathtub, hand showers, and special utensils that can make many tasks easier, even possible.

Color design is an important feature for frail elders. Since elders are better able to discriminate oranges, yellows, and reds, these colors should be used in situations where contrast is important such as on steps. The mentally alert may also be unaware of hazards such as scatter rugs, poor lighting, and the importance of the way in which certain items of furniture are placed (see Appendix B).

The negative features of the home environment should not overshadow evaluating the positive aspects as well. Many arrangements already may be in place that greatly enhance the functioning of the older person. The very fact that the elder has learned to compensate for or gradually accommodate to sensory, motor, and/or cognitive deficits is a plus, particularly if functioning in a certain sphere seems to be going well. The gathering of a clutter of needed items within reach may seem confused or disorganized to the worker but actually be a successful adaptive effort at reorganizing the environment to accommodate to diminished mobility (Miller & Solomon, 1979).

THE SOCIAL ENVIRONMENT

"The social environment comprises the network of human relations at various levels of organization" (Germain, 1979): family, friends, neighbors, small groups in the community or in institutions, and formal organizations or bureaucracies. These interrelated networks strongly affect the individual's behavior and, in turn, are influenced by it. They provide a wide range of affective and instrumental interactions. Litwak and Meyer (1966) divide these networks into face-to-face groups and bureaucracies, akin respectively to the informal, or natural, and formal social systems. They distinguish between them in terms of the tasks they are best able to perform and underscore the important ways in which they link to one another. We shall address face-to-face "natural" groups in this section. In the next section, we shall examine the formal organizations that comprise the service environment of the frail elderly.

NATURAL HELPING NETWORKS

Natural helping networks, or face-to-face groups, are defined by their continuity over time and affectional attributes. In contrast to bureaucracies, natural groups can respond with spontaneity and feeling to the idiosyncratic needs of members. The most important face-to-face group for the frail elder is the family. While most frail elders do not live with a younger nuclear family, i.e. mother, father, and children, they are usually members of an extended family system and, if not widowed, an older nuclear family, i.e. the husband-wife team.

Theoretically, the family is ideally suited to meet many of the needs of the frail elderly. One of its major functions in modern times, in addition to the important tasks of childrearing and maintaining cultural continuity, is to provide emotional support and affection and a variety of personal and housekeeping services. Like other small groups, it is well suited to perform a number of instrumental tasks, particularly if these tasks do not involve a great deal of technical skill. Shopping, chore services, money management, case management, and some nursing and personal care tasks are well met by family members because of their availability to meet needs flexibly (such as at night), motivation to help based on filial bonds, and knowledge of the individual idiosyncratic needs of the elder. By virtue of its structure and history, the family is suited to fill portions or all of the auxiliary role.

The great majority of families respond to the increased and changing needs of the frail elderly and perform affective and instrumental tasks guided by an intuitive knowledge of what would be helpful. This occurs even though the burden may be great. A recent study of 617 family members in the Cleveland area who care for frail elders in their homes found them providing an array of tasks, but with the great burden tending to fall on one caregiver (Poulshock & Noelker, 1982).

It is when there is a lack or breakdown in family support that frail elders usually come to the attention of the formal service system. The problems associated with impairment may be so severe that the burden is too great for the family. Some families are rejecting, abusive, or live far away. In others, members may be too old or emotionally unable to provide the quantity or type of care needed, or there simply may be no family left for a frail elder who has outlived loved ones. There is also the situation of the frail elder who has always eschewed family relationships, the lifelong isolate who upon reaching a state of dependence lacks the social skills to interact with the informal network.

Whatever the reason for breakdown in or dearth of family supports, it is incumbent upon the social worker to seek new networks and try to reestablish old ones. Chapter 10 will discuss strategies of working with family members to enable them to manage their emotions, organize their resources, and move ahead to support the frail elder. Here we shall deal with other face-to-face groups that can be created or strengthened for the elder, substituting for or supplementing family and professional efforts.

For the frail elder living in the community, ties with friends and neighbors can be of immense importance. These friends and neighbors can perform one or more tasks such as shopping or meal preparation and be deeply involved in the auxiliary role. Sometimes they are seen by the elder as "family." These relationships often develop naturally over the years and may reflect appreciation for past favors on the part of the elder. Whatever, the elder who has retained social skills is most successful in sustaining these helpful relationships.

Assessing the Informal Caregiver

The study and assessment should identify the informal supports available to the elder and evaluate their quality. These face-to-face informal relations can potentially provide socialization, concrete services, and perform part or all of the auxiliary role. If connections are already in place, efforts should be made to strengthen these ties within the framework of the elder's changed condition. At times, new neighborhood and friendship ties can be established, particularly in settings where there are tenant groups, church involvement, or other organized volunteer activities. As with family relationships, the status quo in relation to friends and neighbors should not be taken for granted.

Molly Porter, an eighty-year-old "bag lady," was hospitalized for a

*broken hip. She had no visitors and was quite despondent since her usual
routine was interrupted. The social worker discovered that she had spent
most of her time travelling one bus route for hours on end, befriended by
drivers and regular passengers who knew her as "Molly." The worker
contacted them, and a few visited at the hospital, cheering her greatly.*

Relations with relatives, neighbors, and friends are as varied
with the old as with the young. Relationships can be based on
reciprocity, good will, and affection. They can also be exploitive
and hostile. When reciprocity diminishes, as in the case of frailty,
neighbors and friends may not be as helpful as they once were.
The filial ties of the family that undergird the family's responsibility toward the old are not necessarily present with neighbors and
friends unless the relationship extends back in time and has assumed
"family-like" characteristics. These informal arrangements can be
particularly problematic for elders suffering mental impairment.
Their vulnerable condition makes them prey for exploitation,
particularly when friendship and neighborhood ties are tenuous.

When the social worker or another professional provides supervision, the qualifications of informal care providers may be less
important than when their responsibilities are significant. If they
are expected to fill a large share of the auxiliary role, however,
several issues must be addressed: the caregiver's capacity for
empathy, his or her understanding of frailty, a willingness to "risk"
in terms of supporting the elder's remaining competencies, and a
readiness to be flexible in response to the elder's changing needs.
If other services are involved, case coordination skills are required
and a willingness to remain a dependable significant other.

The capacity of the auxiliary role to be a shared one comes in
to play at this juncture. The worker may continue as service
coordinator, leaving others to serve as primary communicators
with the elder, or each of these functions may be shared, with the
worker supplementing the efforts of friend and neighbor.

*Eighty-year-old Mrs. Loman was to be discharged soon following
in-hospital rehabilitation for a broken hip. Homemaker-home health aide
services and shopping were planned for, and her son was ready to visit
from a neighboring city once a month. From the client, the worker
learned the names of friendly neighbors and with the elder's permission*

contacted them to inform them of Mrs. Loman's weakened condition. Three neighbors responded favorably to Mrs. Loman's situation, for they were very fond of her. One chose to visit and another to run supplementary errands. With the worker's encouragement, Mrs. Loman herself contacted a third neighbor to accompany her to the doctor's office. The worker maintained her relationship with the elder visiting once a month for a few months and then decreased her contacts to regular phone calls and occasional visits as Mrs. Loman's condition improved and the son expressed readiness to oversee the plan.

Top priority must be given to the client's feelings and opinions. While family members are usually accepted as caregivers, the frail elder may be very hesitant about involving friends and neighbors. Issues of pride, privacy, and fear of intrusion all come to the fore, and the involvement and participation of the elder in mapping out a service plan are essential. By the same token, the issue should not be averted. A little encouragement and support may result in a mutually satisfactory arrangement (see Chapter 5).

The neighbor, friend, or volunteer is brought into the frail elder's life space to be helpful. As with professionals, their motivations may be varied and potentially destructive to the frail elder. An inordinate need to have a helpless person dependent on one or a need for power and control may dominate the relationship with the elder. Care should be taken to screen out such persons. Potential helpers should be empathic but not possessive or intrusive (Greengross, 1980). Relating empathically to the elder's plight and responding to increased dependence—as we have noted repeatedly in this text—do not have to interfere with remaining areas of autonomous functioning.

Mrs. Frank needed someone to accompany her to the bank each month, as her ambulation was poor. She was, however, fully capable of carrying out all needed banking operations. The neighbor who used her "better judgment" to arrange for direct deposit of social security checks and bill payment by mail was not helpful, robbing the client of an important opportunity for exercising her abilities in money management.

The judgment of the mentally alert elder can be an excellent barometer of such relations. In the case of the mentally impaired, however, the worker may have to step in directly to interview and evaluate each potential helper. As the network broadens into volunteer services that simulate the help of friend and neighbor, supervision is hopefully provided by the sponsoring agency. If not, the worker must remain involved.

The availability of informal help over time must also be examined within the framework of the helper's understanding of frailty. Responsibility is shirked by the social worker if the case of a frail elder is closed because "a natural network" has been established. It is far better for the worker to share in the auxiliary role to the extent of monitoring a situation than to close the case entirely. The frailty of the client—a condition that can worsen rapidly—and changes in the lives of friends and neighbors require this attention.

Helping Friends and Neighbors

In addition to assessing the informal caregiver's capacity to assist the elder, time and effort should be given to sensitization, education, and support of friends and neighbors. The helper should be alerted to the shifting needs of the frail elder calling for a flexible service plan. The need for shopping help, for example, may decrease as an elder's strength increases, but not the need for a friendly contact.

In order to sensitize and educate informal caregivers about the needs of the elder, the worker can selectively share his or her general knowledge about aging and frailty and the particulars of an individual elder's situation as spelled out in the study and assessment.

Confidential, irrelevant, and complex information should not be shared, of course. The informal caregivers, on the other hand, may be privy to much more information about the elder than a worker. It is important that this information is organized in such a way that the behavior of the elder is understood.

The neighbor reported to the worker that Mr. Muller shouted at her a great deal and refused to open the front door sometimes when she dropped by to shop for him. This led to the worker's discovery that Mr. Muller's deafness had worsened. She instructed the neighbor in proper speaking techniques and suggested a phone call before visiting to alert

Mr. Muller, who could hear the telephone ring but not the front door bell.

The worker can also share selectively with informal supports the skills he or she has developed in communicating with a frail elder. Here the worker can serve as a model.

The worker sat close to blind Mrs. Wilson and held her hand as they talked. She permitted the fearful client to touch her face and her clothing. This was reassuring to the client and instructive to the neighbor, who was unaccustomed to this sort of physical contact.

To be avoided are situations where the elder's dependence in concrete matters is perpetuated *only* in order to maintain a social contact. The helper must be able to recognize and respond to both affective and instrumental levels of need and must also be supported in situations that seem risky for the elder.

Mrs. Smith, eighty-five years old, decided that she no longer needed her friend to take her shopping, but did not want to jeopardize the relationship by shopping alone. The friend was fearful that Mrs. Smith would lose her money or be robbed. The worker helped the friend see that this was a risk worth taking, since Mrs. Smith was able to protect her money and at this point only needed companionship.

Friends and neighbors willing to help a mentally impaired elder need a very special type of support from the worker since the elder may offer few gratifications.

Mrs. Clark was ninety-five years old and had lived alone for the past twenty years in a housing project since the death of her husband. While physically healthy, she now had almost no memory and rarely recognized friends and neighbors who helped her out in many ways. The social worker made it a point to visit them and praise them for their help.

Beyond sharing professional knowledge and skills selectively with informal caregivers, the social worker may also want to supplement these efforts with reading materials (see Appendix B). Ongoing education and support also may be provided by special groups for informal care providers organized by churches, social agencies, and other organizations.

THE SERVICE ENVIRONMENT

The service environment, also referred to as the formal support system, is an important part of the social environment, comprising professionals and bureaucracies serving frail elders and families. It is differentiated from the informal support system, which provides the great bulk of services to the elderly and performs other social functions as well.

Social work services are an important part of the service environment and, hopefully, will play an increasingly important role in shaping it in the future. One segment of the service environment is the professional community, chiefly physicians and lawyers in private practice. Another segment comprises the human service organizations in which the social worker may practice (described in Chapter 3) and other organizations that serve the frail elder and family but are not the home setting for a social worker. Just as the social worker's conceptual range must include the informal network in assessing a frail elder's situation, so must it encompass the total service system. In spite of the constraints of agency and professional boundaries, collaborative efforts must be as broad as the life space of the elderly and their families dictates.

The social worker is similar to other service providers in that his or her area of expertise represents but one aspect of the client's total situation, the psychosocial component. The worker differs from them in that his or her role often involves a coordinating function. In this second capacity, as case manager, the worker is accountable not only to the client but to all others engaged in the care of the client. Successful collaboration is based on mastery of a distinct set of principles and skills. Of primary importance are written and verbal communications, which specify clearly and concretely the worker's assessment and plan. Social work jargon and global objectives such as "psychosocial well-being" are to be avoided.

The following is an overview of the service environment of the frail elderly: the professionals and paraprofessionals who serve them in private practice and organizations and the policies and programs that affect service delivery. These are described in tandem with interventions consonant with the auxiliary function model.

Private Practitioners

Professionals in private practice constitute a significant portion of the elder's service environment. They include physicians, lawyers, and—to a lesser extent—social workers, nurse practitioners, and rehabilitation therapists. Physicians and lawyers have the most interaction with frail elders and their families and more often than not need to be involved by the social worker in assessment and planning of particular cases. They may need to be collaborators in problem solving, or their relationship with a frail elder may be the problem that needs to be addressed.

The social worker's goals, however, must be pursued within the context of the other service provider's perspective vis-à-vis the frail elder. The following pages examine the perspectives of several different types of service providers and the ways in which the worker can reconcile social work goals with them.

Physicians

Physicians in private practice form a critical part of the frail elder's service environment. In many communities, the physician is depended on not simply for medical care but for advice in a variety of life decisions. Physicians are often imbued with great powers by older patients, and their advice can have dramatic effects on the life of an elder. It is often the physician who is instrumental in nursing home placement. Ideally, private practitioners should utilize social work services since some of the problems they face with frail elders fall within the realm of social work expertise. Yet, outside of situations in which the elder is hospitalized, few do.

It is incumbent on the social worker to be in touch with the elderly client's physician, whether clinic or private practice based. If a frail elder does not have a physician, it is a primary task of the social worker to make this referral. Reliance on family members to communicate with a physician may not suffice, particularly if they lack knowledge or are intimidated. By the same token, the social worker may be able to turn to a co-worker, such as a nurse, to serve as an intermediary in complex situations.

Contact with the physician involves alerting him or her to the

social worker's or agency's presence in the situation, expressing a willingness to work cooperatively. It might include consulting with the physician about a very specific problem such as drug overuse, or it might involve obtaining more specific information from the physician about an elder's condition. Whatever, the perspective of the physician must be foremost in the mind of the social worker before making this contact.

The physician's perspective is usually influenced by a busy schedule and an absorption with emergency situations which consume a great deal of time. Very often, physicians are not afforded the leisure to review cases and think about all the problems facing their patients. The physician's perspective in some cases also may be influenced by negative attitudes toward the frail elderly. The physician may view the elder's plight as irreversible and treatment efforts as purely palliative. A narrow focus on disease processes leads in some situations to a myopic view of the patient, which in the case of the frail elderly may obscure complex processes. Geriatric and family medicine physicians often have a broader view of the psychosocial situation of an elder.

For the more narrowly focused and/or busy physician, it is nonproductive to try to change the physician's perspective. Rather, the social worker should address the problem as the physician sees it. If the social worker can communicate that he or she can help an elder and family with a care plan, most physicians are only too glad to be relieved of this responsibility.

Specific situations may be a pivotal point for the communication between the social worker and physician. An overwrought elder and family may place many demands on a physician, calling him or her often with "emergencies." Here again, the social worker may be able to partialize and deflect these demands from the physician. A social worker can interpret a physician's orders to a frail elder, particularly one with communication difficulties, and in turn interpret the elder's wishes to the physician. The auxiliary role of the social worker and its interpretative tasks come into strong play here.

The worker telephoned Dr. Price to get more understanding about the medication regimen of her client. It took her a few days to reach the harried doctor, and when she did reach him, he had trouble remembering specifically who the patient was. After quickly looking at the record, he recalled that the client was a troublesome one for him. He had been concerned about her condition and lack of care and the obvious fact that she was not following his orders. The worker pointed out that she was now involved with this case for the very reasons he described and was hoping to offer supervision of the medication regimen and other aspects of the life of the client, who was becoming more confused and unable to manage her life. It was then agreed that the worker would serve as a link between physician and patient.

Lawyers

The lawyer is another important community practitioner for the social worker to interact with, particularly in regard to the impaired frail elder whose mental competency is in question. Lawyers often have power of attorney to manage a frail elder's finances. They may serve as court-appointed guardians when incompetency has been declared and manage all aspects of the frail elder's life. They may be consulted by families in regard to the family's rights in relation to a frail elder.

Social workers, of course, may wish to utilize lawyers in situations where the elder may be endangering his or her life and where legal intervention is needed. Social workers may wish to consult with the lawyer regarding the rights of the client in a situation where these rights may be abrogated by housing managers, relatives, nursing home administrators, etc. Whether the condition of the frail elder or treatment by others determines the need for legal intervention, the relationship between social worker and lawyer must be defined.

The legal perspective relates to the civil rights of clients and the rights of family, neighbors, and the community at large. Action might be taken on behalf of or against a frail elderly client. The interest of the social worker may coincide or conflict with those of the lawyer. Interest in the self-determination of frail elders, their decision-making prerogatives, or their wish to remain in their own homes in the community may overshadow, in the social worker's view, the rights of others and the perspective of the lawyer. Where the lawyer's interest is in the elder's rights, a cooperative relationship can be worked out; but where the actions of the lawyer are, in a sense, against the elder, there may be a direct confrontation.

This confrontation can be avoided if a litigious atmosphere is sidestepped. While mentally impaired elderly clients are not children, their condition places them in a similarly helpless position, and the approach should be akin to that of the family court in relation to juvenile offenders. The common goal, as articulated by advocates of enlightened protective service workers, is the welfare of the elder (Regan, 1977). This may in the long run require legal intervention, but it should follow after efforts to resolve the conflict without force have proved unsuccessful. The social worker might also support temporary legal injunctions that do not permanently abrogate an elder's rights. Paramount to these types of effort is the establishment of a trusting relationship between worker and client.

From the lawyer's perspective, an underlying reason exists for each legal action taken: to provide a safe environment for the elder, protect the elder from dangerous acts that he or she can commit and from abuse or rejection by others, guard the community from the dangerous or distasteful actions of frail elders, or relieve relatives of undue burdens. Each of these goals can possibly be achieved through routes other than legal force, routes lawyers often prefer to take. They are usually willing to give the social worker a chance.

Mr. Fisher had become increasingly unkempt and neglectful of his home and property, and there was a great deal of concern about fire and other hazards. There also seemed to be a garbage problem, which was very offensive to the neighbors, as well as an overabundance of animals on the property, which was frightening to them as well. A group of neighbors finally engaged a lawyer to take action against Mr. Fisher that could result in his eviction. Mr. Fisher, who had been a welfare recipient a number of years ago, remembered enough to call the agency who sent out a worker to visit him. He was frightened and distraught and couldn't understand what was going on. The worker was able to persuade the key neighbors and lawyer to withhold action until he had an opportunity to work with Mr. Fisher over the next few months.

The worker soon discovered that Mr. Fisher was malnourished and in need of medical care. It was through gaining Mr. Fisher's trust and establishing a working alliance with him that medical care was given and his diet was improved, leading to less paranoid behavior. He agreed to have services brought into the home, the property cleaned up, and the animal population weeded out. All parties were content for the time being.

Service Organizations

The variety of social and health care settings in which social workers serve the frail elderly and their families were described in Chapter 3. For the most part, these settings are human service organizations, some who target their services only to the elderly and others who serve the general population. Because of the frail elder's complex and long-term problems, the auxiliary function model calls for extending the social worker's vision beyond organizational boundaries. Thus, we have viewed these organizations along a continuum of care including those that provide acute or occasional services to the elderly, sustained care to elders living in the community, and total care within the institution. This continuum of care was described as a skeletal framework for a long-term care system, which is needed to fully address the needs of the chronically impaired. We noted that this framework is disjointed, bone bare in terms of community resources, and supported by irrational funding streams, which tend to support medical and institutional needs of elders sometimes at the expense of community and social service needs.

It is important for the worker to understand the strengths and weaknesses of the system, for they seriously affect the organizations that serve the elderly and delineate the parameters of the social worker's potential influence. While organizational change initiated by human service professionals is indeed possible and professional vision must be as broad as the client's environment, the limitations of the worker's effectiveness must be understood. We first shall discuss the contradictions and limitations which the social worker must be mindful of and the types of common organizational problems that might be tackled. We are indebted to George Brager and Stephen Holloway (1978), whose text on the subject of organizational change provided a useful framework for this discussion (see Appendix A for other readings).

Contradictions and Limitations

The irrationality characterizing our long-term system, if indeed it can be viewed as a system, is deeply rooted in the values and beliefs of our society. American society's ambivalence in regard to institutional responses to human need is a case in point; on one hand, desiring adequate services and care and, on the other, resenting "freeloaders"—those who depend on public services. The norm of reciprocity and a deep abiding belief in the free enterprise system contributes to this contradiction.

Our long-term care system reflects this ambivalence as illustrated by government funding patterns and eligibility requirements. Medicare and Medicaid are two major funding sources for services to the frail elderly. Medicare expenditures have mushroomed since its inception in 1965, totalling 18.3 billion dollars in 1977 (Brotman, 1979). A government health insurance, it has been embraced as a deserved reward to elders who have contributed during their working years to the social security system. The fact that Medicare largely supports acute hospital and physician's fees speaks to the moral justification for medical care to say nothing of the free enterprise dimensions of American medical practice and its institutional support—the acute hospital.

Medicaid, funded by federal, state, and local governments, is a system of public assistance for the medically indigent. It has grown astronomically totalling almost 7 billion dollars for the elderly in 1977 (Brotman, 1979). Medicaid fills the gap in Medicare insurance for the poor elderly who cannot afford its copayment features. It also supports an extensive system of nursing home care spurred on in the 1960s and 1970s by the crowding of expensive hospital beds by the impaired elderly and a nursing home industry ready to fill the vacuum in services for an exploding population (Vladeck, 1980). The fact that this welfare system has flourished in American society only can be explained by the pressing needs of a frail population who hardly can be viewed as freeloaders and a forward-looking entrepreneurial system of care.

Community services for the frail elderly have not fared as well and tend to be identified with welfare services for the poor.

Their cost comprises a very small percentage of Medicare and Medicaid expenditures. Publicly funded social services under Title XX of the Social Security Act and Title III of the Older American's Act are sadly inadequate, totalling only a small portion of health care expenditures. In terms of social care, society has gone the institutional route which, ironically, promotes much more dependence than community support systems.

Human service organizations that are funded to address the needs of the frail elderly operate under other handicaps. The implicit rationale of many publicly funded programs is social control. While the implicit organizational mandate of social control is usually viewed in relation to "disruptive" social minorities such as the nation's poor (Cloward & Piven, 1971), it is a critical feature of publicly funded services to the frail elderly.

Protective service programs that presumably are mandated to protect impaired vulnerable elders in reality also protect the public from their deviant behavior. Nursing homes accommodate the mentally impaired, warehousing rather than treating a troublesome population. Hospital discharge units mandated to ease the transition from hospital to aftercare are an important tool for expediting economic utilization of hospital beds.

Human service organizations that endure must accommodate these conflicting imperatives either by maintaining ambiguity about their goals, operating from crisis to crisis thus avoiding the need for a clear long-range perspective, or focusing on coordinating functions, which sidestep the issue of inadequate resources. The latter route has been popularly utilized in the aging field, with information and referral and case management systems proliferating.

Within the context of the bewildering contradictions that characterize our system of long-term care, the social worker must address organizational constraints that thwart addressing service needs of the frail elderly and their families. The conflict within the profession as to whether the social worker should function as an autonomous professional or an employee morally bound by agency proscriptions adds to the contradictions. Our text has taken a firm position that the social worker in operationalizing the auxiliary function model must exercise skill regardless of organizational constraints and extend his or her vision beyond agency boundaries to the critical life space of the frail elder. However, what the worker actually might be able to do, given limited agency resources and mandates, is subject to great variation. We have discussed elsewhere the value dilemmas that face the individual social worker and the profession and the need for collective advocacy on behalf of the frail elderly. Short of these efforts, there are organizational problems that can be addressed.

Common Problems and Strategies

It is not difficult to identify the problem areas in organizations. The common experiences of elders and clients utilizing services and professional standards indicate where the need lies. Problems can be with staff, service delivery, and organizational services. Here, each is discussed in conjunction with suggested change strategies.

STAFF ISSUES: NURSES, AIDES, AND VOLUNTEERS. A serious and prevalent problem for staff who serve the frail elderly is that of burnout, or apathy and diminished investment in the job resulting from the stresses of caring for impaired patients and clients. These may be caused by an organizational structure not responsive to the needs of the client group or by personal attitudes. Prejudices that staff bring to the workplace may include a bias against working with the frail elderly and an inbred hopelessness about their plight. In the case of physicians, nurses, and nursing home administrators who are accustomed to operating under the acute care model, the psychosocial needs of frail elders are often overlooked. Staff members also can be ignorant about the aging process and individual and family behavior. In agencies serving clients of all ages, priority may be given to those who are younger and more likely to improve.

The individualized approach of the social worker can be effective with staff and serve as a model for other situations. These could be described as auxiliary functions that utilize educational, persuasive, and interpretive skills on behalf of the elder.

The nursing home administrator wanted to restrict visiting hours for Mrs. Black since she seemed so upset when her daughter visited. The worker pointed out that this had always been the nature of their relationship, and it would be a deprivation to the resident if her daughter visited less.

Nurses comprise the key personnel within institutional settings and are important decision-makers in regard to a frail elder's life. A successful liaison with the social worker, whether working within the institutional setting or outside, is often the key to an effective care plan. It is a more important relationship than with the physician, who is often peripheral to day-to-day care.

The perspective of the nurse will be different from that of the social worker. For some, the primary goal is narrowly related to · the health status and direct physical care of the frail elder. Others have a broader view that encompasses the psychosocial needs of the elder. Often overburdened in their tasks, nurses must not only provide for twenty-four hour direct personal and health care to their impaired and needy patients but they must supervise untrained staff and adhere to a variety of professional and regulatory requirements. Recordkeeping alone can be a burden for a nurse, who often is not spared much time to relate directly to the resident population. Management of behavioral problems and families who are difficult can be particularly trying for the nurse.

Here, the social worker should address the needs of the nurse rather than hoping to change routines and viewpoints. The worker needs to relate social work inputs to the nurse's attempt to get a particular job done. Imagination on the part of the social worker can bring the psychosocial needs of the clients and the needs of the nurse together.

Ninety-year-old Mrs. North was quite mentally impaired, but active physically, requiring little sleep. The nursing staff on the floor did not want to ask for orders that would overmedicate the patient and in turn have a deleterious effect on her functioning, yet they felt compelled to ask. Mrs. North's hyperactivity greatly worried the family and was potentially disruptive on the floor, particularly in the dining room. Family members, in fact, complained to the administrator that the nurses weren't responding to Mrs. North's needs and providing the care and medication she needed.

The social worker was able to match the needs of the nurses, client, and family by broadening the family's understanding of the client's hyperactivity, thus decreasing their anxiety and pressure on staff. She worked out an arrangement with the other residents on the floor wherein

Mrs. North ate the evening meal in her own room, at this time of heightened hyperactivity.

Nurses in the community setting, not under the constraints of institutional requirements, often are more independent in their professional decisions and have a broader perspective of the psychosocial needs of elders. Some nurses in the community perform social work functions, and undoubtedly there are nurses who believe that social workers are performing nursing functions. There indeed is an overlap, and the overlap can lead to conflict. This is not always the case. Visiting nurse associations have social workers on their staffs as consultants whom they utilize well, and of course, there are social agencies with nurses on their staffs with whom they have good working relationships.

With the complexity of needs of the frail elder and the blurring of boundaries between the social, psychological, and physical problems, a role conflict is possible even in the best of circumstances. The task of the social worker is to recognize the overlap and then engage the nurse in identifying the unique tasks of each profession and the common areas that can be shared.

Aides furnish the bulk of hands-on care to the elder in community and institution. The perspective of the homemaker-home health aide, or the nurse's aide in the nursing home is varied. There are many who are deeply committed with unusual capacities for empathic and caring relationships. They can form strong, even possessive, relationships with the frail elder. Usually the lowest paid of service providers with the most onorous tasks to perform, their perspective can also be very negative. Racial discrimination and a lack of agency support can add to this negativism.

These service providers identify social workers as a professional class who are in a position of authority. Social workers can thus be respected and/or resented. Resentment is intensified by an overidentification on the part of social workers with their frail clients who they fear may be abused or neglected by aides. Social workers may also over-identify with family members who are demanding and/or critical of the care offered by aides.

Attempts to ameliorate status differences by pretending they do not exist are neither trusted nor effective. It is important that the social worker not discriminate against these primary caregivers by failing to recognize their needs for information and assistance and their desire to provide quality, expert service. The aide or homemaker needs to have useful information about the client or resident. Also needed is help in dealing with particular management problems and support in relation to families who may be difficult to handle.

The social worker-helper interaction will be determined to a large extent by respective agency affiliations. In some instances, the worker may carry supervisory responsibility for an aide. In others, the social worker has no such authority and assumes more of a linkage function. Whatever the arrangement, lines of responsibility should be clear to all. Needless to say, the worker's assessment and intervention skills are as crucial in establishing a working relationship with these helpers as they are with the elder. Through their regular interaction with the elder, aides are a valuable source of information about the daily, almost imperceptible, important changes of functioning that might not be picked up by the social worker in less frequent visits.

Whether the social worker is affiliated with the provider agency or independent community agency, his or her work includes thoughtful preparation of the aide. The aide should be aware of the elder's need and expectations of care. Feedback should be elicited. The overzealous social worker, closely identified with an elder, may go overboard in describing the client's fine points, making it hard for the aide to express negative feelings and iron out difficulties that later arise. It is usually possible to share a flavor of the client's personality and highlight points of similarity with the aide without divulging confidential information. The social worker can also use his or her knowledge and dynamic understanding of the client to direct the aide toward acceptable interventions. Food preparation and housecleaning may be equally important tasks to home health aides but assume different priorities according to each elder.

Homemaker-home health aides and nurse's aides are often grateful if given direct guidance on how to communicate. A client who is anxious to go outdoors may querulously repeat this request time and time again. The preoccupied aide may respond "later" or not at all, giving rise to further tension. The words or technique that the social worker has found helpful with a particular elder can be shared with the aide. For example, a patient explanation of the sequence of events may be called for. The aide need not always understand all the reasons why a particular response is indicated. If she tries it on faith and it works, her confidence in herself is boosted and with it her positive regard for the elder. Role playing, such as asking the aide to imagine herself in the elder's position and eliciting what response would please her, can also be of value. Needless to say, the social worker's assessment and intervention skills are as crucial in establishing a working relationship with the aide and other staff as they are with the elder.

If aides are being abused by the elder, this must not be viewed by the social worker as a function of "old age" and something to be excused. Empathic concern about this type of treatment and intervention with the elder may be very appropriate.

Mrs. Fulmer shared with the worker her disdain of the nurse's aide, pointing out, "what else can you expect of those kind of people?" Her own mother knew how to handle servants, and this wouldn't have happened if things were as they used to be. The worker thought that there did seem to be situations where Mrs. Fulmer was not getting all the help she needed from the aide, but began to see this might be because of her attitude. She talked with the aides on the floor about Mrs. Fulmer's attitude and was told that they didn't like being treated as servants or demeaned because of their race. The worker suggested that they might actually share their feelings with Mrs. Fulmer if they felt comfortable and the worker would be there with them if they wanted. They chose the latter alternative and a meeting was held between two of the aides, the worker, and Mrs. Fulmer. They shared with her their dislike of being treated as servants. Mrs. Fulmer, who was quite mentally alert in spite of her frailty, heard them out, apologized, and later was able to share with the worker her lack of realization of how things have changed since she was a younger woman.

Staff shortages are a serious problem in organizations, and *volunteers* are often utilized to fill gaps. They also have much to offer on their own. Their status, however, is often ambiguous, and problems arise because of their uncertain role in relation to the elder. Clearly, within the organizational structure a secure and supportive basis must be formed for volunteers. The social worker's individual attention is also important.

The perspective of volunteers who wish to work with the frail elder is no different from that of any other service provider. They see their contribution as meaningful, important, and needed. Thus, the attitude of the social worker must convey recognition of their contribution. This recognition is strengthened by the utilization of volunteers in meaningful roles. They are of particular value when fulfilling the role of friendly visitor or counsellor to a frail elder isolated in community or nursing home (Rowlings, 1981). Like the nurse's aide, the volunteer's status should not be demeaned. Expectations of volunteers should be high and remain high. By the same token, volunteers must be supervised and supported. They may exhibit problems in relation to the frail elderly similar to those of paid staff.

SERVICE DELIVERY PROBLEMS. Serious problems exist in the context and technology of service delivery. The first is deeply rooted in the norms of our society and reflected in government funding patterns and eligibility requirements. The second concerns the quality of services provided to frail elders and families. As with staff problems, these may be amenable to case management interventions consonant with the auxiliary role or may require changes in organizational structure. We shall discuss several of these problems as experienced by the frail elderly.

Poor access to services is a formidable problem for frail elders who are unable to travel to or identify services resources. Centralized services located away from the neighborhood in which elders live is a case in point. Outreach effort in these cases may have to be extensive. Transportation for the elder to get to services or the service provider to reach the elder in his or her home will be necessary if care is to be provided.

The problem of access in rural areas is particularly challenging. The imaginative use of informal supports and other service providers is often helpful. In Norway, for example, postmen who travel the fiords by boat have been enlisted to identify problems with frail elders and even provide some care. Social workers responsible for a particular geographical area may find contacts with local churches, physicians, and neighborhood organizations useful in identifying frail elders and informing them of help that is available.

Fragmentation of services is another serious problem. Few agencies are set up to meet all of the complex needs of the frail elder. Thus, the social worker literally must shop around to put together a service package compatible with the needs of the elder and family. The case coordination component of the auxiliary role is of prime importance here. If family members are not present to support the frail elder, much attention must be given to maintaining a relationship that will enable the client's use of disparate services.

Even within a single agency such as a nursing home, service delivery may be haphazard and uncoordinated, failing to address the elder as a whole person. The mentally impaired elderly, particularly, may have difficulty in translating the many services they receive into a coherent picture for themselves, and here the auxiliary role of the social worker becomes of paramount importance.

Another technological problem in organizations serving the elderly is related to the *quality of care given.* Services may be geared simply to custodial care. This is illustrated by personal and routine nursing services in nursing homes that overlook the interventions needed to encourage maximal functioning on the part of the elder be they restitution, compensation, or a more successful accommodation. The structure of the organization, of course, sets the tone for a custodial or therapeutic approach. Even within structural constraints the social worker, particularly in conjunction with like-minded staff such as rehabilitation therapists and nurses, can have considerable impact on service delivery, case-by-case, or in the aggregate.

STRUCTURAL PROBLEMS. Staff and service delivery problems more often than not are rooted in the structure of an organization: the way in which staff are organized and authority exercised. The major problems, as they relate to frail elderly clients, are faulty staff communication and collaboration, powerlessness of the consumer, rigid organizational boundaries, and inflexible policies and rules.

Staff communication and collaboration within and between organizations is critical in terms of case coordination and the meshing of services to meet the complex needs of frail elders. Yet, inadequate communication and collaboration is one of the most serious and prevalent organizational problems. While the social worker can accomplish much on a one-to-one basis or in informal staff groups, much more can be gained when a variety of legitimized staff linkages are built into the organizational structure.

Meetings are required that bridge various professional and status boundaries within the organization. Within the nursing home, this would require team meetings of all personnel involved in providing services on a floor with the charge of planning for individual residents and improving the quality of floor life. Regular meetings of higher level staff can provide coordination at the appropriate level of authority. The administrator needs to be regularly connected in a meeting format to the various service components of the organization.

In addition to providing information as to what other service providers are doing and why and coordinating a care plan, the meeting format serves as an important framework for the exchange of support between service providers. The social worker with group work skills can go far in expediting the productiveness of such meetings. The worker who is isolated from the formal communication networks of an organization is a far more likely candidate for burnout. Thus, organizational change may be required that loosens rigid hierarchal patterns and creates linkages across staff levels. The autonomy of supervisors and line staff is not necessarily compromised in such situations, if the purpose of these meetings is seen as collaborative and communicative.

The *powerlessness of frail elderly consumers* is a function not only of personal depletions but of the status they are often accorded in the organizational structure. With relatives and friends to serve as advocates, of course, their powerlessness is mitigated; but often, particularly in the nursing home setting, elders are helpless to control aspects of their lives or have an impact on the organization upon which they are so dependent.

Organizational changes that provide for resident (as well as relative) participation in management issues are required. The resident council, certainly a therapeutic tool, is also an important means of protecting the rights of residents and ensuring for them some say in their lives. Resident advocacy will be regarded as a threat by administrators unless the social worker can demonstrate that the organization will benefit from an informed active constituency. Historically, resident groups treated fairly have flocked to the support of their institutions when funding cuts were considered.

Cases of abuse may exist. The auxiliary role of the social worker requires that the situation be addressed. Rather than waiting for crises to arise, the social worker or social work department is well advised to establish in conjunction with the administrator and other department heads, policies and procedures, should such abuse situations arise. Most other staff and administration understand that the social worker is often a confidant of the elder and are receptive to properly channelled feedback. Short of this cooperation, linkages with external advocacy groups may be necessary.

Another formidable organizational problem is that of *rigid agency boundaries* that fail to recognize the fact that the life space of the elder extends beyond the organization. For the social worker within such an organization, outreach and linking efforts may be thwarted because of such policies. For the social worker who wishes to influence another organization, special change strategies may have to be employed. Litwak and Meyer (1966) outline a series of strategies wherein organizations can link to one another in their efforts on behalf of a particular client group. Where there are mutually shared goals, coordinating councils can be set up to bridge organizational boundaries. Where there is a lack of receptivity for such cooperative efforts, special change strategies may need to be employed. This can include aligning oneself with consumer and professional groups.

Inflexible rules and policies pose special problems for service organizations and the social worker. Sometimes this inflexibility is rooted in external (funding) requirements, but at other times may be the result of rigid administrative styles. This inflexibility may affect the intake process into nursing homes preventing the social worker from exploring the various parameters of the elder's life. Rules and regulations may be in effect governing the activities of daily living of residents or the way in which home-delivered services are provided, restricting the freedom of clients and workers to individualize the care plan. Rules, regulations, and policies can exist that subtly place the elder, particularly in agencies that serve all ages, at the low end of the priority list. This type of organizational problem is possibly the most difficult for the line worker to contend with. The higher the social worker is in the agency hierarchy, the greater is the potential for achieving change. While political and environmental forces may conspire to thwart these efforts, the line worker may yet have some power to affect large organizations.

If the agency is so organized that feedback mechanisms are built into the structure, an ongoing process of correction to accommodate changing needs of the population served and problematic situations is possible. In such a case, workers have an opportunity to influence organizational policies, which in turn can enhance future efforts. If such an opportunity is not available in an agency, this is a problem that in and of itself must be addressed. Social workers can consider a variety of ways of having an impact on the system. Organizing in numbers is often effective, if done in a formal, dignified manner, lacking in recrimination and accusations.

A problem-solving approach that addresses a felt problem of administration is more readily received then a flat criticism, since it gives the administrator something to react to and does not put him or her on the defensive.

Board and administrative staff at the Sunshine Nursing Home were becoming increasingly concerned because of the proliferation of family complaints, particularly related to the nursing care and food service. The social work staff prepared a report wherein they suggested organization of a family auxiliary, which they would undertake to channel these concerns, sifting out the legitimate ones from those that were distorted. They also offered to prepare an informational manual for families. The administrator welcomed these suggested changes and offered to attend the meetings of the auxiliary and fund the manual.

A problem related to a community agency was solved in yet another way that spoke to the perspective of all those involved.

A large metropolitan hospital was failing to notify community social workers about discharge plans for their clients, thus creating great difficulties in terms of continuity of care. The hospital social workers maintained that the client was "their case" while a patient in the hospital. When the problem was reformulated in a way to show that the hospital staff was only inhibiting its own discharge potential, a coordinating mechanism was set up for cooperative efforts in the future.

This chapter has provided an overview of the wide variety of environmental interventions the social worker can make on behalf of frail elderly and their families. Our concerns have been with the physical environment and the social environment that encompasses the informal networks and formal organizations having an impact on the lives of the frail elderly. Focus has been placed on problems common to the service environments of the frail elder with suggestions of possible change strategies.

Chapter 10

WORKING WITH THE FAMILY

MARIO TONTI

For many frail elderly the existence of an organized, committed family is the single most important support in life. Such a family provides some or all of the resources, care, and social contacts that will determine the elder's continued life in the community as well as the quality of that life. It is the family who most commonly fills the auxiliary role, performing affective and instrumental tasks for or on behalf of the frail elder.

The family brings to the auxiliary role added dimensions that are highly desirable in most situations. The family can respond quickly and flexibly to the idiosyncratic needs of the elder and interact affectionately and empathically over time. The family also sustains a reciprocity of relationships and roles dating back many years that counterbalance for the elder his or her increased dependence, enhancing self-esteem and perceived competency.

The ability of the family to reciprocate in an auxiliary role is not a given. This ability is based on a number of factors and must be carefully assessed (see Chapter 3). These factors include family resources such as time, energy, dependability, and the pattern of reciprocity established over the years. Some families have a history of caring and support while others may be involved in an ongoing struggle around this issue. Some families may have a good understanding of the aging process and its effects on family life, while others have none at all. The poor health of family members may preclude their being helpful.

This chapter addresses an important role for social workers: working with families to support and maximize their ability to

243

address the needs of frail aged members and fill all or part of the auxiliary role. While a large percentage of families cope with this role without professional assistance, increasing numbers are seeking direct help with planning, providing care, and/or managing the emotional problems precipitated or generated by frailty and impairment. The social worker's task with the family is to set into motion a process whereby areas of depletion within the elder and available resources are identified and a plan of care established compatible to the adaptive capacities of the elder. Appendix A lists basic texts in family therapy that provide essential background and skills for the interventions discussed here.

ASSUMPTIONS

Several important assumptions about the families of the frail aged undergird this chapter:

— While family involvement with the frail elderly is extensive, it is also widely diversified. There are no laws or specific contracts that govern the behavior between adult family members with the exception of the marital relationship. Furthermore, there are no universally accepted norms of filial responsibility. While adults are expected to act responsibly toward their aging parents, they may fulfill this responsibility in varying ways and degrees.

— There are also varying ways in which elders relate to their extended families. Some elders are deeply embedded in the family structure; others are not. While most elders turn to their families at times of crisis and expect the family to be dependable, not all view the family as a direct caregiver.

— Family boundaries are also diverse. Families can be tightly knit and shun seeking or accepting outside help. Other family structures can be loosely defined and open to external inputs.

— A family's adaptation to the frailty of an elder is a process that can span many years or be abrupt, as in the case of a catastrophic illness. The process has its onset with the family's realization that their elder can no longer live independently without some support. During this process, the family and the elder may go through several phases: (1) The elder lives alone and requires increasing contact, which generates the concern of family members. (2) The elder is unable or unwilling to live alone and moves in with a relative (usually a daughter). (3) The family can no longer provide sufficient care for the elder and nursing home placement is made. The transition from one phase to another usually comes with the physical or mental decline of the elder and/or the decline or death of a primary caregiver, such as a spouse or a child.

— Within each of these phases with its own specific tasks, the family must reconcile the elder's functional dependency and increased emotional needs with his or her remaining competencies and ability to contribute to family life. A new family equilibrium is reached as the family reconstitutes itself to perform new tasks and assume new roles.

— This transition is a time of anxiety for many families, for it challenges their usual methods of problem-solving and reactivates unsolved old problems. It can also be a time of learning to solve both old and new family problems.

— As a living system, the family does not operate in isolation. Its ability to maintain its elder in a manner that will be healthy for all family members is related directly to its own resources, i.e. time, health, and energy, and to the services and resources of the local neighborhood, community, state, and country.

FAMILY ISSUES

It is important for the social worker to grasp these assumptions about family behavior. However, it is equally important to realize that families usually do not define the issues generated by an elder's frailty in these terms. While they experience considerable anxiety and conflict, families operate more pragmatically and tend to define issues in terms of the elder's problems, what can be anticipated, who in the family should be involved, what is expected, and how plans are going to be carried out.

What Is Wrong With The Elder?

Whether decline is slow or abrupt, a question very much on the minds of family members is the condition of the elder and its causes. Physical illnesses and impairments are usually understood, but rarely are they unaccompanied by emotional reactions that can baffle the family. When mental impairment is suspected, the family is often in a quandry. Dreaded notions of senility can even precipitate premature mourning reactions.

After Mrs. Grey fell and broke her hip she became temporarily confused and depressed in spite of the excellent prognosis for her complete physical recovery. When her depression did not abate after a few weeks, Mrs. Grey's daughter was certain something else was wrong but did not know where to turn. She was not satisfied with the physician's diagnosis of senility, and found that she was becoming increasingly upset.

Ignorance about the aging process and its concommitant diseases and behaviors is not uncommon among families. It is often compounded by ignorance and disinterest of the professional community. The very old age of a relative does not diminish a family's need for answers.

Unanswered questions about present problems create anxiety about what lies ahead. Although decline is not linear and frail elders are capable of surviving for many years, family members face crises such as an accident, illness, or loss of a significant other, which exacerbate this decline. These crises, part of the lives of frail elders, also generate anxiety, which is a part of the lives of families. To a large degree the ability of a family to tolerate the anxiety around possible crises and maintain flexibility will determine the quality of their relationship with the frail aged member and the quality of his or her life.

Mrs. Adler lived alone in a small apartment. Recently she had fallen and was hospitalized with a broken leg. Her daughter and her husband felt they could no longer take the chance of letting Mrs. Adler live alone since this was the second hospitalization in a year and they were exhausted from worry. The elder, however, felt that after her leg mended she could and wanted to return to her own home. She dismissed her children's anxiety as meddlesome. The daughter did not understand the mother's capability and the greater problem that would result if she could not return home. The result was a considerable amount of tension between mother and children.

Who Is The Family?

Family development is a centripetal process in which husbands and wives spin off from their nuclear families to form new nuclei with their own children repeating these steps. The family is always evolving, but it is never more difficult to define than when parents are in their later years. Distance, time, and events can obfuscate relationships, even close ones between parent and child or brother and sister.

The term "family," as it refers to elders, may extend beyond traditional blood bonds to significant others with available personal resources. Some retired elders who live in communities away from their children include neighbors and friends in their wills. Thus, the close available friend becomes more like a family member than the distant child. The definition of family can also be obscured by events that create schisms in families. Many of the elderly individuals whom we define as isolated or without functional family have, in fact, alienated their biological families.

Mr. Jarvis lives alone in one room in a boarding home and is weakened by years of drinking. He is cared for by two women, one runs the boarding home and the other is a tenant. Mr. Jarvis has been married and has children, but his history of drinking, gambling, and abusiveness toward his family has created a gulf between them that he feels incapable of crossing. He does, however, feel that the two women who bring him meals are "family."

Mr. Jarvis's history of alcoholism that isolates him from his family is a familiar occurrence. Also familiar are situations where the issue is not the lack of available family but rather who in the family is designated as available.

Mrs. Roberts cared for her mother, Mrs. Ames. Recently, her mother deteriorated to such an extent that she could not stay alone at night. Mrs. Roberts wanted to stay with mother in Mrs. Ames's home for three months until her daughter left for college. Then she would have the room to bring her mother into her home. Mrs. Roberts's husband supported her in this plan but felt that spending every night away from him was a great burden. Her brother also lived in town, but he had not been involved in this plan and, therefore, was not available to provide respite for Mrs. Roberts. In a meeting with Mrs. Roberts and her brother, who felt that he had always been overlooked by his mother in favor of the sister, considerable emotion was generated by the issue of who should be "family" to the mother in this situation.

What Do They Expect Of Us?

Closely related to the issue of defining available family is the issue of familial expectations. The continuum of individual familial expectations runs the gamut from the heroic, sometimes self-destructive, sacrifices of one family member (usually a daughter) to provide total care for her elderly parent to the family member who arranges placement in a nursing home at the first sign of an elder's frailty. To a large extent these levels of expectation reflect the familial history of caregiving, the cultural context of the family, and the current situations in the family. However, these patterns are also created by the family's understanding and lack of understanding of their elder's frailty and by the resources available in the community.

The commitments that families make in regard to an elder are very much affected by these expectations. The process by which expectations are transmitted and commitments made within families is complex. Expectations are transmitted over the years as parents and children exercise their own responsibilities and view the options available to older neighbors and relatives. Sometimes the statements are clear, for instance, "Don't let me end up in one of those nursing homes like Aunt May." More often it is the sacrifices one generation makes for another that cement the pattern of caregiving.

These messages can also be unclear. They are mixed by the elder's desire to remain independent on one hand and by the fear of being helpless and alone on the other. Despite the ongoing process of communication about expectations, plans are rarely made by the elder and the family in advance of a crisis. Too often, commitments are made at the time of a hospitalization during which the elder and family realize that a change in the living situation is necessary. At this point, decisions are made based upon layers of familial communications about expectations and all too often without sufficient information about the amount of care needed, the competencies of the elder, and the other available community and family resources. This spring, which uncoils at some point in almost every family's life, often creates a poor fit between the needs of the elder and the family.

Expectations are always problematic when they are not openly and honestly expressed by family members. Never is this more true than when plans are being developed with frail elders for their future care. These expectations often create situations where manipulation and guilt are the primary methods of operating and where the sense of personal competence of all the individuals involved is diminished.

Mr. Darling has suffered a stroke. He was living at home with his wife and was often visited by his two daughters. He was so depressed and withdrawn that the family feared for his health. Mr. Darling had always been a confidant for his daughters, and they spoke about how they missed being able to talk to their father about their lives, plans, and problems. The unspoken expectation of Mr. Darling was that he was too burdened with his own physical difficulties to listen to his daughters. The father's expectation was that no one wanted to share with him since he was no longer of any value to the family. This lack of a valued family communication was closely related to the depression felt by the whole family.

Untested expectations also prevent the family from shifting roles, a vital part of the family's ability to problem-solve during times of crises.

Ms. Thomas lived with her mother and was her mother's primary caregiver. As her mother deteriorated, the amount of time and energy Ms. Thomas had to devote to her mother's care increased. When it was suggested that she involve her younger sister in her mother's care to provide respite for herself, Ms. Thomas responded with the expectation that her sister had never helped and never would; therefore, she would not extend herself to ask her sister for help.

The expectation prohibits Ms. Thomas from obtaining respite, keeps her sister from taking part in her mother's care, and increases the tension between all family members.

How Are We To Do It?

Even families who have identified the elder's needs and their available resources, who are clear about expectations, and who have made initial commitments live in a situation where decline, crisis, and change are the expected norms. Families of the elderly must problem-solve around the changing nature of their involvement with the frail elder.

The changes that families undergo as they recognize frailty in their elders and alter their patterns of intervention often produce emotional turmoil in all family members. Some of this becomes obvious during the process of making care plans for the elder. In some families, the crisis occurs not at this initial stage but rather after plans are made and the family begins to operate within the newly established structure. This delayed crisis is the result of living with or caring for the elder. No matter how well informed or thoughtful the planning process, there is no escaping the fact that actually living with the elder differs from the expectations of that process. Of course, in some families, the variance will be greater than others; but there will be a need for adjusting expectations and plans to the reality of the situation and reestablishing the family balance. The family's capacity for performing the auxiliary role is a critical issue.

Mrs. Vale had lived with her mother for three weeks when she called the agency requesting counseling. She stated that she had no idea how difficult it would be to live with her mother, and she felt unless she got some help she would have to place her mother in a home.

The actual experience in the situation was so different from her expectation that it precipitated a crisis for the daughter. Emotional issues were created by the reawakening of earlier family conflicts and the change in roles and positions in the family.

Mrs. Vale and her mother discussed the struggle they were having in living together. "She treats me like a child," explained the elder, "She hides the salt and won't let me have butter on my bread." "I'm just following doctor's orders," complained Mrs. Vale. "I don't like being my mother's keeper, but I'm responsible if she gets sick from eating salt . . . She acts just like a child and I've no choice but to be as strict with her as she was with us kids."

In this interchange, we see the difficulty of shifting roles for mother and daughter compounded by feelings about past parent/ child relationships. While these issues are a normal part of the adjustments elders and their families must make as their lives move closer together, they have important implications for the family's capacity to meet the affective and instrumental needs of the frail elder.

Families usually define issues in terms of the here and now, although longstanding unsolved family problems and patterns may be lurking close by. Several of these issues have been defined here. Others important to family members may be presented openly or be very much on top of their minds. Whatever the issues defined by the family, they must be addressed directly by the social worker as she or he seeks to involve and/or contract with the family in relation to the situation of a frail elder.

CONTRACTING WITH THE FAMILY

Making a contract is as important with the family as with the elder. It not only involves a contract between family and worker but among family members as well, extending far beyond the worker's involvement. Since the elder is an integral part of the family, the individual contract with the elder may overlap with the family contract, but never be totally subsumed to it. The auxiliary function model of social work practice requires direct one-to-one contact with elders, if only for the purpose of assessment and testing their understanding of the plans being made with and for them. Family information about the elder and themselves is critical, but it places the elder's behavior in the family context. Furthermore, the worker-elder relationship, no matter how shortlived, serves as a baseline for assessing family interaction.

Elderly Mrs. Whitney constantly complained to her daughters about their lack of attention and sensitivity to her fears and helplessness. The daughters in turn seemed immobilized by their own helplessness in reassuring the mother. In individual sessions with the worker, Mrs. Whitney's

anger at her daughters surfaced as well as her willingness to take more
control of her life, giving the worker a clue about her real capabilities.

Contracting with the family describes a process that contributes heavily to the study, assessment, and plan. Data must be collected about family resources and the extent of the commitment family members, including the elder, are willing to make. These findings are interpreted in relation to the elder's situation, resulting in a redefinition of the problems at hand and its manageable components. The transactions may result in new or changed commitments on the part of the elder, family members, and social worker.

Identifying Family Resources

The family as a group may seek help in developing a comprehensive care plan for an elder. More often, their initial request is couched in terms of the issues outlined above or even a request for concrete services or nursing home placement. These families may respond quickly to the worker's redefinition of the problem as a family one and move ahead to deepen their understanding of the elder's needs and make appropriate commitments. This very process may lead to a final decision for nursing home placement; however, it is still in order. An orderly decision-making process is reassuring to family and elder alike, forestalling guilt and recrimination at a later time.

Initial contact may be made, however, by only one family member, immediately highlighting the issue of who is available family, or a family member may be very involved even though the initial request for service may have come from an elder or third party.

A request was made by Mary at the insistence of her husband for
homemaker services for her mother, Mrs. Rose. Mrs. Rose had been
hospitalized six months ago with a stroke that had partially paralyzed her.
Her eldest daughter Mary moved from another city to live nearby and
care for the mother. Although the doctor had prescribed rehabilitation for
Mrs. Rose, none was instituted because Mary felt she could care for all her
needs. In the months that passed, however, Mary had become overwhelmed
with the task of caring for her mother, and her marriage began to suffer.
The social worker's inquiries revealed that Mrs. Rose, a seventy-five-

year-old widow, had six other living children who, according to Mary, were disinterested in the mother, with the exception of a sister Marlene who occasionally helps out. There was a good deal of dissension, however, between Mary and Marlene over "who is in charge." An interview with the mother disclosed that all her children are in contact with her, but she feels badly because she is such a burden on Mary and angry because she only seems to be getting worse.

It became quickly apparent to the social worker in this situation that there was a great deal of family dissension and disorganization in relation to the mother, but the first concern of the worker was to help the elder and the immediately available family member broaden their perspective about available family resources and examine what has prevented them from coming together to plan and help with the mother's care.

It can be difficult to identify the appropriate family members to involve in planning for an aging parent. Claims by adult children that siblings live too far away or are disinterested should never be taken at face value. Generally, it is important to involve family members or even friends who express concern, who will be affected by the decisions to be made, and who have resources to offer. Omissions from the family decision-making process of a member who meets these criteria may result in serious consequences. Probably the most serious omission is the older person whose condition precipitated the family crisis. Without input, the older person may be an unwilling partner to any plan reached. Furthermore, such an omission may undermine feelings of self-worth and only exacerbate the elder's physical and mental problems.

The worker, of course, must meet the family where *it* is. In the case of Mary, alienation between the siblings was so strong and the resentment on the part of the daughter so intense that some time had to be spent with her alone. This enabled Mary and her husband to share their intense feelings and view the situation more objectively. They then were able to reach out to other family members and together as a group move ahead to plan.

The family does not always define itself so easily. While the Rose family was disorganized, they were able to view themselves as "family." From the viewpoint of some elders and their relations, however, there is no family, since contacts may have ceased long ago. These judgments should not be accepted at face value. The task of the social worker is to look beyond what seems to be readily apparent. This may involve extending the concept of family beyond the traditional blood bonds to close friends or neighbors, which was discussed in Chapter 9. It may involve engaging family members who have been out of contact with the elder for an extended period of time.

Patterns of long-standing duration need not be impervious to change. They are often tenuous and sustained simply because family members lack motivation to challenge them. As elders respond to the question of who is available or involved with them, they are presenting the system only as it now stands. The role of the social worker is to explore the possibility of challenging that status quo and work with the elder to change the patterns of involvement. Formerly alienated adult children may have changed their perspective with the passage of time and want to help an elder.

When the social worker got Mr. Jarvis's permission to contact his daughter, the worker found that the daughter had just successfully worked with her own alcoholism, and because of her A.A. experience, felt a need to contact her father. Another child welcomed the chance to reestablish ties with his now sober father.

There are, of course, situations where the elder or relative refuse to be involved with each other, or if so, only tangentially. The elder's and family's right to self-determination must be respected in such circumstances, and formal services to the elder not withheld.

With demonstrated interest and even an initial commitment on the part of family members, the social worker can proceed to arrange a family meeting. Face-to-face gatherings including the elder are preferable but may be impossible because of geographical distance. The goal of full attendance can be adhered to via telephone (maybe even a conference call), correspondence, and an occasional family meeting.

Defining and Partializing the Problem

Against the backdrop of a preliminary assessment of the elder and what is known to date about the family situation, the worker proceeds to help the family define the problem. Certainly the worker should encourage all family members to express their opinions and feelings, thus involving them from the start in an ongoing process.

Fortunately, the members of the Rose family lived sufficiently close to each other that the worker was able to meet with them all in Mary's home, contract with the group as a whole, and attempt to define the problem. There was a great deal of confusion among family members about what the problem was. One brother saw it as Mary's overprotectiveness and solicitousness of the mother and inability to face the fact that Mrs. Rose might need to be in a nursing home. Mrs. Rose viewed the problem as the continuing disinterest and rejection of her children since her husband died. Another brother expressed simple bewilderment at the whole situation and asked for clarification. The other daughter agreed with the first brother that Mary was the major problem.

A number of different problematic situations can be present, each contributing to the family crisis: marital difficulties, sibling rivalries, lack of money, illness on the part of the other members, etc. Agreement must be reached that the problem to be addressed must relate to the elder's situation. If work with the family process is sidetracked into dealing with other issues, it can be stalled interminably or aborted. By the same token, the elder should not become the scapegoat for family problems, which must be viewed as involving all family members.

Without discounting any of these views, the worker was able to show the family that all of these problems had been around for a while, although they had erupted around the increasing dependence of Mrs. Rose. Mrs. Rose, herself, was able to see that she had asked little of her children before her stroke and, thus, could not fault them for not responding spontaneously to her plight. Mary talked of her own overprotective reaction to her own guilty feelings.

The social worker's reframing of the problem from the elder to the entire family opened an important avenue of communication between family members, wherein they could deal with their own expectations and commitments.

The problem as defined should coincide with the worker's assessment, but it must be in language understandable to the family. It simply may be defined in terms of the very typical issues spelled out earlier in the chapter. It may be far more complex, and problem definition may have to be an ongoing, integral part of the problem-solving process. Changes in the elder or family situation will also call for a redefinition.

Outside knowledge is often needed at this juncture, usually in terms of understanding better the elder's condition and what are his or her actual care requirements. Although time consuming, the family's knowledge base must be strengthened in order that ensuing steps are based on a correct assessment of the situation.

The social worker arranged a consultation for the family with Mrs. Rose's physician, who previously had spoken only with Mary, who in turn, was too anxious to absorb the realities of the situation. Mary, her mother, and the siblings were helped to understand the nature of the stroke and that functioning could be greatly enhanced by rehabilitative efforts to strengthen the healthy side of her body. However, they also became aware that Mrs. Rose's functioning would never become fully independent and that something must be done to offer her supportive care for the rest of her life.

The identification and partialization of the family problem and the elder's care needs interweave with the next step in contracting: clarifying expectations and making commitments. Family members may have to discuss their expectations before looking more clearly at the problem. Initial commitments may have to be made for the problem to be fully understood. Whatever the timing or sequence, the important principle remains: educating the family about the reality of the situation and partializing what can appear to be an overwhelming problem is an essential prerequisite to reaching a meaningful family contract.

Clarifying Expectations and Making Commitments

This is the most difficult step in contracting with the family, for it involves family members coming to terms with their own willingness to make a commitment of time or resources. Vague commitments, such as, "I want to help," "I'd be glad to help," must be substituted by family members being very specific about what they are able to do and what they are not able to do.

It is important that this commitment be an honest one. The worker's role is to encourage realistic contributions from family members and avoid pushing family members beyond their capacities. Family members may have to admit personal shortcomings and display less filial devotion than they fantasized they were capable of. Rather than face this confrontation with themselves and others, some family members may drop out of the planning process using a variety of pretexts.

First, the worker will want to monitor and clarify family expectations. As a rule, expectations are best clarified when they are expressed to the appropriate family member. Helping family members make such statements as "what I expect from you is to ..." often has a powerful effect on breaking up family myths and projections.

Mrs. Graves and her children were arguing about how much contact was realistic for the elder to expect from her children. The worker asked Mrs. Graves to go around the room and tell each of her children what she expected from them. Most of these statements, in which she requested contact with her children, were very appropriate and led the way to a commitment by each child to contact her in a manner that she felt would meet her needs. Only her stated expectation of daily visits from her eldest daughter, which before had only been hinted at, brought forth family objections. The children then were able to state to their mother their expectations that she should direct some of her needs to other sources; i.e., lunch program, golden age centers. The family was able to get a commitment from her that she would try to get involved in such programs.

The social worker during the process was involved in (1) clarifying the statement made by the family member, (2) allowing the statement to be revealed completely before being responded to, (3) controlling other family members' interference in the process between the elder and the child, and (4) negotiating between parent and child when there was a discrepancy between expectation and commitment. The role requires that the social worker govern the process taking place in the family meeting so that different kinds of expectations and commitments can be stated between family members. Such clear and appropriate contact, even when unfulfilled (which is almost always true to some extent), provides valuable baseline experience for all family members from which the social worker can help the family cope with the more hidden expectations that interfere with family functioning.

In the second interview with Mrs. Graves and her four children, two of them acknowledged that the two weeks since the first interview had been problem-free in their contact with their mother, while two felt that their mother had still made unrealistic demands. This led to another family discussion of the difference in their expectations of the individual treatment they will receive from their mother.

Expectations cannot always be stated clearly, and at times, the worker's main thrust will be in determining the unspoken expectations at work in problematic family situations. Often, the best clue to the expectation is the behavior that the family is exhibiting. Behavior of family members that otherwise seems puzzling is often directly tied to hidden expectations.

Mrs. Paulis, seventy-nine, and her daughter Mrs. Hyde, sixty, lived together for five years. Mrs. Paulis was afraid to leave the house and terrified of being left alone. When she was left alone, she would cry until her daughter returned. When meeting with the mother and daughter, the worker was curious as to how the daughter expected the mother to act when she was alone. The daughter replied that she expected her to act like an adult and not cry. Later in the interview, the daughter explained that when her mother refused to maintain the prescribed diet she used threats and fear tactics to keep her mother in line. The worker suggested to both mother and daughter that the family seemed to use fear a good deal. The daughter then explained matter of factly that this was the historical method of family operations: in our terms, the familial expectation.

The social worker's role in the initial phase of familial commitments is to try to gauge the appropriateness of those commitments made by family members. Sometimes the issue is overcommitment, which needs to be critically examined by all family members.

The Vale family meeting was being held to plan for Mr. Vale's care during his wife's hospitalization. The room was full of concerned family members, suggesting that people other than themselves care for Mr. Vale. His daughter stood up in anger and said that she would care for her father. The worker stopped the process at this point and found out that Mr. Vale's daughter had several small children and her own health problems and would have been overwhelmed by the extensive health and dietary needs of her father. This discussion slowed the family process and allowed others to make statements about when and how they could care for Mr. Vale. The result was that Mr. Vale's sister moved into his house to care for him.

The issue of undercommitment is more difficult to manage since it is not the social worker's role to suggest that people do more for their family members. The level of appropriate commitment may be raised by reviewing the elder's actual care commitments and disabusing family members of distorted views they may have. Education about the realities of the issue may promote their willingness to assume more responsibility.

Anxiety related to dependency may also reduce family commitments. The social worker can lower anxiety around the dependency issue by structuring the discussion of the elder's needs and the family members' availability. Family anxiety may be exaggerated because of a distorted view of the elder's actual care needs. The worker's knowledge of community resources is an important addition to this discussion, since it presents options and provides respite from family care. The final issue is for the worker to emphasize that there is value in any level of family involvement and that family members have the right to state their unwillingness and/or unavailability to make a commitment to care for an elder. What this framework does is provide the family a *choice* in the extent of commitment and place value on the *willingness* of a family member to make a consistent and reliable commitment to the elder's care.

A social worker was meeting with Mrs. Owen and her three sons to plan for the care of her husband when he returned from the hospital. During the discussion, it became obvious that the sons were unwilling to make a clear commitment to their mother regarding their support of her and her husband. As Mrs. Owen became increasingly angry, her sons withdrew more and more. The worker intervened and asked the sons what prevented them from either making a clear commitment to their mother or a clear refusal. The eldest son said he could only come once a week because of his family responsibility and knew that his mother would be angry at this limited amount of aid. The worker stopped Mrs. Owen from responding angrily to her son and asked the other two sons how much time they could give. They both agreed that they could visit after work and that their wives possibly could help during the day. The worker said that the wives would have to speak for themselves, but that being clear about sharing care for three nights per week would be better than the current lack of decision between them and their mother. The mother quickly agreed saying that she knew they had families but questioned whether she could rely on them to come even one night apiece. The rest of the discussion centered on what the mother needed from the sons and the importance of being able to depend on them. The result was a realistic family care plan in which, with some continued social work intervention, everyone thought of the family as supportive.

Experience has shown that social work intervention at the point of commitment can help family members provide more realistic and longlasting plans for their elders. Such plans take the needs of all family members into consideration and place a value on all levels of family involvement. The outcome is that family members feel they are more in control of their own lives and part of a caring family.

Before commitments are explicitly made, the worker might encourage individual members and/or couples to step back from the family group and carefully examine their own position in relation to the care of aging parents. The worker might note that individuals and couples, particularly in the middle years, have a wide array of commitments in their lives and that it is a normal process to consider the needs of the aging parent in perspective to these other commitments. The worker's legitimization of this process may help ensure realistic commitments on the part of family members, even if the commitment is a heavy one. Family consensus can be reached on a meaningful plan when family members make commitments that are both realistic in terms of their own capabilities and the need of the elder. A commitment of outside resources on part of the social worker may be an important ingredient of this plan.

FAMILY PROBLEM SOLVING

An Ongoing Process

The two previous sections set the stage for family involvement or a change in that involvement with their frail aged members. Problem definition and partializing does not stop even when plans are made with the best intentions and neither does an examination of family resources, expectations, and commitments. The reality of working with families of the frail aged is that they live in a situation where decline, crisis, and change are the expected norms. The focus of this section is on helping families problem-solve around the changing nature of their involvement with their frail elder.

Interaction during this adjustment period is aimed at reestablishing a sense of balance between family members. Again, the cognitive approach is useful in explaining how difficult the adjustment to the reality of this new phase of family life is for all family members. Some workers come to the rescue of the children of the elderly too quickly and empathize with their plight, since they are closer in age to the children than the elder. The reality, however, is that unless the burden of change and adjustment can be spread to all family members the elder too easily will become the scapegoat for the family's distress and lose his or her part in the family's solution.

Mrs. Brown and her daughters requested counseling about Mrs. Brown's mother, Mrs. Fox, who had been living in the Brown's home for six months. Mrs. Brown complained that her mother was disrupting her life terribly. Mrs. Brown's two daughters shared their mother's feelings and said that although they cared a great deal for their grandmother they were concerned about their mother's health. The issue they felt strongest about was Mrs. Fox's expression of fears of dying and her refusal to let Mrs. Brown out of her sight. During the family interview, Mrs. Fox was asked how the past few months had been for her. "Terrible," she replied. "I feel more and more like no one wants to talk to me. They treat me like a chair, a piece of furniture." The mother and daughters quickly retorted that she was miserable to be with and that's why people don't want to be around her. The worker suggested to all of the family that they were going through a rough adjustment period and that they all needed to hear how difficult it was for everybody to deal with the changes. Everybody nodded in agreement and a discussion ensued in which each family member expressed her own reactions to the changes in the family and acknowledged the differences in others.

The social worker's reframing of the problem from the elder to the entire family opened an important avenue of communication between family members. Solutions to the adjustment problems now could be sought with fuller participation of all the involved family members. Even if the elder is confused and cannot be as clear as Mrs. Brown, the impact of caring for a confused elder should be defined as one that affects all family members and not just the primary caregiver.

Mrs. Carr cared for her mother in her home for over a year. During that time, Mrs. Carr's mother had become totally disoriented and confused. This burden had grown to the point that Mrs. Carr called the agency for help. In a meeting with Mrs. Carr, her brother and sister, and her children, the issue was Mrs. Carr's anger at her mother and her family for the burden she was experiencing. The family quickly suggested that she institutionalize her mother and that she was being a martyr by trying to care for her mother. The worker refocused the discussion on what it would mean to each family member if their mother or grandmother were placed in a home. This changed the tone of the session to one in which they all shared a great deal of sadness over the decline of this very significant woman in their lives. The discussion freed Mrs. Carr from the role of being the martyr and enabled more of the family members to be involved in a discussion of what plans could be made for their elder.

Here, again, the worker's ability to define the situation as a family problem allows all sides of the issue to be heard. The worker empathized with the anxiety of the family for their elder and also stated the right of the elder for autonomy. The social worker encouraged a discussion in which each acknowledged the validity of the other's position. This allowed for appropriate compromises between the two generations. The social worker must always be aware of the changing nature of the family's plan for care and help them remain open and flexible.

Family problem-solving is an ongoing process, and the family reenters it over and over again as new situations and problems arise. Many families problem-solve well on their own; for others, an outside resource can greatly expedite the process. Potential breakdowns in the process are numerous. Failure to include meaningful family members in the decision-making process, of individual members or dyads to clearly set their own priorities and express their preferences and commitments, or to obtain prompt information or outside support can contribute to this breakdown. However, these failures do not preclude starting over and trying again. The worker's quiet encouragement and support can help families accept their shortcomings and move on to problem-solve old and new situations.

Roadblocks to Effective Problem Solving

There are additional roadblocks to effective problem solving. Several common situations include keeping secrets, hiding feelings, and asymmetrical relationships.

Keeping Secrets. In family problem solving, open communication is probably the most important principle to adhere to, but also the most difficult. The entire process can be scrupulously adhered to: inclusion of appropriate decision makers, knowledge and information acquisition, consensus on goals satisfactory to everyone, priority setting, etc. However, if certain pieces are left outside the process, the whole endeavor can be undermined by the artificial and unreal flavor it assumes.

The keeping of secrets can occur on the part of individual or family coalitions. They are undertaken usually under the guise of protecting "my children" or protecting "mother." Usually, however, they are undertaken to protect oneself. The keeping of secrets not only hinders the problem-solving process but can further confuse elders with mental impairment (see Chapter 8).

Hiding Feelings. Closely aligned to keeping secrets is hiding feelings. While problem solving is very much a cognitive, task-oriented process, it is difficult to avoid the fact that situations involving aging parents are highly charged emotionally. If family members hide from themselves their upset about the burden being placed upon them, distress over a failing parent, or other negative feelings, they may unwittingly discharge them in irrational ways and abort the problem-solving process.

By the same token, the indiscriminate expression of feelings is highly questionable and even may be destructive. Family problem solving can be helpful in setting these feelings aside and functioning productively on the task at hand. Strong feelings, however, are very normal in these situations and shared by other people. Sometimes an empathic interchange of feelings will not resolve the problems facing the family, however, it may free them to move ahead. Furthermore, the worker has an important clue in understanding what may be impeding decisions, such as fear or anxiety.

The Asymmetrical Relationship. Some members of the family will have more power than others in regard to the decision-making process. Here, perhaps the most powerful person of all is the elder, who legally and morally has the right to make decisions regarding the governing of his or her life. Unless guardianship is obtained by the family, this power is a real one. Perhaps the second most powerful person in the family grouping is the spouse of the elder. Here, again, the law and the strength of the marital relationship creates a powerful dyad.

Other alliances can be very real in the family, throwing weight to a person, dyad, or triad, who can *take action* that is displeasing to the other members. Less powerful persons in this situation can react with anger, frustration, or a wish to escape. It may be preferable for outvoted family members to withdraw temporarily knowing they have contributed to the best of their ability, ready to enter the process again when new problems arise.

Mr. and Mrs. Zoler, in their seventies, lived in an apartment in Miami; their children lived in Chicago. Mrs. Zoler was suffering from advanced emphysema, and much of her care was provided by her devoted, but possessive, husband. They each complained bitterly about each other to their children, but when attempts were made to offer help, the couple found numerous excuses for continuing the status quo. The children finally were able to pull themselves away from the marital struggle and state the conditions of their involvement — that they would discuss problems only in a group.

The Long-Term Care Facility

It would seem that once an elder is placed in a long-term facility family problem-solving becomes a thing of the past. Nothing could be further from the truth, for problems often arise in nursing homes and they often involve the family. These problems may involve an elder's missing family visits and wanting to see more of them, a family's concern and complaints about the care the elder is receiving, or behavior on the part of the family that is deleterious to the elder's care. A common problem is the further deterioration of an elder, which may necessitate transfer to another floor or facility. The problem-solving process is as instrumental here as in other situations. Family members need to gather, the problem must be clearly understood, commitments made, and future family plans spelled out.

The social worker, in this particular situation, becomes a very involved member of the problem-solving process because he or she represents the institution whose expectations and commitments must be fully understood by the family. Just as family members are limited in the commitments they can make and cannot make, so are institutions. While institutions are basically committed to providing good care, cleanliness, and decent food, there are many discretionary areas in which commitments can vary a great deal. These have to be made explicit to residents and families. By the same token, the institution may adjust its commitments in the interest of solving a problem at hand.

The Sanders family, two sons and their wives, was upset that their father, age eighty-five, was becoming increasingly disorganized and confused when they visited. They were particularly upset because the home wished to place him on the floor where he could receive more protection. The family felt that this segregation would only worsen his condition and he would be depressed by living with such sick people. The social worker met with the four family members and gave them each time to ventilate and state their opinion and pointed out the limitations on the institution in terms of caring for this kind of resident. She noted the fact that the elder Mr. Sanders would become increasingly isolated on his present floor since he was being rejected by residents and would have more activities and companionship on the new floor.

With the problem outlined, both sons agreed to fill the social gap by visiting more regularly to aid in the care of their father. They made a commitment to take him to their homes as frequently as possible for visits, take him out on other visits from the home, including other residents when possible, and be helpful to staff in his direct care when they were there. The wives supported their husbands in this commitment. Mr. Sanders was particularly pleased.

With these commitments, the problem was redefined and the social worker, after talking with staff, agreed to make a tentative commitment to keeping Mr. Sanders where he was for the time being. The new plan worked well for nine months, at which time the sons felt that their commitment was too much for them since Mr. Sanders was growing worse, and he was moved to another floor. However, the extension of his time of socialization was a meaningful one for all involved, including the sons and Mr. Sanders.

THE ROLE OF THE SOCIAL WORKER

This chapter has described a chief task of the social worker in working with the family: setting in motion a process whereby areas of depletion within the elder and available resources are identified and a plan of care established compatible to the adaptive capacities of the elder. In addition to organizing concrete family resources for the elder, the social worker seeks to shift the family role to an auxiliary function. The very processes involved in this pursuit presumably benefit the elder. The reduction of family anxiety, reorganization of family resources, and rational planning creates better family atmosphere and care for the elder. Also accrued are the benefits of being cared for by significant others with all of the implicit components of trust, love, and family continuity and reciprocity.

The social worker's role must extend beyond these efforts that in and of themselves do not insure quality care for the elder. Family care may have to be supplemented by formal services—home health aide visits, day care, chore services—if only for purposes of respite. These must supplement family efforts, not supplant them.

Skills in communicating with the elder must also be imparted to the family. The skillful interaction required of the social worker in communicating to the elder is no less important for the family, particularly if they are to assume the auxiliary role. These skills cannot be taken for granted. The social worker must share his or her expertise with family members and even serve as a model.

Mrs. Akins turned off her hearing aid whenever the family gathered, which only enraged family members who felt she was tuning them out. There was much shouting in order to gain Mrs. Akins's attention, which only made the situation worse. When the social worker arrived, she immediately turned off the television set and asked everyone in the room to remain quiet while she spoke to Mrs. Akins. She placed her chair directly in front of Mrs. Akins and on a piece of paper wrote to Mrs. Akins that she would like to talk with her if she would turn on her hearing set and promised that the room would remain quiet and that she would speak distinctly and slowly. Mrs. Akins acquiesced to this request, turned on her set, and a meaningful conversation was carried on. Later, the social worker was able to bring other family members into the discussion but in a way where static and confusion were at a minimum. Each family member, when they spoke to Mrs. Akins, sat directly and closely in front of her and spoke slowly and distinctly.

The skills that the social worker has acquired in establishing a relationship with a frail elder can be imparted to the family. These skills have been described in Chapters 4 through 8 of this text. Explanations and instructions to some families can suffice. Perhaps, the most important ingredient of the worker-client relationship that the social worker can model for the family is a readiness and willingness to engage the frail older person emotionally, affirm the elder's existence and desire to live, and give help and yet provide room and flexibility within the relationship for the elder to exercise his or her remaining competencies, dignity, and self-respect. Particularly in the case of a mentally impaired or emotionally distraught elder, the family can withdraw emotionally or overreact, resulting in a lack of understanding, fear, frustration, and poor communication, even if living under the same roof. Skills that can be shared with the family can be invaluable.

The social worker's role is also extended to utilizing other educational resources. Written materials can be helpful to families. Nurses, home health aides, and rehabilitation therapists can serve as models and instructors. Self-help groups sprouting up around the country can be both supportive and instructive.

This chapter has reviewed the assumptions that underlie our work with the family, the issues as seen by families, and the task of the social worker in implementing the auxiliary function model through mobilizing and organizing family resources. Contracting with the family is an important first step, and problem-solving is an ongoing process that enables families to assume some or part of the auxiliary role and provide concrete services in an organized balanced way. We have stressed that the role of the social worker is an enabling one, but also one in which she or he shares professional skills either through serving as a model for the family or providing information and instruction and utilizing other professional and community resources as well.

EPILOGUE

The Social Worker's Challenge

Our text has focused on the frail elderly and their families: their problems, needs, environments, and the special interventions dictated by their unique circumstances. These closing pages are devoted to the perspective of the social worker: the professional and personal issues faced daily in working with the frail elderly.

On the professional level, our mission and code of ethics compel us to face the challenge of an ever increasing frail population who are placing growing demands on the formal and informal service systems at a time when government responsibility and support are being seriously undermined. We must examine the quality of our response to the frail, as well as the conceptual framework in which we view their problems. These issues cannot be examined only within the realm of theory. On a practical day-to-day level, we face the burden of heavy caseloads and the often conflicting expectations of government, agency, communities, families, and the elders themselves. These must be reconciled with what we view as our professional role, especially in the areas of advocacy, protection, and job management.

COLLECTIVE ADVOCACY

The auxiliary function model has spelled out the components of direct practice with the elder as well as environmental measures that implement the auxiliary function. Advocacy on behalf of individual elders or elder groups has been stressed as an important component of the model. Historically, the profession has not given advocacy on behalf of the old high priority, although individual social workers in leadership positions have spoken out clearly. Improved attitudes in recent years have been reflected in actions by the Committee on Aging of the National Association of Social Workers, which in 1979 issued a strong position paper on long-term care for the chronically impaired elderly (National Association of Social Workers, 1979) and in 1982 joined in leading a successful protest against federal government attempts to dilute nursing home regulations. Concerns about the elderly, however, are not as widely shared as those about the young, the poor, and victims of racial and sexual discrimination.

Yet, all who live long enough will normally encounter impairment and/or frailty, conditions that are unrelenting and not remediable by social change. Our profession must, along with related professions, advocate for needed environmental supports. Medical technology has initiated and responded to the needs of the very old. Social technology must now take its turn if the last years of life are to have quality and dignity.

The need for advocacy becomes more compelling when the various depletions that characterize the frail are taken into account. Frailty in and of itself preempts a strong advocacy role for the old themselves. Unlike the younger adult handicapped who have vigorously defended and fought for their full rights in society, the frail old lack the stamina to storm the gates on their own. Their advocacy role requires a strong partnership with family, ombudsman, lawyer, *and* social worker.

The present political climate makes the need for advocacy critical. The old are being set against the young in the competition for depleting resources. The capping of Medicaid and reductions in food stamps speak to this crisis. As cutbacks are felt, quality of life for the young and old will diminish. The holistic view of the social worker that spans all generations—young and old alike—must be loud and clear. The needy of all ages deserve our concern.

Advocacy on behalf of the frail elderly is not a social work role exclusively. There is one aspect of it, however, that we are uniquely equipped to fill. This pertains to advocacy on behalf of the isolated frail elder, the individual without family or friends, to plead his or her cause. Social isolation is a fact of life for a significant number of elders. While most are imbedded in or related in some way to natural helping networks, there are those who have outlived their peers and children, lacked family and friends, or been alienated from them most of their lives. There are those who, for personal or characterological reasons, have eschewed intimate relationships, an adaptation that was relatively successful in earlier life when they were healthy and strong. The enforced dependency of frailty, however, finds them alone.

It is these frail elders who turn to, or are referred to, the formal system and comprise a disproportionate share of our caseloads. Whether their entry into the system is via the health care route or via the social service route, it is the social worker or other social services personnel who ultimately must care for them. Whether this care is defined in terms of advocacy or protection, it is uniquely a social work role that we cannot shirk. Assumption of the auxiliary role in the absence of other social supports broadly and precisely defines our professional stance.

PROTECTION OF THE CLIENT

The auxiliary function model sets the stage for the particularly difficult professional and ethical issues faced in relation to guardianship and institutional placement. The elder whose judgment is so impaired that a danger is posed to self or others is frequently the focus of professional concern. Although not representative of the majority of the frail, the dilemma presented accounts for our preoccupation.

The dilemma lies in the fact that we, as a profession dedicated to the self-determination of our clients, find ourselves in a position where we may be seeking to abrogate the civil rights of our clients or their freedom in order to offer them protection. We become, in a sense, an arm of the law or society's representative in managing deviant behavior.

Family members, of course, are thrown into similar dilemmas. While they may not be as concerned with issues of self-determination as social workers, many do realize they may be interferring with the rights of another adult and have grave misgivings.

The dilemma may fall short of having to resort to legal action.

Nursing home placement often can be easily accomplished with mentally impaired elders who have insidiously lost control over their lives, and we as social workers, in our role formally or informally as protective services workers, become the instruments of this action.

The challenge before us — as with other client groups — is to be scrupulously aware of their rights, individualize and humanize the protective process, and bring to the situation skilled help that may in the long run avoid the need for legal solution. The auxiliary function model of social work attempts to individualize and humanize the helping process and hopefully help the frail elder function in ways more acceptable to society. It also attempts to sensitize society to the normalcy of frailty. Given patience and time, we believe a relationship can be established with a frail elder wherein fears can be identified, concerns expressed, trust established, and actions taken to which the elder is a willing partner.

JOB MANAGEMENT: OVERLOAD AND BURNOUT

Practicing social workers are often dismayed by well-meaning efforts such as ours to improve their skills, for too frequently they are overwhelmed with large case loads, an elder population in crisis, and family members and community voices that demand that "something be done." This is particularly true for social workers in the public sector and in nursing homes, which, if they have social workers at all, are usually understaffed.

These types of situations undoubtedly are no less true for other client populations; yet, the fact that work with the aging has not been a popular pursuit for social workers has contributed even more to meager staffing patterns. In addition, the frail elderly are often caught in desperate situations that seem to require immediate action. Thus, the worker can be easily beset by many demands.

How is the social worker to cope with large caseloads and still practice skillfully with clients in need? The answer is not an easy one, but some steps can be taken. They are related, first, to handling personal reactions and, second, to organization of the workload. These efforts can be made singly or in conjunction with fellow staff members. Ideally, leadership in such efforts is given by supervisors and administrators.

Workers with the frail elderly and family members in distress often unknowingly pick up their anxieties. Even a routine occurrence will appear an emergency to some clients, not to mention the large number of actual emergencies that occur. The worker who begins with an open door, equally responsive to all elder demands, willing to give up lunch hours, or work overtime in order to see everyone, will not last long.

The time devoted to direct practice must be rationally allocated based on the worker's assessment of who needs immediate attention and who, given calm reassurance, can wait. Often, a brief supportive telephone contact with anxious elders will suffice.

The social worker who is disorganized in his or her work tasks is doubly handicapped when workloads are high. If tasks are performed indiscriminately, it becomes impossible to provide skilled and meaningful service. Tasks should be partialized and prioritized. One approach might be to divide tasks into three general categories: (1) tasks related to the case plan, (2) paperwork tasks required by the agency and regulatory bodies, (3) tasks requested by elders, families, and staff but not related to a case plan.

Tasks related to the case plan are usually considered most important by the social worker, and paper work tasks the least important. Yet paperwork documents professional interventions and conveys the worker's thoughts on a case. It is a basic tool of accountability. It cannot and should not be avoided. The demands and requirements of elders, families, and other staff unrelated to a case plan cannot be ignored lest the worker is viewed as rejecting or insubordinate. The tasks, therefore, most important to the social worker can be easily overshadowed and reduced to rote activity and easy solutions.

A key, if not a solution, lies in apportioning a certain amount of time to each set of tasks and within each category again partializing and setting priorities. This division of labor needs to be shared with others so that effective feedback loops are in place informing management of the real needs that exist but are not met.

The case plan must also be realistic in terms of workload demands. The study and assessment, with increased experience and skill, can be conducted as quickly as the condition of the elder permits. Case plans must tap the strengths of the elder and all available resources in the environment to implement the auxiliary function. The social worker must constantly question, "Am I really needed here?"

Participation in continuing education is helpful in sharpening these organizing skills and in assuring professional enhancement. Burnout is often related to a diminishment in professional self-esteem, the difficulties and moral dilemmas involved in working with the frail and impaired, and large case loads. Burnout can also be allayed by setting aside time for interaction with other staff members for the purpose of sharing experiences and giving mutual aid and support. Agencies organized around ongoing team activities provide an excellent vehicle for such interaction.

At the same time, because day-to-day demands of practice are often draining, it is helpful to cultivate personal outlets for replenishment and pleasure. Sharing with and support of peers and colleagues also offers needed nurturance to the worker, thus enabling him or her to better sustain the frail elder.

PERSONAL INVOLVEMENT

Throughout this text, we have stressed the importance of respect, mutuality in the worker/client relationship, and avoidance of infantilization of the elder regardless of the degree of regression and disability. We have also stressed flexibility on the part of the worker. Emotional closeness, strong empathic responses, and encouragement of a significant degree of emotional dependence may all be warranted.

Empathic responses on part of the worker, however, can be far from easy. A significant generation gap can exist between the worker and elder, and biases and fears about aging can affect, consciously and unconsciously, feelings and behavior.

More than a one-generation gap can exist between client and worker not only in the case of the frail elder but also in relation to family members. The elder can reactivate in some cases the worker's relationship with his or her parents, simply because the client is old enough to be the worker's parent or even grandparent. The balance between independence and dependence that the elder negotiates in the latter stages of life is not dissimilar to the conflicts the young worker may be experiencing in assuming a professional role in the adult world. Thus, often the conflicts inherent in giving and receiving help are present in both worker and client, making it imperative that the worker recognize and separate out personal feelings and needs. How often is the elder's stated wish to "not bother my children" or to be independent unquestionably accepted by a worker struggling from separation from his or her own parents.

A great difficulty, particularly in terms of sharing empathically with an elder, is the striking fact that a younger worker has not yet experienced the life terrain travelled by the elder client. Edna Wasser (1966) notes that "case workers are generally younger and healthier than their elderly clients." They need to "climb inside the client's skin to understand empathically his feelings of psychological need and to form a relationship with him."

The large age differential may touch off other reactions in a worker as well. A worker may experience emotional dependence on an elder because he or she recalls a past relationship of significance. The fact that the frail elderly are often approving and appreciative of worker efforts increases this possibility. Worker dependence on an elder for personal gratification must be recognized and dealt with, because of the burden placed on the elder and because loss of the elder through death will be experienced as abandonment and precipitate a strong grief reaction.

The worker's relationship with authority in his or her private life is also significant. The elderly client sometimes appears as the parent or teacher challenging the ability of the social worker "young enough to be my grandchild" to provide help. Beginning workers, recently emancipated from authority figures at home and school and unsure about their ability to function independently, can err by responding in an angry, defensive, or prematurely reassuring manner. However, the elder's perception is valid and any doubt should be acknowledged. The social worker does not have to display credentials or grasp at surface similarities in their lives to prove an understanding of the elder's problems. A solution cannot be promised, but an attempt to try can. A willingness to help, a readiness to begin, and a desire to learn from the elder can set the stage for effective practice.

The worker may also feel more powerful by treating the frail elder as a child, a form of behavior often legitimized by the impairment or regression of the client. Setting up this role reversal model may also serve to help the worker protect against relating to the client as a potential parent or grandparent. However, it is demeaning and ultimately unfruitful. Such common pitfalls must be guarded against.

Practitioners, regardless of age, must consider other personal reactions inherent in work with the very old. Proximity to illness and death is upsetting to most of us, touching on the deepest human fears. It is easy to become discouraged when the elder's need far outstrips the ability of anyone to help. Anxiety, boredom, impatience, or a premature push to accomplish concrete tasks is often motivated by the worker's attempt to avoid the inescapable pain inherent in the frail elder's situation. A tendency to infantilize or extol elders as a group may further cloud the worker's ability to individualize. Rescue fantasies manifested by an attempt to save elders from illness, pain, and inevitable death and ease the worker's fears are also prevalant. These common reactions must constantly be monitored by the worker, alone, in supervision, or in peer support groups.

On a personal level, our attitudes and feelings about growing old ourselves, about relating to and helping those now in the last stages of life, must be examined if we are to be comfortable and effective in our work. We may choose not to work with this population if these personal issues cannot be resolved, or we may reconcile ourselves to an ongoing struggle. Some days, we are fired to do all we can. Other days, we question if we are of any help at all to elders whose needs appear never ending. Always, we must live with the ambiguity of unresolved (and frequently unresolvable) situations and the high degree of risk intrinsic to the best made plans.

Even with the most experienced, able, and committed workers, doubts are never laid completely at rest. What characterizes their ability to function so well is the perspective in which they are able to place their work. They recognize that the success of practice need not be measured by great changes accomplished but rather by small increments. An abatement of fear, easing of everyday functioning, and reemerging interest in the outside world on the part of the elder may all be occasions for worker pride. To the frail elder for whom life has become a static painful affair, a single intervention may have far reaching and positive consequences.

In practice with the frail elderly, one's time perspective is altered. The importance of service is heightened rather than diminished by the fact that the elder may not have long to live. The satisfaction of enriching the last months or years of a long life with concrete help and personal caring is great. The experience rarely is as depressing as most beginners fear. Rather, it provides a personal growth experience for the worker and deepened understanding and appreciation of life. In the last analysis, worker and frail elder are more alike than different: both aging day-to-day, both imbued with the best and worst of human nature, both mortal.

> *All of us, after all, inevitably spend our lives evolving from an initial to a final state of dependency. If we are fortunate enough to achieve power and relative independence along the way it is a transient and passing glory, and it would be well to keep clearly in mind our inevitable decline as we contract and deal with the helpless and dependent who come within our influence.*
>
> Willard Gaylin (1978)

APPENDICES

Appendix A

BASIC READINGS

Historical and Personal Perspectives

Achenbaum, W. Andrew: *Old Age in the New Land: the American Experience Since 1790*. Baltimore, Johns Hopkins, 1979.

Becker, Ernest: *The Denial of Death*. New York, Free Press, 1973.

Blythe, Ronald: *The View in Winter*. New York, Harcourt Brace Jovanovich, 1979.

Olsen, Tillie: *Tell Me a Riddle*. New York, Delacorte, 1978.

Saul, Shura: *Aging: an Album of People Growing Old*. New York, Wiley, 1974.

Scott-Maxwell, Flora: *Measure of My Days*. New York, Knopf, 1968.

The Physical Environment

Brody, Elaine M.: Community housing for the elderly the program, the people, the decision-making process, and the research. *Gerontologist, 18*:121, 1978.

Costa, Frank J., and Sweet, Marnie: Barrier-free environments for older Americans. *Gerontologist, 16*:404, 1976.

Elderly housing. *Progressive Architecture, 8*:59, 1981.

Hiatt, Lorraine G.: The color and use of color in environments for older people. *Nursing Homes, 30*:18, 1981.

Hiatt, Lorraine G.: Is poor light dimming the sight of nursing home patients? *Nursing Homes, 29*:32, 1980.

Lawton, M. Powell: Assessment, integration, and environments for older people. *Gerontologist, 10*:38, 1970, Pt. 1.

Pastalan, Leon A., and Carson, Daniel H. (eds.): Spatial Behavior of Older People. Ann Arbor, Institute of Gerontology Univ of Michigan-Wayne State Univ, 1970.

Schwartz, Arthur N.: Planning micro-environments for the aged. In Woodruff, Diana S., and Birren, James E. (eds.): *Aging Scientific Perspectives and Social Issues*. New York, Van Nostrand Reinhold, 1975, p 279–294.

Sherman, Edmund, and Newman, Evelyn S.: The meaning of cherished personal possessions for the elderly. *International Journal of Aging and Human Development, 8*:181, 1977–78.

Social Gerontology

Atchley, Robert C.: *The Social Forces of Later Life*, 3d ed. Belmont, Wadsworth, 1980.

Binstock, Robert H., and Shanas, Ethel (eds.): *Handbook of Aging and the Social Sciences*. New York, Van Nostrand Reinhold, 1976.

Hendricks, Jon, and Hendricks, C. Davis: *Aging in Mass Society*, 2d ed. Cambridge, Winthrop, 1981.

Monk, Abraham (ed.): *The Age of Aging*. Buffalo, Prometheus, 1979.

Woodruff, Diana S., and Birren, James E. (eds.): *Aging: Scientific Perspectives and Social Issues*. New York, Van Nostrand Reinhold, 1975.

Biological Aging and Geriatrics

Brocklehurst, J. C. (ed.): *Textbook of Geriatric Medicine and Gerontology*, 2d ed. London, Churchill Livingston, 1978.

Fries, James F. and Crapo, Lawrence M., *Vitality and Aging—Implications of the Rectangular Curve*. San Francisco, W. H. Freeman and Company, 1981.

Finch, Caleb E., and Hayflick, Leonard (eds.): *Handbook of the Biology of Aging*. New York, Van Nostrand Reinhold, 1977.

Behavioral Theory, Psychology and Psychiatry

Bandler, Bernard: The concept of ego supportive psychotherapy. In Parad, Howard J., and Miller, Roger R. (eds.): *Ego-Oriented Casework, Problems and Perspectives*. New York, Family Services Association, 1963, p 27–45.

Birren, James E., and Schaie, K. Warner (eds.): *Handbook of the Psychology of Aging*. New York, Van Nostrand Reinhold, 1977.

Birren, James E., and Sloane, R. Bruce (eds.): *Handbook of Mental Health and Aging*. Englewood Cliffs, Prentice-Hall, 1980.

Busse, Ewald W., and Blazer, Dan G. (eds.): *Handbook of Geriatric Psychiatry*. New York, Van Nostrand Reinhold, 1980.

Busse, Ewald W., and Pfeiffer, Eric: *Mental Illness in Later Life*. Washington, D.C., American Psychiatric Association, 1973.

Butler, Robert N., and Lewis, Myra I.: *Aging and Mental Health*, 3d ed. St. Louis, Mosby, 1982.

Cath, Stanley H.: Some dynamics of middle and later years. *Smith College Studies in Social Work, 33*:97, 1963.

Coelho, George V., Hamburg, David, and Adams, John E. (eds.): *Coping and Adaptation*. New York, Basic, 1974.

Erikson, Erik H.: *Identity and the Life Cycle*. New York, International Universities Press, 1959.

Gladwin, Thomas: Social competence and clinical practice. *Psychiatry, 30*:30, 1967.

Goldfarb, Alvin I.: The psychodynamics of dependency and the search for aid. In Kalish, Richard A. (ed.): *The Dependencies of Old People*. Ann Arbor, Institute of Gerontology. University of Michigan-Wayne State Univ, August, 1969, p 1–15.

Goode, William J.: A theory of role strain. *American Sociological Review,* 25:483, 1960.

Gross, Neal, Mason, Ward S., McEachern, Alexander: *Explorations in Role Analysis,* New York, John Wiley & Sons, Inc., 1966 (see part 1, pages 11–70).

Hartmann, Heinz: *Ego Psychology and the Problem of Adaptation.* New York, International University Press, 1958.

Horner, Althea J.: *Object Relations and the Developing Ego in Therapy.* New York, Aronson, 1979.

Loewenstein, Sophie: An overview of the concept of narcissism. *Social Casework,* 58:136, 1977.

Mechanic, David: Social structure and personal adaptation: some neglected dimensions. In Coelho, George V., Hamburg, David, and Adams, John E. (eds.): *Coping and Adaptation.* New York, Basic, 1974, p 32–46.

Parad, Howard J. (ed.): *Ego Psychology and Dynamic Casework.* New York, Family Service Association, 1958.

Peck, Robert E.: Psychological developments in the second half of life. In Anderson, John E. (ed.): *Psychological Aspects of Aging.* Washington, D.C., American Psychological Association, 1956, p 42–53.

Schulz, Richard: Effects of control and predictability on the physical and psychological well-being of the institutionalized aged. *Journal of Personality and Social Psychology,* 33, 1976, p. 563.

White, Robert W.: *Ego and Reality in Psychoanalytic Theory.* New York, International University Press, 1963.

Zarit, Steven H.: *Aging and Mental Disorders.* New York, Free Press, 1980.

Organizational Structure and Change

Brager, George, and Holloway, Stephen: *Changing Human Service Organizations.* New York, Free Press, 1978.

Hasenfeld, Yeheskel, and English, Richard A. (eds.): *Human Service Organizations.* Ann Arbor, University of Michigan Press, 1974.

Litwak, Eugene, and Meyer, Henry J.: A balance theory of coordination between bureaucratic organizations and community primary groups. *Administrative Science Quarterly,* 11:31, 1966.

Mechanic, David: Sources of power of lower participants in complex organizations. In Cooper, W. W., Leavitt, H. J., and Shelly, M. W. II (eds.): *New Perspectives in Organization Research.* New York, Wiley, 1964, p 136–149.

Patti, Rino J.: Organizational resistance and change: the view from below. *Social Service Review,* 48:367, 1974.

Wax, John: Power theory and institutional change. *Social Service Review,* 45:274, 1971.

Long-Term Care and Rehabilitation

Bonner, Charles D.: *Homburger & Bonner's Medical Care and Rehabilitation of the Aged and Chronically Ill*, 3d ed. Boston, Little, Brown, 1974.

Brody, Elaine M.: *Long-Term Care of Older People: A Practical Guide*. New York, Human Science Press, 1977.

Brody, Elaine M.: Long-term care of the aged: promises and prospects. *Health and Social Work*, 4:29, 1979.

Kastenbaum, Robert, and Candy, Sandra E.: The 4% fallacy: a methodological and empirical critique of extended care facility population statistics. *International Journal of Aging and Human Development*, 4:15, 1973.

National Conference on Social Welfare: *The Report of the Task Force on the Future of Long-Term Care in the United States*. Washington, D.C., U.S. DHEW, February, 1977.

Rusk, Howard A.: *Rehabilitation Medicine*, 4th ed. St. Louis. Mosby, 1977.

Sherwood, Sylvia (ed.): *Long-Term Care: A Handbook for Researchers, Planners, and Providers*. New York, Spectrum, 1975.

Silverstone, Barbara: Long-term care. *Health and Social Work*, 6:28S, Supplement, 1981.

Silverstone, Barbara: Social aspects of aging. In Williams, T. Franklin (ed.): *Rehabilitation in the Aging*. New York, Raven, in press.

Vladeck, Bruce C.: *Unloving Care*. New York, Basic, 1980.

Social Work Theory and Practice

Bartlett, Harriet, M.: *The Common Base of Social Work Practice*. New York, National Association of Social Workers, 1970.

Brody, Elaine M.: *A Social Work Guide for Long-Term Care Facilities*. Rockville, NIMH., 1974.

Burnside, Irene M.: *Working with the Elderly: Group Process and Techniques*. North Scituate, Duxbury, 1978.

Compton, Beulah Roberts, and Galaway, Burt: *Social Work Processes*. Homewood, Dorsey, 1975.

Garrett, Annette: *Interviewing: Its Principles and Techniques*, 3d rev. ed. New York, Family Service Association of America, 1982.

Gaylin, Willard, Glasser, Ira, Marcus, Steven, Rothman, David J.: *Doing Good: the Limits of Benevolence*. New York, Pantheon, 1978.

Germain, Carel: Casework and science: a historical encounter. In Roberts, Robert W., and Nee, Robert H. (eds.): *Theories of Social Casework*. Chicago, University of Chicago Press, 1970, p 3–32.

Germain, Carel B.: General-systems theory and ego psychology: an ecological perspective. *Social Service Review*, 52:535, 1978.

Germain, Carel B. (ed.): *Social Work Practice, People and Environments*. New York, Columbia University Press, 1979.

Germain, Carel B., and Gitterman, Alex: *The Life Model of Social Work Practice*. New York, Columbia University Press, 1980.

Getzel, George, and Mellor, M. Joanna (eds.): *Gerontological Social Work Practice in Long-Term Care*. New York, Haworth, 1983.

Glasser, Paul, Sarri, Rosemary, and Vinter, Robert: *Individual Change Through Small Groups*. New York, Free Press, 1974.

Hartford, Margaret E.: *Groups in Social Work*. New York, Columbia University Press, 1972.

Hartford, Margaret E.: The use of group methods for work with the aged. In Birren, James E. and Sloane, R. Bruce (eds.): *Handbook of Mental Health and Aging*. Englewood Cliffs, Prentice-Hall, 1980, pp. 806–826.

Hartman, Ann: To think about the unthinkable. *Social Casework*, 51:467, 1970.

Hollis, Florence, and Woods, Mary E.: *Casework: a Psychosocial Therapy*, 3d ed. New York, Random, 1981.

Lowy, Louis: *Social Work with the Aging: The Challenge and Promise of the Later Years*. New York, Harper-Row, 1979.

Meyer, Carol H.: *Social Work Practice*, 2d ed. New York, Free Press, 1976.

Meyer, Carol: *Social Work with the Aging*. Washington, D.C., National Association of Social Workers, 1975.

Monk, Abraham: Social work with the aged: principles of practice. *Social Work*, 26:61, 1981.

Perlman, Helen Harris: In quest of coping. *Social Casework*, 56:213, 1975.

Perlman, Helen Harris: *Relationship: The Heart of Helping People*. Chicago, University of Chicago Press, 1979.

Pincus, Allen, and Minahan, Anne: *Social Work Practice: Model and Method*. Itasca, Peacock, 1973.

Reid, William J.: Mapping the knowledge base of social work. *Social Work*, 26:124, 1981.

Reid, William J., and Epstein, Laura: *Task-Centered Casework*. New York, Columbia University Press, 1972.

Rein, Martin, and White, Sheldon H.: Knowledge for practice. *Social Service Review*, 55:1, 1981.

Roberts, Robert W., and Nee, Robert H. (eds.): *Theories of Social Casework*. Chicago, University of Chicago Press, 1971.

Roberts, Robert, and Northern, Helen: *Theories of Social Group Work*. New York, Columbia University Press, 1976.

Schwartz, William, and Zalba, Serapio R. (eds.): *The Practice of Group Work*. New York, Columbia University Press, 1971.

Siporin, Max: *Introduction to Social Work Practice*. New York, Macmillan, 1975.

Siporin, Max: Situational assessment and intervention. *Social Casework*, 53:91, 1972.

Wasser, Edna: *Creative Approaches in Casework with the Aging*. New York, Family Service Association, 1966.

Family Theory and Practice

Ackerman, Nathan W.: *Treating the Troubled Family*. New York, Basic, 1966.

Blenkner, Margaret: Social Work and Family Relationships in Later Life With Some Thoughts on Filial Maturity. In E. Shanas & G. Streib (eds.): *Social Structure & the Family: Generational Relations*. New York, Prentice-Hall, Inc., 1965.

Brody, Elaine, and Spark, Geraldine: Institutionalization of the aged: a family crisis. *Family Process, 5*:76, 1966.

Getzel, George: Social work with family caregivers to the aged. *Social Casework, 62*:4, 1981.

Haley, Jay: *Problem-Solving Therapy*. San Francisco, Jossey-Bass, 1976.

Hartman, Ann: Diagrammatic assessment of family relationships. *Social Casework, 59*:465, 1978.

Kirschner, Charlotte: The aging family in crisis: a problem in living. *Social Casework, 60*:209, 1979.

Minuchin, Salvador: *Families and Family Therapy*. Cambridge, Harvard University Press, 1974.

Rhodes, Sonya L.: A developmental approach to the life cycle of the family. *Social Casework, 58*:301, 1977.

Satir, Virginia: *Conjoint Family Therapy*. Palo Alto, Science and Behavior, 1964.

Schorr, Alvin: "... *thy father and thy mother*... " *a second look at filial responsibility and family policy*. Washington, D.C., U.S. DHHS, July, 1980.

Silverstone, Barbara: The family is here to stay. *Journal of Nursing Administration, 8*:47, 1978.

Troll, Lillian E., Miller, Sheila J., and Atchley, Robert C.: *Families in Later Life*. Belmont, Wadsworth, 1979.

Appendix B

HELPFUL PAMPHLETS AND PUBLICATIONS
FOR ELDERS AND FAMILIES

General

Bumagin, Victoria E., and Hirn, Kathy, F.: *Aging is a Family Affair*. NY Crowell, 1979.

Cohen, Stephen Z., and Gans, Bruce Michael: *The Other Generation Gap*. Chicago. Follett, 1978.

Silverstone, Barbara, and Hyman, Helen Kandel: *You and Your Aging Parent*. New York, Pantheon, 1982.

Arthritis

Publications available from The Arthritis Foundation, 3400 Peachtree Road, N.E., Atlanta, Georgia 30326, or from local chapters of the Foundation.

Arthritis Foundation. Arthritis Health Professionals Section: *Self-Help Manual for Patients with Arthritis*. Atlanta, Arthritis Foundation, 1980.

Arthritis Foundation: *Home Care Programs in Arthritis: A Manual for Patients*. Atlanta, Arthritis Foundation 1969.

Clothing and self-help aids

Bowar, Miriam T.: *Clothing for the Handicapped: Fashion Adaptations for Adults and Children*. Minneapolis, Sister Kenny Institute, 1977.

Davis, Wendy M.: *Aids to Make You Able: Self-Help Devices and Ideas for the Disabled*. New York, Beaufort, 1981.

Hoffman, Adeline M.: *Clothing for the Handicapped, the Aged, and Other People with Special Needs*. Springfield, Charles C Thomas, Publisher, 1979.

Sargent, Jean Vieth: *An Easier Way: A Handbook for the Elderly and Handicapped*. Ames, Iowa State University Press, 1981.

Crime and accident prevention

Davis, Linda J., and Brody, Elaine M.: *Rape and Older Women: A Guide to Prevention and Protection*. Washington, D.C., U.S. GPO, 1979.

Midwest Research Institute: *Crime Prevention Handbook for Senior Citizens*. U.S.

Dept. of Justice. Law Enforcement Administration, June, 1977.

National Institute on Aging: *Age Page: Accidents and the Elderly*. Washington, D.C., U.S. DHHS, July, 1980.

National Retired Teachers Association, American Association of Retired Persons: *Older Americans and the Criminal Justice System*. Washington, D.C., NRTA–AARP, (n.d.) NRTA–AARP, 1909 K Street, N.W., Washington, D.C., 20049.

U.S. Department of Justice, Office of Justice Assistance — Research and Statistics: *Senior Citizens Against Crime: Take a Bite Out of Crime*. U.S. GPO, 1979.

Day-care and homemaker services

Materials available from: National HomeCaring Council, Inc., 67 Irving Place, New York, New York, 10003.

National HomeCaring Council, Inc.: *Help at Home . . . in Personal Care and Rehabilitation*. New York, National HomeCaring Council, Inc., (n.d.).

National HomeCaring Council, Inc.: *Someone I Can Trust*. New York, National HomeCaring Council, Inc., 1979.

National HomeCaring Council, Inc.: *Sometime in Your Life, You or Someone You Know Will Need Homemaker Service*. New York, National HomeCaring Council, Inc., (n.d.).

Smith, Bert Kruger: *Adult Day Care — Extended Family*. Austin, University of Texas. Hogg Foundation for Mental Health, 1981.

Death and dying

Kubler-Ross, Elisabeth: *On Death and Dying*. New York, Macmillan, 1969.

Kubler-Ross, Elisabeth: *Questions and Answers on Death and Dying*. New York, Macmillan, 1974.

Shepard, Martin: *Someone You Love is Dying: A Guide for Helping and Coping*. New York, Harmony, 1975.

Shneidman, Edwin S. (ed.): *Death: Current Perspectives*. New York, Aronson, 1978.

Simpson, Michael A.: *The Facts of Death: A Complete Guide for Being Prepared*. Englewood Cliffs, Prentice-Hall, 1979.

Heart disease

American Heart Association: *After a Heart Attack*. Dallas, American Heart Association, 1979.

Barbarowicz, Pat: *An Active Partnership for the Health of Your Heart (After Your Coronary Bypass Surgery)*. Dallas, American Heart Association, 1976.

Davis, Judy A., and Spillman, Shirley J.: *Cardiac Rehabilitation for the Patient and Family*. Reston, Reston, 1979.

Materials available from: The American Heart Association National Center, 7320 Greenville Avenue, Dallas, Texas, 75231, or local chapters of the Association.

Home nursing

American Red Cross: *Family Health and Home Nursing.* Garden City, Doubleday, 1979.

Parker, Page, and Dietz, Lois N.: *Nursing at Home: a Practical Guide to the Care of the Sick and Invalid in the Home, Plus Self-Help Instructions for the Patient.* New York, Crown, 1980.

Trocchio, Julie: *Home Care for the Elderly.* Boston, CBI Pub, 1980.

Legal

Brown, Robert N., Allo, Clifford B., Freeman, Alan D., and Netzorg, Gordon W.: *The Rights of Older Persons: the Basic ACLU Guide to an Older Person's Rights.* New York, Avon, 1979.

Legal Research and Services for the Elderly: *The Law and Aging Manual.* Washington, D.C., National Council of Senior Citizens, Inc., July, 1976. National Council of Senior Citizens, Inc., 1511 K Street, N.W., Washington, D.C., 20005.

Swisher, Thomas R.: *The Law and You,* 5th ed. Columbus, Ohio State Bar Association, 1981.

Wishard, William R.: *Rights of the Elderly and Retired: A People's Handbook.* San Francisco, Cragmont Pubns, 1978.

Medications

The following publications are part of a teaching program, Elder-Ed: an Education Program for Older Americans. Using Medicines Wisely, available from the National Institute on Drug Abuse.

National Institute on Drug Abuse: *Do's and Don't's of Wise Drug Use.* Washington, D.C., U.S. DHEW, 1979.

National Institute on Drug Abuse: *Keeping Track of Your Medicines.* Washington, D.C., U.S. DHEW, 1979.

National Institute on Drug Abuse: *Saving Money with Generic Medicines: Can You? Should You?* Washington, D.C., U.S. DHEW, 1979.

National Institute on Drug Abuse: *Using Your Medicines Wisely: a Guide for the Elderly.* Washington, D.C., U.S. DHEW, 1979.

Mental disorders

Cohen, Gene D: Fact Sheet: *Depression in the Elderly.* Washington, D.C., U.S. DHHS, NIMH, 1981.

Henig, Robin: *The Myth of Senility.* Garden City, Anchor Press, 1981.

Jury, Mark, and Jury, Dan: *Gramp.* New York, Penguin, 1976.

Mace, Nancy L., and Rabins, Peter V.: *The 36-Hour Day.* Baltimore, Johns Hopkins, 1981.

Thornton, Susan M., and Fraser, Virginia: *Understanding "Senility"—a Layperson's Guide.* Denver, Loretto Heights College, September, 1978. Loretto Heights College, 3001 South Federal Boulevard, Denver, Colorado, 80236.

U.S. Department of Health and Human Services. Public Health Service. National Institute of Health: *Questions and Answers about Alzheimer's Disease.* Bethesda, NIH, June, 1980.

Nursing homes

Burger, Sarah Greene, and D'Erasmo, Martha: *Living in a Nursing Home: a Complete Guide for Residents, their Families and Friends.* New York, Seabury, 1976.

Horn, Linda, and Griesel, Elma: *Nursing Homes: A Citizen's Action Guide.* Boston, Beacon Press, 1977.

U.S. Department of Health, Education, and Welfare. Public Health Service. Office of Nursing Home Affairs: *How to Select a Nursing Home.* Washington, D.C., U.S. GPO, 1977.

Nutrition

Editors of Consumer Reports: *Eating Right for Less for Older People; Consumers' Union Practical Guide to Food and Nutrition.* Mt. Vernon, Consumers' Union, 1975.

MacDonald, Barbara, and Miller, Peggy M.: *To Your Health in Your Second Fifty Years.* Rosemont, National Dairy Council, 1978. National Dairy Council, Rosemont, Illinois, 60018.

Stroke

American Heart Association: *Aphasia and the Family.* Dallas, American Heart Association, 1969.

American Heart Association: *Strike Back at Stroke.* Dallas, American Heart Association (n.d.).

American Heart Association: *Strokes: A Guide for the Family.* Dallas, American Heart Association, (n.d.).

American Heart Association: *Up and Around: a Booklet to Aid the Stroke Patient in Activities of Daily Living.* Dallas, American Heart Association, (n.d.).

Fowler, Roy S., and Fordyce, W. E.: *Stroke: Why Do They Behave That Way?* Dallas, American Heart Association, (n.d.).

Sarno, J. E., and Sarno, M. T.: *Stroke: A Guide for Patients and their Families.* revised ed. New York, McGraw-Hill, 1979.

Smith, Genevieve Waples: *Care of the Patient with a Stroke: A Handbook for the Patient's Family and the Nurse,* 2d ed. New York, Springer, 1976.

Vision and hearing

American Foundation for the Blind: *Facts About Aging and Blindness.* New York, Am Foun Blind, (n.d.). American Foundation for the Blind, Inc., 15 West 16th Street, New York, New York, 10011.

Consumer Reports: How to buy a hearing aid. *Consumer Reports, 41*:346, 1976.

Esterman, Ben: *The Eye Book: A Specialist's Guide to Your Eyes and Their Care.* Arlington, Great Ocean, 1977.

Fleming, Arthur W.: *The Real Truth About Cataracts.* Pittsburgh, Armor, 1980.

Sayre, Joan M.: *Handbook for the Hearing-Impaired Older Adult (An Individualized Program).* Danville, Interstate, 1980.

The following sources produce a wide variety of booklets, brochures, and other documents of interest to the elderly and their families.

NRTA–AARP
1909 K Street, N.W.
Washington, D.C. 20049

New England Gerontology Center
15 Garrison Avenue
Durham, New Hampshire 03824

Public Affairs Committee, Inc.
381 Park Avenue South
New York, New York 10016

U.S. Department of Health and Human Services
200 Independence Avenue, S.W.
Washington, D.C. 20201
Publications available through Regional Offices and Government Printing Office.

Appendix C

COMMON DISEASES OF THE ELDERLY

Some diseases, although they also may occur earlier in life, are much more likely to appear in the later years. Listed below are a number of common diseases that afflict the elderly and some ways in which they may be treated.

Alzheimer's Disease
(Senile Dementia of the Alzheimer's Type)

This is a neurological illness affecting the cerebral cortex — the outer layer of the brain. It affects up to 15 percent of the elderly population and now is recognized as a common cause of severe intellectual impairment in the elderly. At the onset there are only minor symptoms — forgetfulness is one of the most noticeable. As the disease progresses, memory loss increases. Some personality and behavior changes appear: confusion, irritability, restlessness. Judgment, concentration, orientation, and speech may be affected. In severe cases, patients may suffer incontinence and eventually become incapable of caring for themselves. The causes of Alzheimer's disease are not known, nor is there yet a cure, but all victims should be under the care of professionals who can carefully monitor their progress and suggest supportive measures as well as routines that can make life easier for both the patients and their families (see Mental Impairments in Chapter 8).

Arteriosclerosis (Atherosclerosis)

Arteriosclerosis is a general term for hardening of the arteries. Atherosclerosis, one type of arteriosclerosis, causes narrowing and

Adapted with permission from *You and Your Aging Parent*, by Barbara Silverstone and Helen K. Hyman. © 1982, Pantheon Books, a division of Random House, Inc.

closing of a blood vessel due to accumulation of fats, complex carbohydrates, blood and blood products, fibers, tissues, and calcium deposits in its inner wall. Other types of arteriosclerosis are uncommon and will not be discussed.

Arteriosclerosis is also related to hypertension (high blood pressure) and diabetes. The extent of arterial involvement in arteriosclerosis increases with age and can affect all the arteries of the body, especially those of the brain, heart, and lower extremities. Cerebrovascular disease, in which the blood supply to the brain is affected, can result in disturbances in behavior and cognition. It can also result in a "stroke" defined as a clinical event where there is a loss of neurological function (see Motor and Speech Loss in chapter 8).

Arteriosclerosis in the aged is treated by attempting to lower the blood fats by diet when they are significantly elevated. Drugs to lower blood fats at this age are not of proven value. Elevated blood pressure should be treated with a low-salt diet and, when necessary, the milder antihypertensive drugs. Cigarette smoking should be discontinued. A program of supervised physical activity is helpful, as is the control of obesity and diabetes. Surgical procedures to relieve or bypass obstructed blood vessels in the chest, neck, heart, and extremities may be of value after careful work-up and evaluation of the benefits and risks involved.

Arthritis

Arthritis is a general term referring to any degeneration or inflammation of the joints. It is classified according to its acuteness or its chronicity and also according to the joints involved and specific laboratory and x-ray findings. Many older persons suffer from arthritis, some to a mild degree and others severely.

The most common form, called osteoarthritis, involves primarily the weight-bearing joints and is due to the wear-and-tear process that accompanies aging. Osteoporosis, or thinning of the bones with aging, which occurs more often in women, contributes to collapse of the backbone as well as hip and wrist fractures. Inflammatory involvement of the joints, rheumatoid arthritis, is less common in the aged. Gout, a metabolic disease of the joints accompanied by severe pain and signs of inflammation, also may be seen in the aged.

Treatment of arthritis varies with the cause and includes physiotherapy, use of certain anti-inflammatory medications, and orthopedic devices. There are specific drugs for treating gout. The use of female sex hormones for treating osteoporosis may be beneficial, but side effects warrant careful discussion with a physician.

Bronchitis and Lung Disease

Bronchitis is an inflammation of the cells that line the bronchial air tubes. It may be caused by infection, chronic irritation from cigarette smoke, or the inhalation of some harmful substance. Infectious bronchitis may be treated with antibiotics. In the case of chronic bronchitis, cessation of smoking is, of course, imperative. If untreated, chronic bronchitis may progress gradually to pulmonary emphysema.

Pulmonary emphysema, which results when the air sacs in the lungs are distended and damaged, is found often in heavy smokers. The patient suffers from shortness of breath and a cough. Treatment centers around relief of chronic bronchial obstruction by use of devices that help the emphysema patient breathe. A variety of drugs and exercises are of value.

Cancer

Cancer (malignant neoplasm or tumor) is an uncontrolled growth of a tissue or portion of an organ that can spread (mestastasize) to another part of the body. Cancer can occur in the throat, larynx, mouth, gastrointestinal tract, skin, bones, thyroid, bladder, kidney, and so forth. Because cancer symptoms in the aged may be atypical, or may be ignored by the aged patient afficted with other symptoms and often with a poor memory, comprehensive annual examinations are vital for early detection and treatment.

Cancer may be treated with surgery, radiotherapy (x-ray), chemotherapy (medication), or by any combination of the three modalities. Because life expectancy is limited and the growth of many cancers is slow in the aged, there should be careful consideration of the value and potential side effects of potent methods of therapy before they are undertaken.

Congestive Heart Failure

Congestive heart failure occurs when the heart muscle has been so weakened that its pumping performance is impaired and cannot provide sufficient circulation to body tissues. This condition may result from many years of untreated high blood pressure, heart attacks, or rheumatic heart disease. It also may be produced by diseases such as chronic lung disease, anemia, infection, and alcoholism.

Treatment for congestive heart failure is directed at improving the heart's pumping efficiency and eliminating excess fluids. Digitalis derivatives are often used to strengthen the heart muscle, and diuretics and salt restriction remove excess fluid from the body. Treatment of a precipitating disease, such as hypertension, overactivity of the thyroid gland, or anemia, may also be necessary.

Coronary Artery Heart Disease

This disease, which is present in almost all individuals over the age of seventy in the United States, involves atherosclerosis of the arteries that supply blood to the heart muscle. In older persons coronary heart disease is superimposed on a heart where there may be a general decrease in muscle-cell size and efficiency.

A heart attack (myocardial infarction) happens when a portion of the blood supply to the heart muscle is cut off. In the elderly it is not unusual for there to be hardly any symptoms accompanying an infarction, in contrast to the crushing pain experienced by younger persons. Substitution symptoms are also common in the elderly; for example, when the elderly heart fails because of a heart attack, blood may back up behind the left side of the heart into the blood vessels of the lungs, causing shortness of breath instead of chest pain. In other cases, the flow of blood from the weakened heart to the brain is diminished, with resultant dizziness or fainting rather than chest pain.

Modern treatment of the complications of acute myocardial infarction (which include irregular heartbeat and heart failure) with drugs, oxygen, and electrical equipment is saving many lives and enabling the period of bed rest to be shortened. Patients with uncomplicated cases now get up out of bed and into a chair much earlier than before, and cardiac rehabilitation is begun early with good results. Cardiac shock (intractable heart failure), however, remains a difficult problem with a high mortality rate.

Common in individuals with coronary heart disease is angina pectoris. This condition results from a temporary inadequacy in the blood supply to the heart muscle due to coronary heart disease. Angina is characterized by severe but brief pain over the midchest region; the pain may radiate to either or both arms, the back, neck, or jaw. Angina is treated commonly and safely with nitroglycerin.

Diabetes Mellitus

The common form of diabetes in the aged is Type II diabetes, a chronic inherited disease in which a relative deficiency of insulin or a disturbance in the action of insulin interferes with the body's ability to metabolize carbohydrates. (Type I diabetes is often referred to as juvenile-onset diabetes and always requires insulin.) The elderly diabetic may present few or no clinical symptoms of that disease. In fact, complications arising from diabetes may be the first signs of this disease in the elderly. Cataracts, strokes, heart attacks, and gangrene of the legs, for example, are frequent in the diabetic. There is a relatively high incidence of diabetes in the aged, with severe complications involving the larger blood vessels.

Most elderly diabetics require only control of their diet. Loss of weight and avoidance of obesity are essential. Insulin injections are needed by only a small number. Long-term benefits of hypoglycemic medications are not proved, and use of these drugs requires thoughtful discussion with a physician. The foot care of elderly diabetics should be managed by a podiatrist, since their poor circulation and lowered resistance make them prone to infection, which may be followed by the dread complication of gangrene.

Diseases of the Ear

The ear consists of the external, the middle, and the inner ears. Problems in each of them may affect hearing. Any condition that prevents sound from reaching the eardrum can cause a hearing loss. Common problems affecting the external ear include impacted ear wax and swelling of the tissues lining the canal caused by inflammation. Problems that frequently affect the middle ear include fluid accumulation and infection within the inner ear cavity. Hearing losses caused by conditions of the external or middle ear are known as conductive losses, since they affect the pathway by which sound is conducted to the inner ear.

Conductive hearing losses are frequently treatable by a physician. Hearing problems involving the middle ear in the aged are similar to those occurring earlier in life. The most common cause is infection. Hearing loss in the middle ear that is not due to infection can often be corrected by surgery. Lesions of the inner ear, if not too extensive, can be helped by the proper use of hearing aids (see Hearing Loss, Chapter 8).

Another type of hearing loss results from damage to the inner ear. That is sensorineural hearing loss, often called nerve deafness. The inner ear houses the nerve structures that receive the sound waves and transmit them to the brain. In most instances, sensorineural losses are irreversible and are not likely to be helped by hearing aids.

Diseases of the Eye

Cataracts are opaque spots that form in the lens of the eye and interfere with the passage of light rays. Often, the first indication is a blurring and dimming of vision. If the retina is essentially normal, as it often is, the removal of the clouded lens can lead to restoration of a gratifying amount of vision. Surgical advances have made the removal of cataracts comparatively easy, even for the aged and infirm. Cataract removal can be performed under local anesthesia. Many surgeons now allow patients out of bed the day after the operation. Since the lens is needed for focusing, special glasses or contact lenses are required after it has been removed. The use of lens implants following cataract removal is controversial and requires careful discussion with an ophthalmologist (see Loss of Vision, Chapter 8).

Glaucoma, a major cause of blindness, is characterized by increased pressure in the eyeball. The disease develops slowly and painlessly, but it can be arrested if detected early enough. Thorough evaluation by an ophthalmologist is needed to determine who will benefit from surgery and who requires appropriate therapy with eyedrops and drugs. Routine determination of the pressure in the eyes of aged individuals is essential for the detection of glaucoma before symptoms, and at times irreversible damage, develop. Such determinations, as part of annual comprehensive examinations or in large-scale screening drives for glaucoma alone, are of great value.

Macular disease is a degeneration of the area of the retina that permits perception of fine details, such as print. The cause is unknown. When it has considerably progressed, older persons with poor sight may be helped with low-vision aids such as magnifying devices.

Hypertension

Hypertension, otherwise known as high blood pressure, when present over long periods of time can lead to arterial disease and eventually to heart failure, stroke, or kidney failure. In the elderly, high blood pressure is unlikely to be of recent origin, and much of the damage to the arterial system has already been done.

Hypertension in the aged should be treated by moderate dietary salt restriction and, if necessary, by drugs. Only the milder drugs should be used in the aged, since the more powerful ones can cause sudden and severe lowering of blood pressure, which may lead to fainting spells or even strokes or heart attacks—the very complications such drugs are used to prevent.

Neuritis

Neuritis is a disease of the peripheral and cranial nerves characterized by inflammation and degeneration of the nerve fibers. It can lead to loss of conduction of nerve impulses and consequently to varying degrees of paralysis and loss of feeling reflexes. Although the term neuritis implies inflammation, this is not invariably present. Neuritis may affect a single nerve or involve several nerve trunks.

Diagnostic work-up by a neurologist is indicated. Treatment of specific causes, such as diabetes, pernicious anemia, or alcoholism, may be helpful.

BIBLIOGRAPHY

Achenbaum, W. Andrew: *Old Age in the New Land: The American Experience Since 1790*. Baltimore, Johns Hopkins, 1979.

Ackerman, Nathan W.: *Treating the Troubled Family*. New York, Basic, 1966.

Adams, Johnny M.: Behavioral contracting: an effective method of intervention with the elderly nursing home patient. *Journal of Gerontological Social Work*, *1*:235, 1979.

American Hospital Association. Society for Hospital Social Work Directors. Committee on Discharge Planning: *Discharge Planning*. Chicago, American Hospital, September, 1980.

Atchley, Robert C.: *The Social Forces of Later Life*, 3d ed. Belmont, Wadsworth, 1980.

Austin, Michael J., and Kosberg, Jordan I.: Nursing home decision-makers and the social service needs of residents. *Social Work in Health Care*, *1*:447, 1976.

Austin, Michael J., and Kosberg, Jordon I.: Social service programming in nursing homes. *Health and Social Work*, *1*:39, 1976.

Austin, Michael J., and Kosberg, Jordon I.: Social work consultation to nursing homes: a study. *Health and Social Work*, *3*:60, 1978.

Axelrod, Terry B.: Innovative roles for social workers in home-care programs. *Health and Social Work*, *3*:48, 1978.

Bandler, Bernard: The concept of ego supportive psychotherapy. In Parad, Howard J., and Miller, Roger R. (eds.): *Ego-Oriented Casework, Problems and Perspectives*. New York, Family Service Association, 1963, pp. 27–45.

Bartlett, Harriet M.: *The Common Base of Social Work Practice*. New York, National Association of Social Workers, 1970.

Becker, Ernest: *The Denial of Death*. New York, Free Press, 1973.

Bell, William G., and Olsen, William T.: An overview of public transportation and the elderly: new directions for social policy. *Gerontologist*, *14*:324, 1974.

Bellack, Leopold, and Karasu, Toksoz B.: *Geriatric Psychiatry*. New York, Grune, 1976.

Bennett, Ruth (ed.): *Aging, Isolation and Resocialization*. New York, Van Nostrand Reinhold, 1980.

Berkman, Barbara: Knowledge base needs for effective social work practice in health. *Journal of Education for Social Work*, *17*:85, 1981.

Berkman, Barbara Gordon, and Rehr, Helen: Social needs of the hospitalized elderly: a classification. *Social Work, 17*:80, 1972.

Bertalanffy, Ludwig von: *General Systems Theory.* New York, Braziller, 1968.

Binstock, Robert H., and Shanas, Ethel (eds.): *Handbook of Aging and the Social Sciences.* New York, Van Nostrand Reinhold, 1976.

Birren, James E., and Schaie, K. Warner (eds): *Handbook of the Psychology of Aging.* New York, Van Nostrand Reinhold, 1977.

Blenkner, Margaret: The normal dependencies of aging. In Kalish, Richard A. (ed.): *The Dependencies of Old People.* Ann Arbor, Institute of Gerontology. University of Michigan-Wayne State University, August, 1969, pp. 27–38.

Blenkner, Margaret: Social Work and Family Relationships in Later Life With Some Thoughts on Filial Maturity. In E. Shanas & E. Streib (eds.): *Social Structure & the Family: Generational Relations.* New York, Prentice-Hall, Inc., 1965.

Blythe, Ronald: *The View in Winter.* New York, Harcourt Brace Jovanovich, 1979.

Bonner, J. P., Sacia, J. M., Rowlands, E., and Snouffer, K.: Medical social services in home health agency: luxury or necessity? *Home Health Review, 1*:28, 1978.

Borup, Jerry H., Gallego, Daniel T., and Heffernan, Pamela G.: Relocation: its effect on health, functioning and mortality. *Gerontologist, 20*:468, 1980.

Brager, George, and Holloway, Stephen: *Changing Human Service Organizations Politics and Practice.* New York, Free Press, 1978.

Brennan, Eileen, and Weick, Ann: Theories of adult development: creating a context for practice. *Social Casework, 62*:13, 1981.

Brocklehurst, J. C. (ed.): *Textbook of Geriatric Medicine and Gerontology,* 2d ed. London, Churchill Livingston, 1978.

Brody, Elaine M.: *Long-Term Care of Older People: A Practical Guide.* New York, Human Science Press, 1977.

Brody, Elaine M.: Long-term care of the aged: promises and prospects. *Health and Social Work, 4*:29, 1979.

Brody, Elaine M.: *A Social Work Guide for Long-Term Care Facilities.* Rockville, NIMH, 1974.

Brody, Elaine M., Cole, Charlotte, Moss, Miriam: Individualizing therapy for the mentally impaired aged. *Social Casework, 54*:453, 1973.

Brody, Elaine, and Spark, Geraldine: Institutionalization of the aged: a family crisis. *Family Process, 5*:76, 1966.

Brotman, Herman B.: Every ninth American. In Special Committee on Aging. United States Senate: *Developments in Aging: 1978.* Washington, D.C., U.S. GPO., 1979, Pt 1, pp. xv–xxxii.

Buckley, Walter (ed.): *Modern Systems Research for the Behavioral Scientist: a Sourcebook.* Chicago, Aldine, 1968.

Burnside, Irene Mortenson: Symptomatic behaviors in the elderly. In Birren, James E., and Sloane, R. Bruce (eds.): *Handbook of Mental Health and Aging.* Englewood Cliffs, Prentice-Hall 1980, pp. 719–744.

Burnside, Irene M.: *Working with the Elderly: Group Process and Techniques.* North Scituate, Duxbury, 1978.

Busse, Ewald, and Blazer, Dan: Disorders related to biological functioning. In Busse, Ewald W., and Blazer, Dan G. (eds.): *Handbook of Geriatric Psychiatry.* New York, Van Nostrand Reinhold, 1980, pp. 390–414.

Busse, Ewald W., and Pfeiffer, Eric: *Mental Illness in Later Life.* Washington, D.C., American Psychiatric Association, 1973.

Butler, Robert N.: The life review: an interpretation of reminiscence in the aged. *Psychiatry, 26*:65, 1963.

Butler, Robert N., and Lewis, Myra I.: *Aging and Mental Health,* 3d ed. St. Louis, Mosby, 1982.

Cantor, Marjorie H.: The elderly in the inner city, some implications of the effect of culture on life styles. (Paper presented to the Institute on Gerontology and Graduate Education for Social Work, Fordham University, Lincoln Center campus, March, 1973.)

Cantor, Marjorie: Life space and the social support system of the inner city elderly of New York. *Gerontologist, 15*:23, 1975.

Carter, James H.: Recognizing psychiatric symptoms in black Americans. *Geriatrics, 29*:95, 1974.

Cath, Stanley H.: Some dynamics of middle and later years. *Smith College Studies in Social Work, 33*:97, 1963.

Cloward, Richard A., and Piven, Frances Fox: *Regulating the Poor, the Functions of Public Welfare.* New York, Vintage, 1971.

Coelho, George V., Hamburg, David, and Adams, John E. (eds.): *Coping and Adaptation.* New York, Basic, 1974.

Cohen, Margery G.: Alternative to institutional care of the aged. *Social Casework, 54*:447, 1973.

Compton, Beulah Roberts, and Galaway, Burt: *Social Work Processes.* Homewood, Dorsey, 1975.

Congressional Budget Office. United States Congress: *Long-Term Care for the Elderly and Disabled.* Washington, D.C., U.S. GPO., February, 1977.

Costa, Frank J., and Sweet, Marnie: Barrier-free environments for older Americans. *Gerontologist, 16*:404, 1976.

Cross-Andrew, Susannah, and Zimmer, Anna: *Incentives to families caring for disabled elderly: research and demonstration project to strengthen the natural supports system.* (Paper Presented at 30th Annual Meeting of Gerontological Society, San Francisco, November, 1977.)

Cumming, Elaine: Engagement with an old theory. *International Journal of Aging and Human Development, 6*:187, 1975.

Dierking, Barbara, Brown, Margot, Fortune, Anne E.: Task-centered treatment for the elderly: a clinical trial. *Journal of Gerontological Social Work, 2*:225, 1980.

Dobrof, Rose, and Litwak, Eugene: *Maintenance of Family Ties of Long-Term Care Patients: Theory and Guide to Practice.* Washington, D.C., U.S. DHHS, 1977.

Downey, Rachel: *An exploration of case management roles: coordinator, advocate, counselor.* Working Paper, Social Policy Laboratory. Los Angeles, Ethel Percy Andrus Gerontology Center, 1979.

Drachman, David A.: An approach to the neurology of aging. In Birren, James E., and Sloane, R. Bruce (eds.): *Handbook of Mental Health and Aging*. Englewood Cliffs, Prentice-Hall, 1980, p. 501–519.

Dubos, Rene: *Man Adapting*. New Haven, Yale University Press, 1965.

Eisdorfer, Carl: Paranoia and schizophrenic disorders in later life. In Busse, Ewald W., and Blazer, Dan G. (eds.): *Handbook of Geriatric Psychiatry*. New York, Van Nostrand Reinhold, 1980, pp. 329–337.

Elderly housing. *Progressive Architecture, 8*:59, 1981.

Erikson, Erik H.: *Identity and the Life Cycle*. New York, International Universities Press, 1959.

Faffer, Jaclynn I.: Casework with the chronically ill—a population that does not "get better." *Social Casework, 62*:372, 1981.

Finch, Caleb E., and Hayflick, Leonard: *Handbook of the Biology of Aging*. New York, Van Nostrand Reinhold, 1977.

Finestone, Samuel, Lowry, Fern, Whiteman, Martin, and Lukoff, Irving: *Social Casework and Blindness*. New York, American Foundation for the Blind, March, 1960.

Fisch, L.: Special senses: the aging auditory system. In Brocklehurst, J. C. (ed.): *Textbook of Geriatric Medicine and Gerontology*, 2d ed. London, Churchill Livingston, 1978, p 276–290.

Fox, Renee: The sting of death in American society. *Social Service Review, 55*:42, 1981.

Frank, Margaret Galdston: Clinical social work: past, present and future, challenges and dilemmas. *Smith College Studies in Social Work, 50*:193, 1980.

Freeland, Mark, Calat, George, and Schendler, Carol Ellen: Projections of national health expenditures, 1980, 1985, and 1990. *Health Care Financing Review, 1*:1, 1980.

Fries, James F. and Crapo, Lawrence M., *Vitality and Aging—Implications of the Rectangular Curve*. San Francisco, W. H. Freeman and Company, 1981.

Gaitz, Charles M., and Varner, Roy V.: Adjustment disorders of late life: stress disorders. In Busse, Ewald W., and Blazer, Dan G. (eds.): *Handbook of Geriatric Psychiatry*. New York, Van Nostrand Reinhold, 1980, pp. 381–389.

Ganter, Grace, and Yeakel, Margaret: *Human Behavior and the Social Environment*. New York, Columbia University Press, 1980.

Garland, James A., Jones, Hubert E., Kolodny, Ralph: A model for stages of development in social work groups. In Bernstein, Saul (ed.): *Explorations in Group Work: Essays in Theory and Practice*. Boston, Charles River, 1976, p. 17–71.

Garner, J. Dianne, and Mercer, Susan O.: Social work practice in long-term care facilities: implications of the current model. *Journal of Gerontological Social Work, 3*:71, 1980.

Garrett, Annette: *Interviewing: Its Principles and Techniques*, 3rd. rev. ed., New York, Family Service Association, 1982.

Gaylin, Willard, Glasser, Ira, Marcus, Steven, Rothman, David J.: *Doing Good: The*

Limits of Benevolence. New York, Pantheon, 1978.

Geherke, J. R., and Wattenberg, S. H.: Assessing social services in nursing homes. *Health and Social Work*, 6:14, 1981.

Gelfand, Donald E., and Olsen, Jody K.: *The Aging Network Programs and Services*. New York, Springer, 1980.

Germain, Carel: Casework and science: a historical encounter. In Roberts, Robert W., and Nee, Robert H. (eds.): *Theories of Social Casework*. Chicago, University of Chicago Press, 1970, p. 3–32.

Germain, Carel B.: An ecological perspective in casework practice. *Social Casework*, 54:323, 1973.

Germain, Carel B.: General-systems theory and ego psychology: an ecological perspective. *Social Service Review,* 52:535, 1978.

Germain, Carel B. (Ed.): *Social Work Practice, People and Environments*. New York, Columbia University Press, 1979.

Germain, Carel B.: Time: an ecological variable in social work practice. *Social Casework*, 57:419, 1976.

Germain, Carel B., and Gitterman, Alex: *The Life Model of Social Work Practice*. New York, Columbia University Press, 1980.

Getzel, George: Helping elderly couples in crisis. *Social Casework*, in press.

Getzel, George, and Mellor, M. Joanna (eds.): *Gerontological Social Work Practice in Long-Term Care*. New York, Haworth, 1983.

Getzel, George: Social Work With Family Caregivers to the Aged. *Social Casework*, 62:4, 1981.

Getzel, George S.: Old people, poetry, and groups. *Journal of Gerontological Social Work*, 3:77, 1980.

Glasser, Paul, Sarri, Rosemary, and Vinter, Robert: *Individual Change through Small Groups*. New York, Free Press, 1974.

Goldfarb, Alvin I.: Patient-doctor relationship in treatment of aged persons. *Geriatrics*, 19:18, 1964.

Goldfarb, Alvin I.: The psychodynamics of dependency and the search for aid. In Kalish, Richard A. (ed.): *The Dependencies of Old People*. Ann Arbor, Institute of Gerontology. University of Michigan-Wayne State University, August, 1969, pp. 1–15.

Gordon, William E.: Knowledge and value: their distinction and relationship in clarifying social work practice. *Social Work*, 10:32, 1965.

Gotestam, K. Gunnar: Behavioral and dynamic psychotherapy with the elderly. In Birren, James E., and Sloane, R. Bruce (Eds.): *Handbook of Mental Health and Aging*. Englewood Cliffs, Prentice-Hall, 1980, pp. 775–805.

Greengross, Sally: Ageing and the community counsellor. In Hobman, David (Ed.): *The Impact of Ageing*. New York, St. Martin's, 1981, pp. 176–191.

Gross, Neal, Mason, Ward S., McEachern, Alexander W.: *Explorations in Role Analysis*, New York, John Wiley & Sons, Inc., 1966 (see part 1, pages 11–70).

Gubrium, Jaber F.: *The Myth of the Golden Years*. Springfield, Charles C Thomas, Publisher, 1973.

Haley, Jay: *Problem-Solving Therapy*. San Francisco, Jossey-Bass, 1976.

Hamilton, Gordon: *Theory and Practice of Social Case Work*, 2nd ed. New York, Columbia University Press, 1951.

Harris, Diana K., and Cole, William E.: *Sociology of Aging*. Boston, Houghton Mifflin, 1980.

Harris, Phyllis B.: Being old: a confrontation group with nursing home residents. *Health and Social Work*, 4:152, 1979.

Hartford, Margaret E.: *Groups in Social Work*. New York, Columbia University Press, 1972.

Hartford, Margaret E.: The use of group methods for work with the aged. In Birren, James E., and Sloane, R. Bruce (eds.): *Handbook of Mental Health and Aging*. Englewood Cliffs, Prentice-Hall, 1980, pp. 806–826.

Hartmann, Heinz: *Ego Psychology and the Problem of Adaptation*. New York, International University Press, 1958.

Hasenfeld, Yeheskel, and English, Richard A. (eds): *Human Service Organizations*. Ann Arbor, University of Michigan Press, 1974.

Helphand, Margaret, and Porter, Catherine M.: The family group within the nursing home: maintaining family ties of long-term residents. *Journal of Gerontological Social Work*, 4:51, 1981.

Hendin, Herbert: *Suicide in America*. New York, Norton, 1982.

Hendricks, Jon, and Hendricks, C. Davis: *Aging in Mass Society*, 2d ed. Cambridge, Winthrop, 1981.

Hiatt, Lorraine G.: The color and use of color in environments for older people. *Nursing Homes*, 30:18, 1981.

Hiatt, Lorraine G.: Is poor light dimming the sight of nursing home patients? *Nursing Homes*, 29:32, 1980.

Hollis, Florence and Woods, Mary E.: *Casework: A Psychosocial Therapy*, 3rd ed. New York, Random, 1981.

Hooker, Carol E.: Learned Helplessness. *Social Work*, 21:194, 1976.

Horner, Althea J.: *Object Relations and the Developing Ego in Therapy*. New York, Aronson, 1979.

Hubbard, Richard W., Santos, John F., and Santos, Mary Alice: Alcohol and older adults: overt and covert influences. *Social Casework*, 60:166, 1979.

Jorgensen, Lou Ann B., and Kane, Robert L.: Social work in the nursing home: a need and an opportunity. *Social Work in Health Care*, 1:471, 1976.

Kahana, Eva: Matching environments to needs of the aged: a conceptual scheme. In Gubrium, Jaber (Ed.): *Late Life: Recent Developments in the Sociology of Aging*. Springfield, Charles C Thomas Publisher, 1974, pp. 201–214.

Kahana, Eva, Liang, Jersey, and Felton, Barbara J.: Alternative models of person-environment fit: prediction of morale in three homes for the aged. *Journal of Gerontology*, 35:584, 1980.

Kalish, Richard A. (Ed.): *The Dependencies of Old People*. Ann Arbor, Institute of Gerontology. University of Michigan-Wayne State University, August, 1969.

Kane, Rosalie A.: Look to the record. *Social Work*, 19:412, 1974.

Kastenbaum, Robert: Death, dying and bereavement in old age: new developments and their possible implications for psychological care. *Aged Care and Services Review,* 1:1, 1978.

Kastenbaum, Robert, and Candy, Sandra E.: The 4% fallacy: a methodological and empirical critique of extended care facility population statistics. *International Journal of Aging and Human Development,* 4:15, 1973.

Kirschner, Charlotte: The aging family in crisis: a problem in living. *Social Casework,* 60:209, 1979.

Kosberg, Jordan I.: The nursing home: a social work paradox. *Social Work,* 18:104, 1973.

Kulys, Regina, and Tobin, Sheldon S.: Older people and their 'responsible others.' *Social Work,* 25:138, 1980.

Laszlo, Ervin (ed.): *The Relevance of General Systems Theory.* New York, Braziller, 1972.

Laszlo, Ervin (ed.): *The Systems View of the World.* New York, Braziller, 1972.

Lawton, M. Powell: Assessment, integration, and environments for older people. *Gerontologist,* 10:38, 1970, Pt I.

Lawton, M. Powell: *Planning and Managing Housing for the Elderly.* New York, Wiley, 1975.

Lawton, M. Powell: Social ecology and the health of older people. *American Journal of Public Health,* 64:257, 1974.

Lawton, M. Powell, and Nahemow, Lucille: Ecology and the aging process. In Eisdorfer, Carl, and Lawton, M. Powell (eds.): *The Psychology of Adult Development and Aging.* Washington, D.C., American Psychological Association, 1973, pp. 619–674.

Lazarus, Lawrence W., and Weinberg, Jack: Treatment in the ambulatory care setting. In Busse, Ewald W., and Blazer, Dan G. (eds.): *Handbook of Geriatric Psychiatry.* New York, Van Nostrand Reinhold, 1980, pp. 427–452.

Leichter, Hope Jensen, and Mitchell, William: *Kinship and Casework.* New York, Russell Sage, 1967.

Leighton, D. A.: Special senses: aging of the eye. In Brocklehurst, J. C. (ed.): *Textbook of Geriatric Medicine and Gerontology,* 2d ed. London, Churchill Livingston, 1978, pp. 267–276.

Lewis, Kenneth: Practical illustrations of nurse-social worker collaboration and teamwork in a long-term health care facility. *Journal of Gerontological Nursing,* 5:34, 1979.

Lieberman, Morton A.: Relocation research and social policy. *Gerontologist,* 14:49A, 1974.

Liton, Judith, and Olstein, Sara C.: Therapeutic aspects of reminiscence. *Social Casework,* 50:263, 1969.

Litwak, Eugene, and Meyer, Henry: A balance theory of coordination between bureaucratic organizations and community primary groups. *Administrative Science Quarterly* 11:35, 1966.

Litwak, Eugene, and Szelenyi, Evan: Primary group structures and their functions: kin, neighbors and friends. *American Sociological Review,* 34:465, 1969.

Loewenstein, Sophie: An overview of the concept of narcissism. *Social Casework,* *58*:136, 1977.

Lowy, Louis: Mental health services in the community. In Birren, James E., and Sloane, R. Bruce (Eds.): *Handbook of Mental Health and Aging.* Englewood Cliffs, Prentice-Hall, 1980, pp. 827–853.

Lowy, Louis: *Social Work with the Aging: The Challenge and Promise of the Later Years.* New York, Harper-Row, 1979.

Mace, Nancy L., and Rabins, Peter V.: *The 36-Hour Day.* Baltimore, Johns Hopkins, 1981.

Marsh, Gail R.: Perceptual changes with aging. In Busse, Ewald W., and Blazer, Dan G. (eds.): *Handbook of Geriatric Psychiatry.* New York, Van Nostrand Reinhold, 1980, p. 147–168.

Martens, Wilma M., and Holmstrup, Elizabeth: Problem-oriented recording. *Social Casework, 55*:554, 1974.

Mechanic, David: Social structure and personal adaptation: some neglected dimensions. In Coelho, George V., Hamburg, David, and Adams, John E. (eds.): *Coping and Adaptation.* New York, Basic, 1974, pp. 32–46.

Mechanic, David: Sources of power of lower participants in complex organizations. In Cooper, W. W., Leavitt, H. J., and Shelly, M. W., II (eds.): *New Perspectives in Organization Research.* New York, Wiley, 1964, pp. 136–149.

Meyer, Carol H.: Purposes and boundaries — casework fifty years later. *Social Casework, 54*:268, 1973.

Meyer, Carol H.: *Social Work Practice,* 2nd ed. New York, Free Press, 1976.

Meyer, Carol H.: Social work purpose: status by choice or coercion? *Social Work, 26*:69, 1981.

Meyer, Carol: *Social Work with the Aging.* Washington, D.C., National Association of Social Workers, 1975.

Meyer, Carol H.: What directions for direct practice? *Social Work, 24*:267, 1979.

Meyerhoff, Barbara: *Number Our Days.* New York, S & S, 1980.

Miller, Irving, and Solomon, Renee: The Development of group services for the elderly. In Germain, Carel B. (ed.): *Social Work Practice: People and Environments.* New York, Columbia University Press, 1979, pp. 74–106.

Minuchin, Salvador: *Families and Family Therapy.* Cambridge, Harvard University Press, 1974.

Moen, Elizabeth: The reluctance of the elderly to accept help. *Social Problems, 25*:293, 1978.

Monk, Abraham: Family supports in old age. *Social Work, 24*:533, 1979.

Monk, Abraham: Social work with the aged: principles of practice. *Social Work, 26*:61, 1981.

National Association of Social Workers: *Code of Ethics.* Washington, D.C., National Association of Social Workers, 1975. July, 1980.

National Association of Social Workers. Committee on Aging: *Long-Term Care for the Elderly, Chronically Ill and Disabled: A Position Paper.* Washington, D.C., National Association of Social Workers, 1975. April, 1979.

National Conference on Social Welfare: *The Report of the Task Force on the Future of Long-Term Care in the United States.* Washington, D.C., U.S. DHEW, February, 1977.

Newsome, Barbara L. (ed.): *Insights on the Minority Elderly.* Washington, D.C., National Center on Black Aged, 1977.

Novick, L. J.: The function of the social worker in the long term hospital. *Long Term Health Care Services Administrative Quarterly, 3*:181, 1979.

Olsen, Tillie: *Tell Me a Riddle.* New York, Delacorte, 1978.

Parad, Howard J. (ed.): *Crisis Intervention: Selected Readings.* New York, Family Service, 1965.

Parad, Howard J. (ed.): *Ego Psychology and Dynamic Casework.* New York, Family Service, 1958.

Pastalan, Leon A., and Carson, Daniel H. (eds.): *Spatial Behavior of Older People.* Ann Arbor, Institute of Gerontology. University of Michigan-Wayne State University, 1970.

Patti, Rino J.: Organizational resistance and change: the view from below. *Social Service Review, 48*:367, 1974.

Peck, Robert E.: Psychological developments in the second half of life. In Anderson, John E. (Ed.): *Psychological Aspects of Aging.* Washington, D.C., American Psychological Association, 1956, pp. 42–53.

Perlman, Helen Harris: In quest of coping. *Social Casework, 56*:213, 1975.

Perlman, Helen Harris: *Relationship: The Heart of Helping People.* Chicago, University of Chicago Press, 1979.

Perlman, Helen Harris: *Social Casework: A Problem-Solving Process.* Chicago, University of Chicago Press, 1957.

Peterson, James A.: Social-psychological aspects of death and dying and mental health. In Birren, James E., and Sloane, R. Bruce (eds.): *Handbook of Mental Health and Aging.* Englewood Cliffs, Prentice-Hall, 1980, pp. 922–942.

Pfeiffer, Eric (ed.): *Multidimensional Functional Assessment: The OARS Methodology. A Manual.* Durham, Center for the Study of Aging & Human Development, 1977.

Pfeiffer, Eric: The psychosocial evaluation of the elderly patient. In Busse, Ewald W., and Blazer, Dan G. (eds.): *Handbook of Geriatric Psychiatry.* New York, Van Nostrand Reinhold, 1980, pp. 275–284.

Pincus, Allen: Reminiscence in aging and its implications for social work practice. *Social Work, 15*:47, 1970.

Pincus, Allen: Toward a developmental view of aging for social work. *Social Work, 12*:33, 1967.

Pincus, Allen, and Minahan, Anne: *Social Work Practice: Model and Method.* Itasca, Peacock, 1973.

Poulshock, S. Walter, and Noelker, Linda: *The Effects on Families of Caring for Impaired Elderly in Residence. Final Report to the Administration on Aging.* Cleveland, The Benjamin Rose Institute, October, 1982.

Rapaport, Lydia: Crisis intervention as a mode of brief treatment. In Roberts,

Robert W., and Nee, Robert H. (eds.): *Theories of Social Casework*. Chicago, University of Chicago Press, 1971, p. 265–311.

Raskind, Murray A., and Storrie, Michael C.: The organic mental disorders. In Busse, Ewald W., and Blazer, Dan G. (eds.): *Handbook of Geriatric Psychiatry*. New York, Van Nostrand Reinhold, 1980, pp. 305–328.

Regan, John: *Intervention through adult protective services programs*. (Paper presented at the Annual Meeting of the Gerontological Society, San Francisco, November, 1977.)

Reid, William J.: Mapping the knowledge base of social work. *Social Work*, 26:124, 1981.

Reid, William J., and Epstein, Laura: *Task-Centered Casework*. New York, Columbia University Press, 1972.

Reid, William J., and Epstein, Laura: *Task-Centered Practice*. New York, Columbia University Press, 1977.

Reid, William J., and Shyne, Ann W.: *Brief and Extended Casework*. New York, Columbia University Press, 1969.

Rein, Martin, and White, Sheldon H.: Knowledge for practice. *Social Service Review,* 55:1, 1981.

Rhodes, Sonya L.: A developmental approach to the life cycle of the family. *Social Casework*, 58:301, 1977.

Roberts, Robert, and Northern, Helen: *Theories of Social Group Work*. New York, Columbia University Press, 1976.

Roberts, Robert W., and Nee, Robert H. (eds.): *Theories of Social Casework*. Chicago, University Chicago Press, 1971.

Rodin, Judith, and Langer, Ellen: Aging labels: the decline of control and the fall of self-esteem. *Journal of Social Issues*, 36:12, 1980.

Rosin, A. and Glatt, M. M.: Alcohol excess in the elderly. *Quarterly Journal of Studies in Alcoholism*, 32:53, 1971.

Rowlings, Cherry: The social worker and the problems of ageing. In Hobman, David (ed.): *The Impact of Ageing*. New York, St. Martin's, 1981, pp. 158–175.

Satir, Virginia: *Conjoint Family Therapy*. Palo Alto, Science and Behavior, 1964.

Saul, Shura: *Aging: An Album of People Growing Old*. New York, Wiley, 1974.

Schorr, Alvin: *"... thy father and thy mother ... " a second look at filial responsibility and family policy*. Washington, D.C., U.S. DHHS, July, 1980.

Schulz, Richard: Effects of control and predictability on the physical and psychological well-being of the institutionalized aged. *Journal of Personality and Social Psychology,* 33:563, 1976.

Schwartz, Arthur N.: Planning micro-environments for the aged. In Woodruff, Diana S., and Birren, James E. (eds.): *Aging Scientific Perspectives and Social Issues*. New York, Van Nostrand Reinhold, 1975, pp. 279–294.

Schwartz, William, and Zalba, Serapio R. (eds.): *The Practice of Group Work*. New York, Columbia University Press, 1971.

Scott-Maxwell, Flora: *Measure of My Days*. New York, Knopf, 1968.

Shanas, Ethel: The family as a social support system in old age. *Gerontologist,* *19*:169, 1979.

Shapiro, Joan: *Communities of the Alone.* New York, Associated Press, 1970.

Shapiro, Joan H.: Single room occupancy: community of the alone. *Social Work,* *11*:24, 1966.

Sherman, Edmund, and Newman, Evelyn S.: The meaning of cherished personal possessions for the elderly. *International Journal of Aging and Human Development,* *8*:181, 1977–78.

Sherwood, Sylvia (ed.): *Long-Term Care: A Handbook for Researchers, Planners, and Providers.* New York Spectrum, 1975.

Silverstone, Barbara: Beyond the one to one treatment relationship. In Bellack, Leopold, and Karasu, Toksaz B. (eds.): *Geriatric Psychiatry.* New York, Grune, 1976, pp. 207–224.

Silverstone, Barbara: Differential aspects of assessment and intervention in social work practice with the elderly and their families. *Journal of Sociology and Social Welfare,* *5*:823, 1978.

Silverstone, Barbara: The effects of introducing a heterosexual living space. *Gerontologist,* *15*:83, 1975.

Silverstone, Barbara: The family is here to stay. *Journal of Nursing Administration,* *8*:47, 1978.

Silverstone, Barbara: Family relationships of the elderly: problems and implications for helping professionals. *Aged Care & Services Review,* *1*:1, 1978.

Silverstone, Barbara: Issues for the middle generation: responsibility, adjustment, and growth. In Ragan, Pauline I. (ed.): *Aging Parents.* Los Angeles, Ethel Percy Andrus Gerontology Center, 1979, pp. 107–115.

Silverstone, Barbara: Long-term care. *Health and Social Work,* *6*:28S, Supplement, 1981.

Silverstone, Barbara: A program of intensified stimulation and response facilitation for the senile aged. *Gerontologist,* *11*:341, 1971.

Silverstone, Barbara: Providing social services in the long term care setting. In Wasser, Lois Jenkins (ed): *Long-Term Care of the Aging: A Socially Responsible Approach.* Washington, D.C., American Association of Homes for the Aging, 1979, pp. 49–54.

Silverstone, Barbara: Social aspects of aging. In Williams, T. Franklin (ed.): *Rehabilitation in the Aging.* New York, Raven, 1983.

Silverstone, Barbara M.: *Establishing Resident Councils.* New York, Federation of Protestant Welfare Agencies. Division on Aging, January, 1977.

Silverstone, Barbara M.: Multilevels and options in chronic care: myth or reality? *Bulletin of the New York Academy of Medicine,* *54*:271, 1978.

Silverstone, Barbara, and Burack-Weiss, Ann: The social work function in nursing homes and home care. In Getzel, George S., and Mellor, M. Joanna (eds.): *Gerontological Social Work Practice in Long-Term Care.* New York, Haworth, 1983.

Silverstone, Barbara, and Hyman, Helen Kandel: *You and Your Aging Parent.* New York, Pantheon, 1983.

Page 312 — Bibliography

312 Bibliography

Silverstone, Barbara, and Miller, Sarah: Isolation in the aged: individual dynamics, community and family involvement. Journal of Geriatric Psychiatry, 13:27, 1980.
Simos, Bertha G.: Adult children and their aging parents. Social Work, 18:78, 1973.
Siporin, Max: Introduction to Social Work Practice. New York, Macmillan, 1975.
Siporin, Max: Situational assessment and intervention. Social Casework, 53:91, 1972.
Smith, Kristen F., and Bengston, Vern L.: Positive consequences of institutionalization: solidarity between elderly parents and their middle-aged children. Gerontologist, 19:438, 1979.
Sorensen, Glorian (ed.): Older Persons and Service Providers: An Instructor's Training Guide. New York, Human Science Press, 1981.
Spikes, James: Grief, death, and dying. In Busse, Ewald W., and Blazer, Dan G. (eds.): Handbook of Geriatric Psychiatry. New York, Van Nostrand Reinhold, 1980, pp. 415–426.
Steinberg, Raymond M., and Carter, Genevieve W.: Case Management and the Elderly, A Handbook for Planning and Administering Programs. Lexington, MA, Lexington Books, 1983.
Stevenson, Olive: Caring and dependency. In Hobman, David (ed.): The Impact of Ageing. New York, St. Martin's, 1981, pp. 128–142.
Tobin, Sheldon S., and Lieberman, Morton A.: Last Home for the Aged. San Francisco, Jossey-Bass, 1976.
Towle, Charlotte: Common Human Needs, rev. ed. New York, National Association of Social Workers, 1965.
Troll, Lillian E., Miller, Sheila J., and Atchley, Robert C.: Families in Later Life. Belmont, Wadsworth, 1979.
Turner, Francis J. (ed.): Social Work Treatment: Interlocking Theoretical Approaches. New York, Free Press, 1974.
United States Bureau of the Census: Marital Status and Living Arrangements: March, 1979. (Current Population Reports, Series P-20, No. 349) February, 1980.
United States Dept. of Health and Human Services. Health Care Financing Administration. Health Standards and Quality Bureau. Patient Care Management Manual. 1982.
United States Department of Health and Human Services: The Need for Long-Term Care Information and Issues: A Chartbook of the Federal Council on Aging. Washington, D.C., U.S. DHHS, 1981.
Urbanowski, Martha L.: Recording to measure effectiveness. Social Casework, 55:546, 1974.
Verwoerdt, Adrian: Anxiety, dissociative and personality disorders in the elderly. In Busse, Ewald W., and Blazer, Dan G. (eds.): Handbook of Geriatric Psychiatry. New York, Van Nostrand Reinhold, 1980, pp. 368–380.
Vladeck, Bruce C.: Unloving Care. New York, Basic Books, 1980.
Wasser, Edna: Creative Approaches in Casework with the Aging. New York, Family Service Association of America, 1966.

Wax, John: Power theory and institutional change. *Social Service Review,* 45:274, 1971.

Weissman, Harold H.: Clients, staff and researchers: their role in management information systems. *Administration in Social Work,* 1:43, 1977.

Welford, A. T.: Sensory, perceptual, and motor processes in older adults. In Birren, James E., and Sloane, R. Bruce (eds.): *Handbook of Mental Health and Aging.* Englewood Cliffs, Prentice-Hall, 1980, pp. 192–213.

Wetzel, Janice Wood: Interventions with the depressed elderly in institutions. *Social Casework,* 61:234, 1980.

Whanger, Alan D.: Nutrition, diet, and exercise. In Busse, Ewald W., and Blazer, Dan G. (Eds.): *Handbook of Geriatric Psychiatry.* New York, Van Nostrand Reinhold, 1980, pp. 473–497.

White, Robert W.: *Ego and Reality in Psychoanalytic·Theory.* New York. International University Press, 1963.

White, Robert W.: Motivation reconsidered: the concept of competence. *Psychological Review,* 66:297, 1959.

White, Robert W.: Strategies of adaptation: an attempt at systematic description. In Coelho, George V., Hamburg, David, and Adams, John E. (eds.): *Coping and Adaptation.* New York, Basic, pp. 47–68.

Whittington, Ronaele R.: Social services for a nursing home: a collaborative approach. *Health and Social Work,* 2:170, 1977.

Woodruff, Diana S., and Birren, James E. (eds.): *Aging Scientific Perspectives and Social Issues.* New York, Van Nostrand Reinhold, 1975.

Wyckoff, Hogie: *Solving Problems Together.* New York, Grove, 1980.

Zarit, Steven H.: *Aging and Mental Disorders.* New York, Free Press, 1980.

Zastrow, Charles: *The Practice of Social Work.* Homewood, Dorsey, 1981.

Zuk, Gerald H., and Boszormenyi-Nagy, Ivan (eds.): *Family Therapy and Disturbed Families.* Palo Alto, Science and Behavioral Press, 1967.

Zung, William W. K.: Affective disorders. In Busse, Ewald E., and Blazer, Dan G. (eds.): *Handbook of Geriatric Psychiatry.* New York, Van Nostrand Reinhold, 1980, pp. 338–367.

INDEX

315